The Dissertation

The dissertation is one of the most demanding yet potentially most stimulating components of an architectural course. This classic text provides a complete guide to what to do, how to do it, when to do it and what the major pitfalls are.

This is a comprehensive guide to all that an architecture student might need to know about undertaking the dissertation. The book provides a plain guide through the whole process of starting, writing, preparing and submitting a dissertation with minimum stress and frustration.

The third edition has been revised throughout to bring the text completely up to date for a new generation of students. Crucially, five new and complete dissertations demonstrate and exemplify all the advice and issues raised in the main text. These dissertations are on subjects from the UK, USA, Europe and Africa and offer remarkable insights into how to get it just right.

Professor Iain Borden is an architectural historian and urban commentator. He is currently Vice-Dean for Communications at The Bartlett, University College London (UCL), UK, where he is also Professor of Architecture and Urban Culture. He graduated from the University of Newcastle-upon-Tyne, UK, in 1985 and went on to complete a masters degree at the University of California, Los Angeles, USA, and a masters degree and a PhD at UCL. He is an Honorary Fellow of the Royal Institute of British Architects.

Katerina Rüedi Ray is the Director of the School of Art at Bowling Green State University, USA. From 1996 to 2002 she was the Director of the School of Architecture at the University of Illinois at Chicago, USA. She studied architecture at the Architectural Association in London, UK, and has a masters and a doctoral degree in architecture from the University of London. She taught architectural design and theory in the UK at the Architectural Association, The Bartlett and Kingston University before taking up her positions in America.

'"Architecture made of words" is how the authors of *The Dissertation* describe their subject. Students are guided through the whole process, from choosing a subject right through to troubleshooting and trying to publish. Borden and Rüedi Ray are full of sage advice and helpful tips and, most usefully, their new edition provides five real dissertations demonstrating the variety of research and writing possible. Lucid and sensible, this is an essential guide for all architectural students.'

- Professor Mark Crinson, University of Manchester, UK

'An invaluable reference guide packed with useful advice and supported with inspiring and informative examples. This book should be required reading for anyone about to navigate the challenges of writing a dissertation.'

- C. Greig Crysler, Associate Professor of Architecture and Arcus Chair, College of Environmental Design, University of California, Berkeley, USA

The Dissertation

A Guide for Architecture Students

Third Edition

Iain Borden and Katerina Rüedi Ray

Routledge
Taylor & Francis Group

LONDON AND NEW YORK

First edition published 2000
by Architectural Press

Second edition published 2006
by Architectural Press

Third edition published 2014
by Routledge
2 Park Square, Milton Park, Abingdon, Oxon OX14 4RN

and by Routledge
711 Third Avenue, New York, NY 10017

Routledge is an imprint of the Taylor & Francis Group, an informa business

© 2014 Iain Borden and Katerina Rüedi Ray

The right of Iain Borden and Katerina Rüedi Ray to be identified as authors of this work has been asserted by them in accordance with sections 77 and 78 of the Copyright, Designs and Patents Act 1988.

British Library Cataloguing in Publication Data
A catalogue record for this book is available from the British Library

Library of Congress Cataloging in Publication Data
Borden, Iain.
  The dissertation : a guide for architecture students / Iain Borden and Katerina Rüedi Ray.—Third Edition.
    pages cm
  Includes bibliographical references and index.
  ISBN 978-0-415-72536-1 (pb : alk. paper)—ISBN 978-1-315-79525-6 (ebook : alk. paper)   1. Architecture—Authorship—Style manuals.   2. Architecture—Study and teaching (Graduate)—United States—Handbooks, manuals, etc.   3. Architecture—Research—Methodology—Handbooks, manuals, etc.   4. Dissertations, Academic—Style manuals.   5. Dissertations, Academic—Abstracts.   I. Rüedi, Katerina. II. Title.
  NA2108.B67 2014
  808.06'672—dc23   2013040185

ISBN: 978-0-415-72536-1 (pbk)
ISBN: 978-1-315-79525-6 (ebk)

Typeset in Palatino
by Keystroke, Station Road, Codsall, Wolverhampton

Printed and bound in Great Britain by
TJ International Ltd, Padstow, Cornwall

Contents

Acknowledgements

Katerina Rüedi Ray offers her sincere thanks to Deborah Fausch for her extensive help and encouragement, and to Pamela Franco for her advice, both of the School of Art History at the University of Illinois at Chicago in the late 1990s. Thanks also to Sherry Bates for his role in developing the agenda of the Image/Text dissertation group at the Bartlett School of Architecture, UCL, to Alex Zambelli for his role as a teaching colleague, and to Peter Cook and Stephen Gage for their support for the programme.

Iain Borden wishes to thank the tutors and students at the Bartlett School of Architecture, UCL, many of whom have made numerous comments and suggestions for the various editions of this book.

We also wish to acknowledge Nezar AlSayyad, Greig Crysler, Katherine MacInnes, Miranda Housden, Leonie Milliner, Nancy West, Ian Latham and the late Katherine Shonfield, as well as Francis Ford at Routledge. Special thanks are due to Ruth Kamen, former Director of the British Architectural Library at the RIBA, and to Caroline Fletcher and Suzanne Tonkins of the Environmental Studies library at UCL.

Many thanks in particular to Joseph Godlewski, Ocean Howell, Mairi Johnson, Joanna Rapp and Amy Thomas for very kindly agreeing to allow their work to be included in this publication.

1   Introduction

Why Write a Dissertation?

As a student of architecture, the major part of your education is always going to be the design of buildings as executed through drawings, models, digital images, prototyping and other kinds of visual representation. Together with the workspace of the architectural studio, the presentation of designs followed by a challenging crit or jury, and the submission of a carefully wrought portfolio are undoubtedly the main elements of an architectural education.

Yet as anyone who has ever tried to explain architecture quickly realizes, architecture is not only about images and models. Words, too, are an integral part of what architecture is all about. Architecture is textual as well as visual and spatial. Most obviously, words are a necessary explanation of what kind of architecture is referred to in drawings and models, and if you don't believe that words are essential, try explaining your designs without speaking at all. Words are also a way of exploring new territories, new ideas, new kinds of architecture – from the Roman architectural theorist Vitruvius to present day bloggers such as Geoff Manaugh, some of the most important and influential works of architecture have been books and other kinds of writing.[1] Indeed, without these words there would be no buildings, no architects and no architectural study.

A dissertation is architecture made of words. It is a way of conceiving and producing architecture through sentences, paragraphs and considered argument. It is an arena in which to alternatively explain, explore, challenge, theorize or imagine architecture. A dissertation can therefore be about many different kinds of subject, from the study of the *oeuvre* of a single architect to tentative speculation about the relation, for example, between shoe design and architectural culture. Most importantly, though, it is a place where, just as in your architectural designs, you have the opportunity not only to learn about architecture but also make a contribution to what we all think about it; the architectural dissertation is your chance to explore what you believe and aspire to, and to present those thoughts to others.

One other thing. A dissertation is a common requirement of many professional architectural courses worldwide, including the vast majority of the various ARB/RIBA Part 1 and Part 2 accredited programmes in the United Kingdom and some professional MArch programmes in the USA. In the UK, universities also often require you to pass your dissertation independently of your design and other architectural studies – no dissertation, no degree! The dissertation can therefore be part of the requirement for all those seeking accreditation or licensing from or membership of their appropriate professional body, such as the National Architectural Accrediting Board (NAAB), National Council of Architectural Registration Boards (NCARB) and the American Institute of Architects (AIA) in the USA, or the Architects Registration Board (ARB) and the Royal Institute of British Architects (RIBA) in the UK, or the Royal Australian Institute of Architects (RAIA) in Australia. If no dissertation means no degree, then it can also mean no professional qualification. For those wanting to be professional architects, doing the dissertation is in many countries not a matter of choice.

The Guidebook

This guidebook provides a guide to the whole process of starting, writing, preparing and submitting a dissertation. It also offers some advice on what to do after the dissertation. It explains carefully what to do, how to do it, when to do it and what the major pitfalls are to avoid. Each university and architectural programme does, of course, have its own rules and requirements, and you are strongly advised to check everything said here with what your own institution expects. Nonetheless, if you follow the guidance in this book, and if you add to it your own intelligent and rigorous efforts, you should go on to produce a dissertation of the best possible standard. It is also aimed directly at students undertaking a professionally oriented architecture degree, and will also be of most use to those who are undertaking a masters-level dissertation in architectural history and theory or related subject. It is not, however, directly aimed at those under an MPhil or PhD research degree, who will often wish to consider the methodological nature of their research in considerably more detail than is discussed in this publication.

The book, following this introduction, is divided into six more chapters. These follow the general chronological procedure by which a dissertation is normally undertaken.

Chapter 2 (*Starting*) describes what to do when first beginning to work on a dissertation. It explains what kind of study a dissertation is, how to select and assess a potential dissertation subject and how to choose a supervisor to work with. It also explains the importance of writing a proposal.

Chapter 3 (*Researching*) identifies what research is, and briefly outlines some of the main kinds of approach that architectural historians and theorists have adopted in order to work within the discipline. On a more practical note, this chapter also explains what you actually have to do in order to research an architectural dissertation: research techniques, working methods, libraries and archives are all covered. A special section, extended in this edition, deals with the internet and other digital resources, all of which offer particular opportunities and challenges for the architectural student.

Chapter 4 (*Writing*) deals with the processes of writing a dissertation, and how to go from the blank sheet of paper or bare screen to a complete first draft. Advice on how to organize and structure a dissertation (including what to include in an 'Introduction' and 'Conclusion') is complemented with tips on working methods, illustrations, referencing, bibliographies, how to avoid plagiarism, submitting a draft and the use of computers. This chapter also suggests how you might change the format of a dissertation into a multimedia or other non-conventional form of submission – indeed, these are kinds of dissertation which have recently been the subject of much discussion, development and innovation.

Chapter 5 (*Presenting*) covers the important process of finishing off, printing and binding a dissertation, and generally making sure that it looks as good as possible while meeting all scholarly requirements. This chapter also explains how tutors commonly assess dissertations.

Chapter 6 (*Afterwards*) moves into the future, when the dissertation has been submitted and assessed. If you have done very well, you may want to consider further study or research in this field, and some suggestions are made about the kinds of courses which you might consider. You may also want to prepare your dissertation for publication, and similar suggestions are made as to how you could do this. This chapter also offers some 'troubleshooting' advice if you are faced with serious difficulties during the production of your dissertation or if you disagree with the result that you have been given.

In Chapter 7 (*Dissertation Examples*) you will also find numerous examples of prize-winning dissertations previously completed by architecture students. In this new edition of this book, we focus on some of the very best work of all, showing a variety of examples of student work as they have been published in prestigious, internationally regarded academic journals of architecture.

4 The Dissertation

Reference

1 Vitruvius, *The Ten Books on Architecture* (New York: Dover, 1960); and Geoff Manaugh, *Bldgblog Book: Architectural Conjecture, Urban Speculation, Landscape Futures* (San Francisco: Chronicle Books, 2009).

2 Starting

What is a Dissertation?

The first thing you need to know about a dissertation is what it is not. Unless you are undertaking a PhD, your dissertation is not going to be like a book, for reasons of time as much as anything else. Consider for one moment that a typical book is commonly something about 80,000 to 100,000 words in length, and can easily take three years or more to write and produce – a PhD is about the same. By contrast, a thesis for an MPhil is typically around 40,000 words, and takes two years to complete, while a dissertation for a graduate architectural course in the USA or a postgraduate architectural course in the UK can be anything from 5,000 to 25,000 words. In practice, an architectural dissertation is often only around 10,000 words (as with most of the details in this book, you should always check the specific requirements of your own institution), and has normally to be completed within one academic year, or nine months. Many students therefore have about the same space and time available as a more experienced author would have to write a single book chapter, or a long article in an academic journal. This situation is even more complex in that many universities will now also accept dissertations which make extensive use of visual material, with some appropriate amendments then being made to the overall number of words.

The dissertation is not, therefore, the appropriate place to try to sum up everything that you have ever thought or believed about architecture – you simply do not have the time, or the number of words, or the number of images at your disposal to cram everything in. Instead, the dissertation is a place in which to enquire into an architectural subject which is of interest to yourself. It is a conscious and deliberate attempt to identify, define, explore and articulate a subject of some relevance both to the architectural discourse and to your own development as an architectural designer and thinker.

A dissertation is, then, a kind of staging post – an opportunity to step outside the studio or to straddle between studio and other areas of architectural exploration, and to focus for a relatively short period of time on a particular aspect of architecture that appeals to you, and which you think would be of benefit when thinking about what architecture is now and might become in the future.

Selecting a Dissertation Subject

One of the biggest problems facing any architecture student when starting a dissertation is what subject they should choose to study. In the past, some schools of architecture have had very specific guidance on this matter, such as the stipulation that the dissertation must be about a single building by a well-known architect. However, such requirements are nowadays quite unusual, and today most architecture schools will allow just about any subject as long as it has some bearing on architecture. You can, for example, get some kind of idea of the potential range of subjects by looking at the "Dissertations" section of the website for the RIBA President's Medals Students Awards (www. presidentsmedals.com), which includes descriptions of dissertation work on individual architects such as Mies van der Rohe, Sverre Fehn and Peter Zumthor, general thematics such as ecology, political power and public grief, individual buildings such as the Braun A.G. Factory, Casa Malaparte and the Buyukada Museum, specific aspects of architectural theory from skew bridges and Piranesian perspective to fictional imaginations, architecture in countries as varied as Chile, Dubai, Lebanon, Northern Ireland and Turkey, and time periods from ancient Rome to the Baroque to the present day.

Evidently the options are very wide indeed, and to begin, then, you have to locate a subject which you want to explore and which you can begin to talk about. The first thing you need to realize here is that, unlike many other essay assignments that you may have been given, your tutor is not going to tell you what to do. Rather, the whole point of the dissertation is that you, yourself, should come up with a topic.

Where, then, might you locate that subject? The following are several places where you might look.

Yourself

What are your interests in architecture? One of the easy mistakes to make about architecture is for you to assume that what you are interested in is also what interests everyone else. Consequently, you might erroneously assume that what you know about architecture is already understood by everyone else, and thus that you should not write a dissertation about it. This is rarely the case. Indeed, one of the great joys about architecture is that it is capable of being thought about in a near-infinite number of ways. So have faith in the fact that what you are interested in will no doubt be shared by some but not all others, and this is your opportunity to convince everyone else of its importance to architecture. The dissertation is, after all, a place of individual work, so give vent to your own obsessions, preoccupations and personal strengths.

How, then, can you identify your own interests? One of the simplest things you can do is to try writing down a few key interests: The way buildings weather over time? The idea of memory? The different kinds of people who inhabit architecture? Advanced-technological or prototyping systems? Political meanings of buildings? The interrelation between word and images? A particular architect's life and work? Have a kind of brainstorming session with yourself and see what you come up with. It is also a very good idea to talk to some friends who are in the same position and ask them to tell you what they think you are interested in, and vice versa.

Your Portfolio

The portfolio you have produced in the design studio over the years is in many ways a record of yourself, your architectural thoughts and how they have developed. Get out those designs and ask what the key themes are within them. Alternatively, what is absent from these projects but which you might like to spend some time thinking about?

One particular question that you may want to bear in mind is the connection between your design work and your dissertation subject. For some students, the dissertation is an opportunity to take a theme from their designs and to explore this in great depth in the dissertation. For others, the reverse is true, and the dissertation is seen as an opportunity to do something entirely divorced from the studio which may only later inform design work, or may remain entirely independent of it. For most, it is probably somewhere in between these two extremes – and many students therefore pick something related to their architectural design interests, but without making it a slave to these studio projects. By the way, although most architecture schools have very broad definitions of an acceptable dissertation, the one kind of subject that many do entirely ban is the dissertation about yourself: writing directly solely about your own design work is not normally acceptable. However, some of the developments in those dissertation which artfully blend both design-based and word-based work may relate very strongly indeed to the student's own studio work. The essential thing to bear in mind here is that the word-based work should not be simply a commentary on your design-based work, and nor should the design-based work be simply the supporting visual evidence for the word-based work. Rather words and designs should be used as equivalent and interrelated ways of exploring the same subject matter.

Other Work

You will probably have already completed a number of different history and theory essays, and maybe even a previous dissertation. As with your portfolio, look at this work and ask what the issues are that you have discussed previously, and what this tells you about your preoccupations. Alternatively, what have you already covered and what might you like to move away from? If you have already written about, for example, contemporary architecture, perhaps it would be a good time to explore something older, such as nineteenth-century ornamentation in architecture, or perhaps something outside the immediate architectural profession, such as the way architecture has been represented in cinema (and vice versa).

Books

What are the books you already own, and which are most attractive to you in the school's library? What kinds of subject do they tend to focus on? Also, what kind of thing have you always wanted to read about but never been able to find? One good trick is to deliberately attempt a kind of parallel study of a chapter you like. For example, if you are impressed with Alice T. Friedman's analysis of the role of the female client in the design of the Schröder House,[1] how might a different building be subjected to the same kind of analysis? Or how might one consider recent architectural drawings in a manner similar to which Mario Carpo has investigated those of the Mannerist architect Serlio?[2] Or how might you construct a theoretical argument similar to (or oppositional to) that advanced by Jeremy Till regarding contingent conditions for architecture?[3]

Magazines, Periodicals and Blogs

These are particularly useful for two reasons. First, browsing through the most recent issues and postings will confirm to you what are the most up-to-date debates and issues under discussion, and you may want to take an active position within debates on, for example, sustainable communities, filmic architectures or rethinking the work of Lebbeus Woods. Of course, just because there are suddenly lots of articles on, for example, parametric surfaces, architecture as icons or the work of Cedric Price does not mean that you should necessarily do the same – indeed, these things can often help you decide *against* as much as towards choosing a particular subject.

Second, many extended research journal articles are about 6,000–8,000 words (sometimes shorter), and so are often not too different from the kind of 10,000-word dissertation that many students undertake. For those undertaking a longer study, the magazine or journal article is about the same length as a typical section or chapter. With these comparisons in mind, take some time to note the range and organization of the argument, the kind of depth that you will need to go into, and the types of evidence and documentation referred to.

Everyday Life

Architecture does not exist only in the studio and architectural school, but is also out there in the city, on the streets, on the roads, in the suburbs, in the landscape. In addition, it has a virtual, mediated existence in the specialist architectural press, on television, in movies, on the internet and on the radio. Here the scope of subjects you might find is truly vast, ranging from how architecture is photographed in different professional magazines, to its role in public spaces or private ways of life, to how it is represented in films or on the world wide web. If you are short of a subject, take a stroll down the nearest busy street, go to the cinema or art galley, drive across an unknown landscape, or take a quick flight to a strange and overseas city.

Other People

Talk to other students in your programme, and with your friends and family. Ask them to listen to what you are thinking about. It may not even matter what they say in response – simply saying something out loud a few times will often make you realize more clearly what you are working towards. Listen to their responses as well though – these may help you see issues which you may not have thought about.

Seminars, Lectures, Conferences, Internet Debates

As you will discover when researching your dissertation (see Chapter 3), most of the information you will need is not contained in books in the library – for the simple reason that these contain work that has already been completed and published. By contrast, seminars, lectures, conferences and internet debates (from generalist sites such as Facebook and LinkedIn to architecture specific blogs such as Archidose, Bldgblog, Contemporist, Design Observer, Dezeen, Eikongraphia and Unhappy Hipsters) are places where architectural thinkers often talk about work in progress, about tentative proposals and strange ideas that are in development. So you can often get clues as to new concepts and lines of thinking from these less formal, more speculative arenas. They are also places where people sometimes talk about exactly how it was that they came to arrive at a subject, how they are developing it, and what problems have arisen on the way.

Tutors

The people who help guide your dissertation can also be enormously helpful at this stage. Don't be afraid to go along with your initial thoughts and ask their advice. One useful thing that you can do is to come up with a number of different proposals, say three or four, and quickly run through the merits of each in turn. Above all, remember that the initial ideas should always come from you, so that your tutor has something to respond to and make suggestions about.

It is also sometimes a good idea, if you have the opportunity, to talk to more than one tutor or professor about your ideas. Even if a particular tutor is not formally part of the dissertation programme, if you think someone might be useful, you can always ask her or his advice – most will be flattered to be asked, so don't be shy. You can also ask your tutor whether there is anyone else that they recommend you talk to. Contrary to what you might think, your tutor will not be upset if you ask someone else's opinion about your dissertation.

Assessing a Dissertation Subject

Rather than just thinking of one topic and launching straight into it, you should aim to identify, say, three to five potential subjects for your dissertation, even if some of them seem hardly feasible. You are then in a position to assess each one of these proposed subjects in turn. Doing this will help you understand the range of different studies that you might undertake, and hence pick the one most appropriate to your own interests and situation.

Going through this process may also be of some help at a later stage in the dissertation, when mid-way through the research and writing process you begin – as everyone does at some point – to have a few doubts about whether you are studying the right thing. If you have carefully assessed the subject early on, you can then remind yourself of this fact, and press on with relative confidence that, yes, you are indeed doing the right thing.

In evaluating a potential dissertation subject, try to identify four things:

- *Objects of study.* What are the particular objects that you are going to look at? A dissertation may be highly philosophical or it may be highly empirical, but it will always have to be *about* something. So what exactly are you going to study: what buildings and architects, books and other media, specific events and historical periods, ideas and concepts? What exactly are you going to talk about and refer to?
- *Interpretive possibilities.* Not only do you have to find something to study, but you also have to know that there is something to

say about it. What can you say about architecture in relation to Hopkins' Velodrome for the London 2012 Olympics, billboards in Mexico City, psychoanalytic readings of bathrooms, or symbolism in Thai temples? In general, small objects can have large questions asked of them, while big objects need to have much more precise lines of enquiry; for example, you might be able to study the life of a single architect, such as the Californian modernist Ralph Rapson, but not of a whole city such as Beijing. Alternatively, you might be able to explore the idea of spatial diagramming in the layout of colonial cities in Latin America, but that might prove too constraining for a study of a single building. In short you need to know:

1 What kinds of issues and questions you want to investigate.
2 How these issues relate to your chosen objects of study.
3 How much, or how little, this will give you to discuss.

- *Nature of the investigation.* One of the things you need to know early on is what kind of study you want to produce: descriptive or explanatory history? Critical history or interpretation? Speculative theory or philosophical musings? Chapter 3 gives some more guidance on the difference between these types of approach, but for now you should at least have some idea of the approach you want to adopt. In other words, do you want to write a documentary account, to find causes and explanations, to try to say something rather unusual about your subject, to write something that is only distantly related to architecture, or to speculate in a creative, propositional or hypothetical manner? All these may be possible.

- *Academic context.* Although no dissertation can be wholly original, your research should contain a significant element of research and interpretation that is unique to yourself. In order to do this, you first have to have an idea of what has already been studied in relation to your proposed dissertation subject and, therefore, of how your own line of enquiry will make an original contribution to the understanding of this topic. In short, who else has already explored this subject, and what do they say or propose about it? Is this a subject that has already been exhaustively covered, and/or can you add something relatively new?

If you apply each of these four criteria to your proposed dissertation subject(s), and come up with some responses, you will very rapidly come to realize what is feasible and what is not.

There are also some very practical issues that you must consider if you are to get off on the right footing. Some of these may seem somewhat trite when viewed in the context of the intellectual parameters of an architectural dissertation, but they are in fact extremely important. Making a mistake here could seriously derail your project.

Size and Scope of Subject

As already explained, you have to carefully match the objects of your study with the conceptual questions you wish to ask of it. This rapidly becomes a matter of the time available to you, the effort you can put into it (which has to be balanced with your other studies) and the words available to write it all out. Can you really cover in depth the decorative schema of all the Renaissance churches of Italy, or the way architecture is used in every single one of Franz Kafka's novels? Can you assess all Merleau-Ponty's philosophy and relate it to the entire history of twentieth-century architecture? Conversely, is there really enough to say about a single Morphosis beach house, or about one film by Sam Mendes?

Bear in mind also that if you choose to do a comparative study – say, the historic marketplaces of Nottingham compared to their equivalents in the French *bastides* cities – then you will have to undertake double the amount of research and writing than if you studied just one of these places. Conversely, in a dissertation about, say, the idea of memory and architecture, comparing the work of, for example, architect Daniel Libeskind with that of artist Maya Lin, might help you to develop interpretations about monuments and memorialization that otherwise would have escaped you.

Availability and Access to Sources

To study something properly then at some point, no matter how many ideas you already have of your own, you are going to have to look at some other material: books, archives, buildings, films, internet sites, individuals etc. are all possible sources. However, not all of these may be open to you, or even exist at all. For example, if you want to write a study of the Peter Jones department store in London, is there a company archive that has information on the building, and will the company let you look at it? (Answer: yes and maybe.) Will you be able to visit and get inside Zaha Hadid's new house for Naomi Campbell in Moscow? (Answer: probably not.) Where will you find information about graffiti art? (Answer: you will need to look just outside the university library.) Will Greg Lynn, Toyo Ito or Jacques Herzog respond to your request for an interview? (Answer: you might be lucky.) Does Mies van der Rohe's Barcelona Pavilion still exist? (Answer: it depends on how you consider the authenticity of the re-creation.) Although you cannot foresee at the outset of your research exactly what sources you will be able to use, you need to have some idea that there is a reasonable variety of material to study.

Time

Chapter 3 offers more advice about time-planning, but for the moment bear in mind that some projects take up more time than others: in particular, interviews may have to be planned many weeks or months in advance, cities in other parts of the country (or the world) take time to visit, and archives may require advance negotiations before access is granted or documents can be reproduced. As with sources, you need to have a general ideas as to whether you have enough time for the kind of research which your dissertation research will entail.

Costs

There are always cost implications in any research, if only for occasional photocopying. Some projects, however, are inherently more expensive than others. If you are planning to go to Chile or New Zealand, can you afford the travel expense? Would Chicago, Cologne or Chester be cheaper than Cairo? Other projects which can prove expensive sometimes include those involving films (rare films, unavailable on video or DVD, may have to be viewed at national film archives with screening charges) or the study of rare photographs or drawings (you may not have to pay copyright charges for reproduction – see Chapter 4 – but you may well have to pay for staff to make copies or prints). Once again, make sure that you understand the cost implications of your research study before getting too deeply committed.

Personal Strengths and Weaknesses

A dissertation should always be challenging, and you will no doubt be wanting to stretch yourself intellectually, but you should also be aware of your own limits. One of the mistakes that architecture students sometimes make is that they think they can be an expert in anything they care to turn their hand to. Sometimes this is true. Sometimes, unsurprisingly, it is not. Thus while you may want to study the depiction of architecture in the works of Thomas Hardy while using the techniques of the Russian formalist school of literary theory, or apply the philosophical speculations of Michel Serres to digital architecture, beware that you are not trained in literary criticism or the philosophy of science and that you may, consequently, find such topics very difficult. Alternatively, if you happen, say, to speak Norwegian as well as English, and have a good knowledge of poetry, you may be able to undertake a study on the relation between the work of Olaf Bull and Alvar Aalto that would be quite beyond the reach of most other architecture students. In many ways this is simple common sense. Try to devise a dissertation project which will best develop and exploit your own personal capabilities. This does not mean only intellectual strengths and weaknesses, there may be other more personal aspects that you may want to consider:

1   *Interviewing.* Do you enjoy meeting and talking to people? If so, an interview-based project would obviously be a good idea.

Conversely, if you are the kind of person who is happy digging around in archives, maybe a library-based project would be more appropriate.

2   *Contacts.* Who are the people you know? Does a family friend work at the Burj Khalifa in Dubai? Did you once work for IBM or OMA?

3   *Languages.* What languages do you speak? Is your French good enough to read those Yona Friedman or Henri Lefebvre texts that are yet to be translated? Does your fluency in Japanese help with a study of Shogunal and Daimyo gateway buildings?

4   *Travel.* Which are the cities and buildings you have visited? How many people can honestly say that they have experienced Shanghai at first hand? Does your first-hand knowledge of New Bedford or New Harmony offer any opportunities?

5   *City of residence.* Where do you live? If you are studying in Glasgow, or come from Stockholm, studying some aspect of Mackintosh or Asplund might be more feasible.

6   *Technical equipment.* Do you own, or have access to, the right technical resources? Such things as high-speed broadband internet access, a good-quality digital camera or voice-recording machine might be required for particular kinds of dissertation research.

In general, take a review of your life – where you are, where you have been, who you know – and make good use of what you have.

Risk

It has to be said that some kinds of dissertation are inherently more 'risky' than others – by which is meant those dissertations which might fail, or which may not be as good as they could be, because of factors which are often outside of the control of the student. Four of the most high-risk dissertation projects are:

1   *Historical research that tries to prove something.* For example, if you want to show beyond all doubt that Piranesi was under the influence of opium when he prepared the Carceri drawings, that may be difficult to demonstrate convincingly. It would be better here to choose a dissertation question that seeks to show how the Carceri drawings *might* be interpreted as drug-inspired or otherwise fantastical invention.

2   *Research that relies on other people or a particular set of data.* If your whole dissertation requires Norman Foster to grant you two hours of his time for an extended interview, or on the existence of original photographs of the construction of Palau Guell, you may be disappointed. As the proverb says, don't put all your eggs in one basket. You will usually do better to choose a dissertation

which draws upon a range of different sources. This way, not only are you more likely to get a substantial amount of information, but you will also get information of different types and shades of opinion, which will greatly enrich the interpretations you can offer.

3 *Dissertations that make extremely unlikely connections.* If you try to show that architects' eye spectacles are directly related to the design of their buildings, you may, or may not, make a highly original contribution to the history of fashion and architecture. If you want to undertake an unusual connection, make sure that you have something meaningful to say.

4 *Dissertations that are purely speculative.* If you write in a purely philosophical manner, you may end up saying little of great originality, or even of much sense. Again, make sure that you have something meaningful to say.

A balance of objects, interpretations and theorization will always help protect against these kinds of risk. Your supervisor can always advise you as to which kind of topic is most likely to succeed.

Choosing and Working with a Supervisor

Not every school of architecture lets you choose your supervisor, often for reasons of staffing and/or other matters of practicality. Others, however, do let you make some kind of choice, and this can be an important advantage. To help you make your choice, you might like to consider the following.

Knowledge

Obviously it is a good idea if your tutor knows something about the kind of dissertation you want to write. However, just like you, even a large group of tutors cannot between them be an expert and authority on absolutely everything, and they consequently cannot be expected to be able to give you highly detailed advice about every subject that you might want to undertake.

This is particularly true with a dissertation, which at its best can be a highly original study and so, by definition, lies beyond the knowledge of most other people. You should therefore not be surprised if your supervisor sometimes seems to know less about your study than you do. Conversely, it sometimes can be a little daunting, even occasionally unhelpful, to have a supervisor who does know a great deal about your particular subject. In either case, your supervisor is not there to instruct you – that is, to tell you what to think and do – but to guide you through the project by discussing and testing your ideas and thus making sure that you explore different avenues of thought and structure your argument to the best possible advantage.

So when choosing your supervisor, in terms of their knowledge all you need to do is try to make sure that there is a general match in interests: someone who has written about medieval architecture might be useful for a study of Scottish castles, or someone who knows about critical theory may be suitable if you are interested in the ideas of Michel Foucault. Beyond this, you should not have too many problems.

Personal Relations

It does help if you get on with your supervisor well enough to feel free to express your ideas. The way that a dissertation is 'taught' is, after all, usually through one-to-one tutorials at which you talk as much if not more than your supervisor. So the more relaxed you feel, often the better the conversations that ensue.

Experience and Reputation

Famous historians and theorists are always attractive options, and if you are lucky enough to have someone particularly renowned in their field, by all means go ahead and capitalize on your good fortune. Beware, however, that such people are not always the best supervisors. Just because they themselves think profoundly and write beautifully does not mean that they will necessarily help you to do the same. They may also be less accessible, being constantly called to other conferences, teaching at another institution, or just plain busy.

However, less well-known or comparatively less experienced tutors may be much more keen to engage with you on your subject, and have the time and inclination to discuss your ideas with you at great length. They may also be more aware of new and interesting developments in architectural thinking. Then again, they might not!

The thing to remember when choosing a supervisor is not to prejudge anyone, particularly by their books or their appearance. Talk to them informally, go to one of their lectures, talk to other students about their experiences – all these things can help you find the right person to work with.

Working with a Supervisor

Remember that your supervisor is very likely to be very busy, not only with other students on your programme but also with other courses, projects and administration. In short, you will only have a limited amount of access to her or him. There are, however, a number of ways in which you can make sure you get the most out of their time:

1   *Be punctual.* If you have a 30-minute tutorial, turning up 15 minutes late will mean that you immediately lose half of that time. If you cannot turn up to a pre-arranged tutorial, contact the tutor

in advance and ask to arrange another appointment. Conversely, if you always see your supervisor at the appointed time, you will get more and better advice.

2 *Ask questions.* Probably you should not try to take control of the tutorial yourself, nor should you expect your supervisor to do all the running. Prepare some questions or issues which you would like to discuss, or at the very least think in advance about what you have done and what you can describe about your subject and research.

3 *Allow time for feedback.* If you give your supervisor something to read, you should allow them at least a few days and often a week or more to do so. Otherwise you may well not get the quality of feedback which you would like.

4 *Provide drafts in a suitable format.* Check with your supervisor if they would like to see draft work in sections or in larger components of the dissertation. And do they prefer to receive this digitally as emailed text documents or pdf files, or as hard-copy printouts?

5 *Use your supervisor.* Seeing your supervisor regularly is one of the best ways of making sure that your dissertation is of the very highest possible standard, yet you would be surprised how many students see their supervisor as little as possible, and sometimes only when they are summoned. Although your supervisor will probably ask to see you if you have been invisible for a long period, in general it is normally up to you to arrange tutorials. Find out what the system is for doing this, and do so as regularly as possible whenever you have something to discuss. Indeed, signing up for a tutorial is often a good way to make sure that you have done something more on your dissertation by that date. Some universities now also require students to keep a 'log book' or similar record of when they met with their supervisor, what was discussed and what was the agreed next course of action.

Writing a Proposal

Once you have selected your dissertation topic, assessed that it is indeed a feasible project, and met with your supervisor, it is often a good idea to write a detailed outline of the proposed study. The purpose of this is to give yourself a clear and definite idea of what you are going to do, how you are going to do it and when you are going to do it. It will also form the basis of a form of 'contract' that you make with your supervisor as to what you undertake to complete.

Dissertation proposals can take many forms, and often different universities have very specific instructions as to what a proposal should include. In general, however, your proposal should contain the following:

- *Title and subject matter.* Here you should give the title and subtitle of the dissertation. Try to be as specific as possible about what you are actually going to look at; for example, 'John Entenza and the *Arts & Architecture* magazine, 1945–1955' is more useful than 'Modern architecture in the United States'. You may be tempted at this stage to immediately give the dissertation a seductive title, and a more descriptive subtitle, such as 'Inference and Impossibility: the Influence of Roman architecture in Budapest'. This kind of title may be acceptable for the final submission, but may not be a good idea for a working title – after all, you have yet to complete the research, and your ideas may well change during this process.
- *Statement of research problem.* This is the most important part of the proposal and should include:
  1 *Identification of the objects of study.* What buildings, which architects, which cities and/or whose films do you intend to study?
  2 *The significance of what you are investigating.* What is interesting about it, and what ideas do you intend to pursue?
  3 *The kind of approach adopted.* How are you exploring and assessing the subject, and with what methodology?
  4 *Academic context.* Who else has written about this subject already, and what kinds of things have they said? How does your proposed study differ from these?

  Note: You do not normally need to produce a sample or extract of your dissertation text at this stage, but in fact the 'statement of research problem' can often go on to form the basis for the introduction to your final text.
- *Contents list.* You should list here the titles of each of the main 'chapters' of your dissertation. Bear in mind that although students and tutors alike often refer to these as chapters, it is in fact better to think of them as sections – remember that your whole dissertation may well be roughly equal in length to one chapter in a book, so each chapter of your dissertation therefore corresponds to one subsection of a book chapter.
- *Sources.* You need to state here where you are getting your information from. List the main libraries, archives, key texts, people, buildings, websites etc. that are of use to your project.
- *Timetable.* Give some indication of time. How far have you progressed with the work? When will the rest be done? If there are key events which need to take place – such as an interview, an art event, or a research field trip – make sure to identify these also.

The proposal is not, therefore, an actual part of your dissertation, but forms the main specification for what it is going to be and how you propose to do it. It should probably be no longer than 1,000 words or two to three pages of documentation, and can easily be shorter.

Once you have written your proposal, make two copies, keep one for yourself on file and give one to your supervisor. This can be a useful discussion document, and help make your tutorial as productive as possible, so ask your supervisor to respond with ideas and suggestions as to how your ideas and work plan might be improved.

References

1   Alice T. Friedman, 'Not a Muse: the Client's Role at the Rietveld Schröder House', Diane Agrest, Patricia Conway and Leslie Kanes Weisman (eds), *The Sex of Architecture* (New York: Harry N. Abrams, 1996), pp. 217–32.
2   Mario Carpo, 'Architectural Drawing in the Age of its Mechanical Reproduction: Serlio', in *Architecture in the Age of Printing: Orality, Writing, Typography, and Printed Images in the History of Architectural Theory* (Cambridge, Mass.: MIT Press, 2001), pp. 42–55.
3   Jeremy Till, *Architecture Depends* (Cambridge, Mass.: MIT Press, 2009).

3 Researching

What is Research?

Exactly what research is can be a contentious issue – ask any two academics, and you will probably get two rather different descriptions. In particular, there is often some kind of narrow-mindedness about what constitutes 'proper' research – those with a scientific background may insist that research is only research when it proves or disproves the answer to a stated hypothesis, while, similarly, architectural historians of a certain kind (now increasingly rare) may insist that research is only research when it uncovers new facts about a specific building or architect. In addition, there are differences in the definition of research in US institutions, where some doctoral programmes in architecture are located in schools of art history, architecture or even in programmes specializing in subjects such as gerontology or social factors and architecture. This can extend to the privileging of constructed aspects of architecture in one institution (such as being studied through orthographic architectural drawings) or architecture as an artistic artefact (such as being studied through photographs). Advanced programmes in design will emphasize still other issues, and vary between the USA, the UK and other countries. If you wish to read about this in more depth, see the extended discussion in Jane Rendell's article, 'Architectural Research and Disciplinarity', in *ARQ* (*Architecture Research Quarterly*), v.8, n.2 (2005).

As you might guess from all this, architectural research can adopt all manner of different forms and approaches, and to some extent you do not have to know exactly what research 'is'. However, there are a number of characteristics common to most if not all good architectural dissertations, which you would do well to bear in mind.

An architectural dissertation should rely on research that:

- is original, in that it is undertaken by yourself, yet which also
- acknowledges other people's ideas and work as appropriate.

'Originality' can thus mean examining material never before studied or providing new interpretations of well-known material. The process by which you do this should entail:

- the study of some specific architectural objects, e.g. persons, ideas, buildings or drawings, and/or
- the application of some interpretive or analytical framework, particularly one which explores a particular theme or asks a specific question about architecture
- the writing or other exploration of these ideas in a way that conveys your investigation to yourself and to others.

The result is then a dissertation which:

- provides new information and/or interpretations about architecture, and which thus
- allows you to learn more yourself about architecture, and which also
- makes a contribution to architectural knowledge in general.

Historical and Critical Methodology

One of the most difficult things for architecture students to get to grips with is a sense of the methodology that they might adopt when writing about architecture. When producing an essay or shorter piece of writing this is less important, but for a larger research study the very best kind of work not only says something original about architecture but also explicitly and clearly understands exactly how those comments and that originality have been produced.

This problem is compounded by the fact that many architectural thinkers and writers have themselves adopted a wide variety of different approaches over the years. To give you some idea of this range, and of the kinds of challenge they would pose, one could identify (and this list is far from exhaustive) the following strains of exploration in the last 50 years or so (which are not necessarily mutually exclusive).

Empiricism

This is the idea that history can be constructed simply by setting out the facts, with the historian maintaining an 'objective' distance from their subject. Henry Russell Hitchcock's *Architecture: Nineteenth and Twentieth*

Centuries is a good example of this kind of approach, which often does little more than describe the building and state the building's date and architect.[1] Challenges here include:

- Would you be content with this relatively limited approach?
- Can you be sure that the facts that you will uncover will be new and original pieces of information?
- Can you be objective about architecture?
- How do you know that the facts you select are the important ones?

Iconography and Iconology?

First developed in relation to art history by German art historians, the iconographic and iconological approach to architecture tries to identify particular ideas or themes as they recur in buildings over time. For example, Colin Rowe's famous essay *The Mathematics of the Ideal Villa* makes comparisons between the use of proportions by Palladio and Le Corbusier.[2] Studies with a similar methodology include Erwin Panofsky, *Gothic Architecture and Scholasticism*,[3] and Robert Venturi, Denise Scott Brown and Stephen Izenour, *Learning from Las Vegas*.[4] Challenges here include:

- How familiar are you with this kind of technique?
- Are you willing to conduct highly focused research on one particular aspect of architecture?
- How will you show the connection between different kinds and periods of architecture?

Hegelian History and Theory

Influenced by the ideas of the German nineteenth-century philosopher G.W.F. Hegel, the Hegelian tradition pervades a large part of architectural history. Some of its most pertinent traits include ideas of progress (architecture is getting 'better'), that this progress is being achieved by specific individual architects (often male) in particular countries (often in the West), and that this architecture somehow represents a 'spirit of the age' or *zeitgeist* that pervades a particular historical period. For extreme versions of this kind of thinking, see Nikolaus Pevsner's *Pioneers of Modern Movement*,[5] any of Charles Jencks' innumerable attempts to capture the latest '-ism' in architecture,[6] or Heinrich Wölfflin's idea of the *kunstwerk* in *Renaissance and Baroque*.[7] Challenges here include:

- Do you believe in the fundamental concepts behind this approach?

- If so, how will you justify your selection of architecture and your interpretation of it?
- How do you define the *zeitgeist* for your chosen subject?
- How is this *zeitgeist* manifested in a physical and visual medium?

Social History

Many architectural writers have paid attention to the social context of architecture. Historians such as Marc Girouard or Spiro Kostof, for example, have both looked at the way people have commissioned, constructed and lived in buildings as well as how these buildings have been designed.[8] Other writers such as Anthony Vidler have combined this with a Hegelian methodology, as in his study of the eighteenth-century French architect Claude-Nicolas Ledoux.[9] Challenges here include:

- What kind of context do you wish to look at? For example, party politics, gender issues, patronage, class relations, building occupancy? How will you justify this context over any other?
- Where will you gain your information from?
- How will you write about these kinds of events?
- Can architecture be entirely explained by its context, or are there criteria and goals particular to architecture that context does not explain?

Politicized History and Theory

Some architectural historians are concerned not only with relating architecture to wider conditions and circumstances outside the architectural profession but also with interpreting that context in relation to a particular political philosophy or position. Two of the most obvious instances of this have been the Marxist studies of Manfredo Tafuri and other Italian writers,[10] who have focused on notions of ideology and revolution, and a large number of feminist studies which seek to explore not only the role of gender relations in architecture but also the possibility for female and male emancipation from those roles.[11] Challenges here include:

- What particular political philosophy do you wish to refer to? For example, classical Marxism, structural Marxism, Anglo-American feminism, psychoanalytic feminism?
- How familiar are you with these concepts?
- How can you show the relevance of these ideas for architecture?
- Are you interested in using the analytical method of the writer you have chosen, or only in demonstrating the theory (these goals may not be the same)?

Operative History, Theory and Criticism

Operative criticism or history is the term deployed by Tafuri for those architectural historians and critics who deliberately seek to use their writings in order to support the case for a particular kind of contemporary architecture today. Again, this kind of writing is particularly pervasive within architectural discourse, and can range from straightforward hagiographic biographies that simply praise a particular architect's work, such as Mary Lutyens's account of the work of her own father, Edwin Lutyens,[12] or those which construct a view of architectural history which by implication supports certain kinds of architecture today, such as Reyner Banham's advocacy of a technological modernism in *Theory and Design in the First Machine Age* and which has done much to support high-tech architecture,[13] or Sigfried Giedion's *Space, Time and Architecture* which performed the same task for much of the modern movement.[14] Challenges here include:

- Do you wish to write in support of a particular architect or kind of architecture? Do you wish to be an advocate of Bruce Goff and organicism, Kenzo Tange and metabolism, or of the work of, say, Fumihiko Maki, Glenn Murcutt, Peter Zumthor, Herzog de Meuron, Paulo Mendes da Rocha, Kazuyo Sejima or Wang Shu?
- If so, why?
- How will you maintain a critical distance from the subject?

Theorized and Interdisciplinary Studies

Historians and critics today often make increasing reference to theories and disciplines from outside architecture. For example, to give but the briefest of glimpses into this very substantial and varied field, you will find elements of semiology in the work of Mark Gottdiener,[15] Derridean post-structuralism and literary theory in that of Jennifer Bloomer,[16] psychoanalysis in Anthony Vidler, Joel Sanders and Diana Fuss,[17] phenomenology in Juhani Pallasmaa and Jorge Otero-Pailos,[18] urban geography in Ross King,[19] post-colonial theory in Zeynep Çelik and Abidin Kusno,[20] etc. This is a growing area in architectural research which has emerged as architectural writers have begun to look to other disciplines to find interpretative frameworks, research methods, primary sources and secondary literature in order to explain architectural issues – see, for example, the wide range of theorized approaches adopted by the contributors to Iain Borden and Jane Rendell (eds), *InterSections: Architectural Histories and Critical Theories*.[21] It is unlikely that you will have time in one of the shorter kinds of architectural dissertation study to familiarize yourself extremely thoroughly with theoretical sources from another discipline. However, if you are undertaking a specialist architectural history or theory programme at masters or for a higher research degree, or if you have a first degree in another discipline, then you may well find that you have much of the knowledge you need. Challenges here include:

- As with politicized writings, to which particular theory do you wish to refer?
- How familiar are you with these concepts?
- How can you show the relevance of these ideas for architecture and for the particular time and place you are studying?
- What role do these ideas play in your work? For example, do you wish to demonstrate Michel Foucault's ideas about power, use a conceptual category of Foucault's such as that of heterotopia, or use his analytical methods?

Social Science

Some architectural historians also make an attempt to use the various methods of social science to examine some point about architecture. For example, Alice Coleman made extensive use of social science survey techniques in her attack on social housing, *Utopia on Trial*,[22] as did Anthony King in his work on the bungalow,[23] while those such as Kim Dovey and Thomas Markus have incorporated elements of space syntax methodology into their studies of building plans.[24] Challenges here include:

- What particular techniques do you want to adopt?
- Will you have the time and resources to carry them out?
- Will they show what you want them to show?
- What point of view about architecture does the use of these methods imply?

Personal Writing

Another kind of architectural writing is the highly personal one, where the author takes a highly subjective and often quite poetic approach to architecture. Examples here range from the journalistic invective of Michael Sorkin[25] to the thoughtful musings of Paul Shepheard,[26] the more philosophical writings of Jun'ichiro Tanizaki,[27] and the complex theoretically informed and interdisciplinary constructions of Jane Rendell.[28] Challenges here include:

- How can you make this interesting and relevant for others to read?
- What style of writing will you adopt?
- How can you make this acceptable as a dissertation at your particular school of architecture?
- How precisely do you satisfy the 'original contribution to knowledge' criterion often employed to assess the validity of a dissertation? Personal is not necessarily the same as original.

Visually Based Studies

These range from studies which are largely design-based explorations, to those which use photographs, diagrams and other visual forms of analysis (such as Robert Venturi, Denise Scott-Brown and Stephen Izenour's *Learning From Las Vegas*) to intersections of multiple texts, images and graphic design (such as Rem Koolhaas and Bruce Mau's *SMLXL*). Obviously there is an extraordinarily wide range of visual and creative strategy possible here. Challenges here are similar to those for 'Personal Writing' above, and also include:

- Which visual strategy will you adopt?
- How does this visual strategy relate to the textual strategy of the dissertation?
- How will the visual material contribute to the understanding or interpretation of the subject matter?
- How will you differentiate your dissertation from studio-based work?

All these different methods may seem a little daunting at first, but they are not meant to be overly problematic for you when thinking about your dissertation. You certainly do not have to understand all these methods before starting your own dissertation, but it is important that you know why you have chosen a particular theoretical framework.

Apart from the specialist and directed questions that the different methodologies identified above can help pose, there are also a number of very simple questions that you might ask of your subject. Some may not be relevant to your subject, but nonetheless often the most apparently straightforward enquiry can lead to the most intriguing of answers. Such questions, and again the list is far from exhaustive, might include:

- Questions of production:
  - How was this architecture constructed?
  - Who was involved?
  - Where is it? Why is this?
  - When was it built?
  - How was it paid for? Who paid for it? Why?
  - Has it been altered after its original construction? When? Why?
  - What were the main intentions of the architects and other producers?
  - Where did these ideas come from?
  - What is the function of the architecture?
  - Who benefited from this architecture? In what way?
- Questions of interpretation:
  - What kinds of design ideas can be related to this architecture?
  - What ideas from outside of architecture can be related to it?

- o How are these ideas manifested in the architecture? Are they visible?
- o How does this architecture compare with other examples of its type? How is it different?
- o What is it trying to avoid? What is it trying to prove or show?
- o What have people said about this architecture? Why was this?
- o What is the significance of this architecture when it was built?
- o Has this significance changed over the years?
- o What is its significance today?
- Questions of reception and experience:
  - o What is the architecture like to look at?
  - o Can you experience the architecture other than by looking?
  - o Is it different on the inside?
  - o Is it different when you move around?
  - o Is it different in the flesh from its representation in books and articles?
  - o How do other media (e.g. films, novels, video games, the internet) represent this architecture?
  - o Who are the different people who have experienced this architecture over time?
  - o How will you convey your own experience of the architecture?
- Questions of use:
  - o What was the intended use of the architecture?
  - o What was the actual use?
  - o Who used it? Were there different groups of users? How did they differ from one another?
  - o When was it used? Did use change over time? How and why? What is the use of the architecture today?

Research Techniques

Apart from the more cerebral questions of methodology, there are also a number of much more practical but nonetheless important research techniques which can be useful when researching your dissertation.

Note-taking

The biggest question when making notes is what to note down. The short answer to this is to note down only what is directly relevant to your dissertation subject. So if you were exploring the experience of verticality in modernist staircases, you would certainly want to note down anything that talked about movement up and down the staircase of, for example, the De La Warr Pavilion. You would probably want to note down details about the concrete and steel construction, but would ignore details about all the other buildings designed by the architects,

Erich Mendelsohn and Serge Chermayeff. This is where your carefully prepared dissertation proposal comes into play – keep this with you at all times, mentally if not physically, and you can then assess everything that you come across in terms of where it fits into your proposal. If it doesn't fit, don't bother taking notes.

Other questions of note-taking include whether to take an exact transcription or quotation from the source, or whether to paraphrase it in your own words. Generally speaking, you should aim for the latter, and reserve quotations only for particularly pertinent phrases, sentences or statements. If you do take quotations, you should check them very carefully as it is very easy to make small errors when transcribing a quotation. You should also distinguish very clearly in your notes what is a quotation, what is a paraphrasing by you, and what are your own thoughts and observations (see below for an example of how to do this). Remember to write down all the relevant published information about the source. When taking notes, always include the page number (see below).

Recording Notes

Whenever you find a relevant piece of information, make an observation or have a new thought, there is one, absolutely essential thing that you simply must do: write it down. This may sound obvious, but it is very tempting to say to yourself that you will make a note later on, or just remember it. However, more often than not, you won't, or you will fret unnecessarily trying to remember whatever it is that you found earlier on!

In general, therefore, the main principle is to gather information and thoughts as you go along. Given the time restraints of a normal architectural dissertation programme, you will probably not have enough time to return to the same place twice, so treat each session as a one-off opportunity. Go somewhere (a book, a library, a person), get what you want, make good but concise notes, leave.

Remember that this applies to your own interpretive thoughts as well as to factual information. If you have a thought of your own about your subject, write this down too. You can do this either in your regular notes, in which case you need some kind of notation system (e.g. your initials) to signify to yourself that this is one of your own thoughts and not someone else's, or in a separate 'ideas book' (see below).

Some people still use a paper-based note-taking system, or perhaps a journal or diary, where you collect all your thoughts and notes in one place. However, the vast majority find it easiest to keep their notes using a laptop or tablet device, and to collate all these in one folder. This means that your notes can be easily referred to at a later date to suit the development of your ideas and the structure of your dissertation. However, beware that you are running the risk of losing all your work if your laptop or tablet goes missing. With any digital device, you should *always* make a backup at the end of each day, which should solve this problem. Indeed, many researchers now use a kind of ongoing backup system, uploading their data to a cloud-based server on a continuous basis. If you wish to pursue this kind of arrangement, you should investigate the kinds of service offered by the likes of Backblaze, Carbonite, CrashPlan, DropBox, Google Drive, HiDrive, LiveData, Mozy and Norton.

If you are using a laptop or other portable computer, one other thing to check, particularly if you are travelling a long distance, is that the archive or library in which you are going to research has suitable power sockets into which you can plug. Few portable computers have adequate batteries on which you could rely for a full day of research.

However you decide to keep your notes, another useful thing to do is to carry a smaller paper-based 'ideas book' with you at all times, or use a smart-phone to fulfil the same role. That way, if something suddenly occurs to you, you can always quickly jot it down.

Filing Materials

You will amass large quantities of information which you must be able to retrieve later. You can choose to file your notes by author or by broad subject categories relevant to your research topic. Whichever system you choose, keep all your research material together in one, easily accessible place, where they are logically stored and arranged.

Photocopying

It is often very tempting to make photocopies or scans of things in libraries and archives. However, remember that copying texts is not the same as reading or thinking about them! Just because you have managed to collect a pile of photocopies 50 cm high on new museums in Shanghai and Minneapolis does not mean that you have done much real work on this subject. In general, try to keep photocopying at a minimum. This will help your bank balance as much as anything else.

Photocopies are, however, very useful in particular circumstances:

- Long quotations, of half a page or more, can be more quickly recorded using a photocopy, and also may help prevent transcription errors (see above).
- Tables, lists of figures and other lengthy pieces of factual information may also be best recorded by photocopy.
- Illustrations may also be usefully photocopied (see below). Line drawings and diagrams photocopy well, while for photographs, renderings and more complex images you may need to use a colour or laser copier.
- Some archives are open only for short periods of time, offer limited access, or close for holidays etc. If you find yourself running out

of time in this way, try photocopying as much as you can, to take away and read later – although note that not all libraries and archives will allow this, so check in advance if you think you going to want to do this.

Illustrations

As with other kinds of information, you should try to gather as many of the illustrations that you think you will need as you go along. There are five ways in which you might do this:

1 *Sketching*. If you are good at freehand or tracing, you may find it easiest to sketch illustrations. Beware, however, that they will lack a certain historical authenticity when you come to include them in your final dissertation, although this may not matter depending on the nature of your subject.

2 *Photocopying*. Generally this is the easiest way to copy illustrations to a standard good enough for nearly all dissertations – this is particularly true if you can use a high-quality laser or colour copier. Beware, however, that although the first copy you make may look good enough, any second- or third-generation copies will rapidly deteriorate in quality. You may therefore need to make more than one first-generation reproduction, particularly if you want to keep one dissertation for yourself while the others are kept by the university.

3 *Photography*. Some libraries or archives will let you take photographs of material in their collections (although many will not). To do this well you will need a good-quality digital camera and possibly also one with a close-up/macro facility. Things to note here include:

   - Digital images or normal prints will be easier and cheaper to scan or copy later on so that you can include them in your dissertation, but make sure you use a high enough resolution.
   - Digital cameras are less directly affected than old film-based cameras by colour-casting, but be aware that colour accuracy is still very difficult under artificial light conditions.
   - If you are using a macro lens, you may also need a tripod or copy-stand in order to keep things steady.
   - Shoot from above, and keep the image as flat as possible, parallel to the camera and in the centre of the shot. A piece of non-reflective glass or Perspex placed over the image in order to flatten it out can help here. Beware of using a wide angle setting in order to fit the image in, as this can distort the image considerably.
   - If you are taking images from a video, DVD, television or computer screen, you should black out the room completely

as annoying reflections in the monitor can very easily stray into the shot. You should use a shutter speed of 1/15 second or slower (i.e. 1/8 and not 1/60), as this will help avoid the black banding that often occurs when taking images from television or monitor screens.

4 *Scanning.* If you can take books or other materials out of the library or archive, you could scan images directly into a digital format. Most scanners produce results good enough for a dissertation.

5 *Official reproductions.* Some archives and libraries will only allow illustrations to be reproduced by their own official reproduction service, either as photocopies, photographs or digital scans. Beware that ordering images in this way can be not only quite expensive but can also take up to several weeks or even months to arrive. Plan in advance. Note that some archives and libraries also charge a separate copyright fee for publishing the illustration concerned – but this should not apply to you as a university dissertation is not normally classified as a published work (see Chapter 5).

Interviews, Surveys and Questionnaires

Many students wish to conduct interviews or other forms of survey as part of their research. Although not an essential part of all architectural dissertations, in some circumstances and when done properly these can be an extremely good way of gaining primary data that are completely original to your own study. If you are conducting a large number of interviews such as a survey of opinion, it may be worth checking with your institution whether it is necessary for your interview subjects to sign an agreement consenting to the interview. Some institutions nowadays also operate a research ethics policy for any research involving human subjects, covering matters of safety, consent, autonomy and privacy. Such issues are not normally relevant to most architecture dissertations, but if in doubt make sure that you ask your supervisor.

Interviews can be difficult things to get right, but with a little foresight and advanced planning most problems can be avoided. If you are thinking of or intending to use interviews in your research you should consider the following.

- *Data targets.* What information do you wish to find out? Are there particular quantitative data which you need (such as the percentages of architecture students who are female or male, broken down by architecture school and by year), or are they of a more general kind (such as different students' perception of whether being female or male makes a difference to the kinds of designs they produce)?
- *Interview set.* Which people are you going to ask? How many? A lot, or are there just a few key people? Does it matter if some of them do not agree to participate?

- *Format.* What kind of format do you want to adopt? A statistical survey, a structured interview with exactly the same questions asked of all participants, or a much more general and open discussion format?
- *Approach.* How will you conduct the interviews? Depending on the format, you have a number of different ways in which you might conduct an interview or survey. Perhaps the easiest is to send a questionnaire to people by email and/or to set up some kind of online questionnaire, and perhaps using an internet-based service such as those offered by the likes of SurveyMonkey, FluidSurveys, FreeOnlineSurveys, InstantSurvey and Zoomerang. However, you should be aware that the response rate to this kind of questionnaire is typically very low, for recipients will often have neither the time nor the inclination to reply, or they will have every intention of doing so but somehow never quite get around to it. If you do send out a questionnaire, one trick is to say clearly and politely at the top how little time it should take to complete a response – asking a few, well-directed questions that take no more than 5–10 minutes to answer is usually about right. Do check with your institution whether it has guidelines on the conduct of interviews – this is likely to be the case if you are in the USA.

Other ways of conducting interviews include speaking to people you meet in the street or at a building if this is appropriate to your study. If you want to explore ideas of what a building means to different people, say for the Neue Staatsgalerie in Stuttgart, you could interview visitors, guards, curators and anyone else that you can engage in conversation. Again, for large numbers of interviewees you may need to check with your institution for procedures.

Interviews conducted via telephone and/or Skype (or other video chat systems such as FaceTime, Google Hangouts, Oovoo) can also be an excellent way of reaching some individuals, but make sure that they have time to talk to you before launching into your questions. If you are going to phone or Skype someone, writing to them in advance and letting them know what you are doing is often considered to be a polite course of action. This is particularly the case with Skype-style interviews, when you will probably need to email in advance to set up a convenient time.

Of course, the main way of conducting an interview is to have a one-to-one and face-to-face meeting. If you wish to do this, you should keep the following in mind:

1 *Plan.* Arrange the interview well in advance, and check a day or so before the interview itself that everything is okay. This is particularly important if you are going to be travelling any great

distance. It is also often a good idea to give the interviewee your mobile phone number, so that they can contact you easily in case of any last minute changes in arrangements.

2   *Research.* Make sure you have done much of your other research in advance. An interviewee will probably not be very happy if you are clearly not well prepared, and if you have not bothered to read published material, existing interviews that are on the internet, etc.

3   *Control.* Take control of the interview yourself, and do not expect your interviewee to just perform (unless, of course, that is clearly how they prefer to operate!). Prepare some questions in advance and use these to run the interview – if you then move on to discuss other subjects, that is fine, but try to cover what you came to find out.

4   *Record.* Ask your interviewee if you can record the conversation. He or she may need to sign an agreement – check with your institution before you ask for the interview – but usually just asking someone for their permission is enough. Make sure that you have a good recorder and microphone, that you know how to use it and that you have enough batteries, tapes, disk space, etc. If you cannot record the interview, keep good notes.

5   *Limit.* Keep the interview relatively short, and don't go on for too long: 30–45 minutes is normally more than enough.

6   *Thank.* Write or email and thank your interviewee for their time a day or so afterwards. You may also want to offer to send them a copy of your dissertation when it is completed.

7   *Review.* Listen to the interview recording, or review your notes, as soon as possible. If you have a tape or digital recording, you can either transcribe the whole thing (although this can be very time consuming), or make a list of the issues covered and use the machine or digital counter to identify where on the recording they occur.

8   *Follow-up.* You may find that as your research progresses you have additional questions for your interview subjects. Often, these supplementary questions can be broached by a follow-up email, telephone or Skype call at a later date.

Visiting Architecture

Actually going to visit a building, city or other piece of architecture can often be an extremely good, not to say essential way of finding more out about a building. However many images, plans, descriptions, theories, websites and DVDs you study, architecture is always different in the flesh. If you intend to visit architecture as part of your research, in order to make the best use of this experience you should consider the following issues.

- *Data targets.* What do you want to find out? Do you need to find out particular information, such as aspects of construction or sense of space, or is your visit more general in nature?
- *Interview set.* What people do you want to meet? The building manager or owner? Users?
- *Access.* When is the architecture open to the general public? Do you need to make another kind of arrangement? What will you be allowed to see? Can the architecture be easily viewed from the exterior? Where from? What can you see? When can you arrange a field trip? How much will it cost? From whom do you need permission to visit?
- *Records.* What records can you make of your visit? Will you be allowed to take photographs? Might video, sketches, or notes be better than photography? Can you obtain documentation while you are there (photographs, plans, visitor guides, other information)? Should you have information beforehand to help you understand the building and know what you want to record?
- *Experience.* What kind of experience have you gained from your visit? Was the architecture different in various parts, and/or when you were moving? Were you allowed to see everything? How might your experience of the architecture differ from that of other people, particularly non-architects?

Recording Sources

Not only is it important to keep good notes of your subject material, it is also essential to maintain a meticulous record of where the information has come from. Thus for every single piece of information you need to note down the archive, book or article details, name of illustration. etc. In general, you need to have all the information that you will have to include in your footnotes, references and bibliography (see Chapter 4). In particular, you need to note page numbers as well as publication details for all information, and especially for quotations, paraphrased notes, facts and other precise data. Note that this applies to illustrations and diagrams as well as textual material. For example, part of a set of notes might look something like this:

Source
Georg Simmel, 'The Metropolis and Mental Life', P.K. Hatt and A.J. Reiss (eds), *Cities and Society: the Revised Reader in Urban Sociology* (New York: Free Press, 1951), pp. 635–46.
Notes
GS – Sees cities as a place of punctuality. [637–8]

Quote – 'If all clocks and watches in Berlin would suddenly go wrong in different ways, even if only by an hour, all economic life and communication of the city would be disrupted for a long time.'
[638]

IB – does this apply to all cities, or just to Berlin??

GS – Quantitative nature of the metropolis leads to: [645]

* individual independence
* elaboration of individuality itself   [646]

IB – might this relate to Loos's interior designs for bourgeois houses in Vienna? See Ronstaid article for more on this.

Here, the source gives publication details, the numbers in square brackets on the right-hand side give the appropriate page numbers, while a notation system shows what is a paraphrasing of Simmel (GS), what is a quote (Quote) and what are the researcher's own thoughts or question (in this case, IB).

Deploying this kind of system methodically and consistently may seem like overkill at this stage, but be assured it will save you an enormous amount of effort and potential trouble later on. This is particularly true when you are trying to avoid unintentional plagiarism (see below).

Reviewing Thoughts

One of the most important things you can do when researching your dissertation is to think about the subject as you go along – that is, do not just be content to collect facts and information, but actively consider what it is that you are finding out during the research process. To help with this process there are a number of things that you might try doing:

* *Write it down.* Write down any thoughts you might have. As stated above, jot down any particular ideas or questions among your notes (in which case take care to distinguish your own ideas from everything else), or in a separate place.
* *Reviewing notes.* Review your notes regularly by taking 30 minutes or so at the end of each research session to go over what you have noted and, once again, take care to write down any reflections you have on this. Some people even find it useful to keep a kind of diary, noting down where they have been and what they have thought.
* *Write as you go.* Although it is often, of course, very difficult to write major parts of your dissertation until you have done at least

some of the research, as soon as you are in the position to write something, do so. These pieces of writing do not have to be very long – just enough for you to get some thoughts down on paper. Doing this will help to keep your thought processes active. You can also give some of this writing to your supervisor as something to discuss. And when you come to write the dissertation proper, you will often find that you have already done much of the thinking and writing.

- *Talk as you go.* Above all, talk to other people about your work, and not just to your supervisor (see below). Different people can often have very valuable things to contribute to your work, and often about matters which you may never have thought about on your own. Talking about your work, as with writing small excerpts, also helps you to keep your thought processes active and enquiring.
- *Review and reflect.* Refer back to your initial ideas and reasons for dealing with the subject. Every now and then, perhaps once a week or so, you should refer back to your proposal. This will help keep you focused on what you are doing, and also remind you of what stage you have reached in the overall project.

Timetable

Apart from doctoral and higher research degrees, nearly all dissertation programmes are run on fairly strict time schedules, at the end of which there is one, immovable date: the submission deadline. In general, therefore, you only have a limited amount of time to come up with your subject, begin researching, discuss things with your supervisor and other relevant people, complete the research, write a draft, make changes, produce the final document and hand in. All this has to be done in a limited period – for many graduate programmes this period of time may often be only 6–12 months, or even less.

In order to cope with these time demands, draw up a timetable showing the main periods of:

- research
- writing
- draft submission
- draft revisions
- deadline for final submission.

You should also include:

- term/semester dates
- important dates such as field trips, special archive trips, scheduled interviews
- dates when your supervisor or advisory faculty are – and are not – available

- important personal dates such as birthdays, personal vacations, family events with which you will not want to have a work clash.

Libraries and Archives

Where to find information is, of course, one of the single most important questions for any dissertation project. Exactly where you can find what you want will vary dramatically according to the architectural subject you have chosen, but there are nonetheless some simple rules and guidance that can help you.

In researching your dissertation, there is one thing to bear in mind: unlike most other essays and assignments, what you are doing is an original piece of research and it is therefore very unlikely that you going to find everything you need in standard, published books sitting on the shelves in the library. Instead, at the very least you are probably going have to look at articles in the academic and professional architectural press, as well as conduct primary research yourself in archives, through interviews, surveys, etc. Some of these have already been discussed above. What follows is particularly related to libraries and archives.

Bear in mind that you may also need to use a foreign language and foreign archives to access some primary sources of information. In the USA, for this reason, many advanced-level programmes require the study of a second language besides English. In the UK, this may require taking special classes. You will also need to plan carefully with respect to time, transportation, accommodation and budget. You may need letters of recommendation or reference from your institution to obtain advance permission to use the archive as well as a general letter confirming who you are and what your research topic is. These documents can be particularly helpful if you need access to sources which you discover only after arriving at the research destination. It helps if these letters are in the language of the country you are visiting. It is also important that you remember to carry your student identity card with you, as this may allow you to enter other archives and buildings that you discover while in your foreign research location.

Books

Most architecture schools have reasonably well-stocked libraries containing a variety of older and more recent publications, some of which will undoubtedly be of good use to you. This is where you should start looking. In particular you should investigate the following.

Reference Books

There are a number of publications which give general introductions to architecture and architects, and in which you will find some initial references, buildings, architects or other subjects which you might want to follow up. These include:

Avery Obituary Index of Architects (Boston: G.K. Hall, second edition, 1980).

Markus Sebastian Braun and Chris van Uffelen, Atlas of World Architecture (Salenstein: Braun, 2012).

Centre Canadien d'Architecture, Guide des Archives d'Architecture du CCA (Montreal: CCA, 1992).

E. Beresford Chancellor, The Lives of the British Architects from William of Wykeham to Sir William Chambers (London: Duckworth, 1909).

H.M. Colvin, A Biographical Dictionary of British Architects, 1600– 1840 (New Haven: Yale University Press, 1995).

Nadine Covert (ed.), Architecture on Screen: Films and Videos on Architecture, Landscape Architecture, Historic Preservation, City and Regional Planning (New York: G.K. Hall, 1993).

James Stephen Curl, A Dictionary of Architecture and Landscape Architecture (Oxford: OUP, 2006).

Alison Felstead, Jonathan Franklin and Leslie Pinfield, Directory of British Architects, 1834–1900 (London: Mansell, 1993).

John Fleming, Hugh Honour and Nikolaus Pevsner, The Penguin Dictionary of Architecture and Landscape Architecture (London: Penguin, fifth edition, 1998).

A. Stuart Gray, Edwardian Architecture: a Biographical Dictionary (Ware: Wordsworth, 1988).

Pedro Guedes (ed.), The Macmillan Encyclopaedia of Architecture and Technological Change (London: Macmillan, 1979).

Joseph Gwilt, The Encyclopedia of Architecture, Historical, Theoretical and Practical (New York: Bonanza, revised edition, 1982).

John Harvey, English Mediaeval Architects: a Biographical Dictionary down to 1550 (Hulverstone Manor: Pinhorns, revised edition, 1987).

Ruth Kamen, British and Irish Architectural History: a Bibliography and Guide to Sources of Information (London: Architectural Press, 1981).

James H. Maclean and John S. Scott, The Penguin Dictionary of Building (London: Penguin, fourth edition, 1993).

Tom Martinson, The Atlas of American Architecture (New York, Rizzoli, 2009).

Ann Lee Morgan and Colin Naylor (eds), Contemporary Architects (Chicago: St James, second edition, 1987).

Adolf K. Placzek (ed.), Macmillan Encyclopaedia of Architects (New York: Free Press, 1982).

Dennis Sharp (ed.), *Sources of Modern Architecture: a Critical Bibliography* (London: Granada, second edition, 1981).

Jack Travis (ed.), *African-American Architects in Current Practice* (New York: Princeton Architectural Press, 1991).

20th-Century World Architecture: the Phaidon Atlas (London: Phaidon, 2011).

Willem Van Vliet (ed.), *The Encyclopedia of Housing* (Thousand Oaks: Sage, 1998).

Randall Van Vynckt (ed.), *International Dictionary of Architects and Architecture* (Detroit: St. James Press, 1993).

Marcel Vellinga, Paul Oliver and Alexander Bridge, *Atlas of Vernacular Architecture of the World* (London: Routledge, 2007).

Arnold Whittick (ed.), *The Encyclopedia of Planning* (Huntington: R.E. Krieger, 1980).

Joseph A. Wilkes (ed.), *Encyclopedia of Architecture: Design, Engineering & Construction* (London: Wiley, five volumes, 1988–90).

In addition, there are also now an increasing number of readers, introductions and other related books which deal with architecture-related articles or provide other overviews of the subject. These can be useful for finding 'classic' articles on architecture and city studies, and for gaining an insight into terminology. These include:

Architectural Theory: from Renaissance to the Present; 89 essays on 117 treatises (London: Taschen, 2003).

Andrew Ballantyne (ed.), *Architecture Theory: a Reader in Philosophy and Culture* (London: Continuum, 2005).

Eugenie Birch (ed.), *The Urban and Regional Planning Reader*, (London: Routledge, 2008).

William W. Braham and Jonathan A. Hale (eds), *Rethinking Technology: a Reader in Architectural Theory* (London: Routledge, 2006).

Neil Brenner and Roger Keil (eds), *The Global Cities Reader* (London: Routledge, 2005).

Gary Bridge and Sophie Watson (eds), *The Blackwell City Reader* (Oxford: Blackwell Publishers, 2002).

Michael Bull and Les Back (eds), *The Auditory Culture Reader* (Oxford: Berg, 2003).

Matthew Carmona and Steve Tiesdell (eds), *Urban Design Reader* (Oxford: Architectural Press, 2006).

Mario Carpo (ed.), *The Digital Turn in Architecture 1992–2012* (Chichester: John Wiley, 2012).

Ulrich Conrads, *Programmes and Manifestos on 20th-Century Architecture* (London: Lund Humphries, 1970).

Greig Crysler, Stephen Cairns and Hilde Heynen (eds), *The Sage Handbook of Architectural Theory* (London: Sage, 2012).

Keith L. Eggener (ed.), *American Architectural History: a Contemporary Reader* (London: Routledge, 2004).

Caroline van Eck and Christy Anderson (eds), *British Architectural Theory, 1540–1750: an Anthology of Texts* (Aldershot: Ashgate, 2003).

Adrian Forty, *Words and Buildings: a Vocabulary of Modern Architecture* (London: Thames & Hudson, 2000).

K. Michael Hays (ed.), *Oppositions Reader: Selected Readings from a Journal for Ideas and Criticism in Architecture, 1973–1984* (London: Academy Editions, 1992).

K. Michael Hays (ed.), *Architectural Theory Since 1968* (Cambridge, Mass.: MIT, 1998).

Michael Hensel, Achim Menges and Christopher Hight (eds), *Space Reader: Heterogeneous Space in Architecture* (Chichester: John Wiley, 2009).

Charles Jencks and Karl Kropf (eds), *Theories and Manifestos of Contemporary Architecture* (London: Academy Editions, 1997).

Charles Jencks (ed.), *The Post-modern Reader* (Chichester: John Wiley, second edition, 2010).

Hanno-Walter Kruft, *A History of Architectural Theory: From Vitruvius to the Present* (London: Zwemmer, 1994).

Michael Larice and Elizabeth Macdonald (eds) *The Urban Design Reader* (London: Routledge, 2006).

Neil Leach (ed.), *Rethinking Architecture: a Reader in Cultural Theory* (London: Routledge, 1997).

Richard LeGates and Frederic Stout (eds), *The City Reader* (London: Routledge, fifth edition, 2011).

Setha M. Low, *Theorizing the City: the New Urban Anthropology Reader* (New Brunswick: Rutgers University Press, 1999).

Brian McGrath, *Urban Ecologies Reader* (Chichester: John Wiley, 2012).

Harry Francis Mallgrave (ed.), *Architectural Theory: an Anthology from Vitruvius to 1870* (Oxford: Blackwell, 2005).

Harry Francis Mallgrave and Christina Contandriopoulos (eds), *Architectural Theory: an Anthology from 1871 to 2005* (Oxford: Blackwell, 2008).

Harry Francis Mallgrave and David Goodman (eds), *An Introduction to Architectural Theory: 1968 to the Present* (Oxford: Blackwell, 2011).

Malcolm Miles and Tim Hall with Iain Borden (eds), *The City Cultures Reader* (London: Routledge, revised edition, 2003).

Kate Nesbitt (ed.), *Theorizing a New Agenda for Architecture: an Anthology of Architectural Theory 1965–1995* (New York: Princeton Architectural Press, 1996).

Joan Ockman (ed.), *Architecture Culture 1943–1968* (New York: Rizzoli, 1993).

Jane Rendell, Barbara Penner and Iain Borden (eds), *Gender Space Architecture: an Interdisciplinary Introduction* (London: Routledge, 1999).

Neil Spiller (ed.), *Cyber Reader: Critical Writings for the Digital Era* (London: Phaidon, 2002).

A. Krista Sykes, *Constructing a New Agenda for Architecture: Architectural Theory 1993–2009* (New York: Princeton Architectural Press, 2010).

Simon Swaffield (ed.), *Theory in Landscape Architecture: a Reader*, (Philadelphia: University of Pennsylvania Press, 2002).

Charles Waldheim (ed.), *The Landscape Urbanism Reader* (New York: Princeton Architectural Press, 2006).

Stephen M. Wheeler and Timothy Beatley (eds), *Sustainable Urban Development Reader* (London: Routledge, 2008).

You will also find a number of similar such readers in related or transdisciplinary fields, such as cultural studies, postcolonialism, anthropology, art history.

General Book Catalogues

Use your library computer or internet access to search by title, subject and keyword for books on your subject. Libraries sometimes list books in only one of these formats, so check all three. This can be a laborious process, so be patient and take your time. In order to make your task more efficient, make a careful note of all the references which look like they might be interesting, and then go to the shelves and check them all in one go. You can also now interrogate online library catalogues semi-automatically, using purpose-designed reference manager software such as EndNote.

When you have found a book on the shelf, take a few minutes to look at other things filed in the same part of the library that might also be of use to you.

When you make notes from the books you have found, you should always also look at their bibliographies and footnotes. This is a very good way to track down more obscure sources, such as chapters in edited books or articles in journals.

Journals and Magazines

Much of the information you need is likely to be located in architecture journals, magazines and the trade press. Be warned that tracking down articles on a particular subject is a notoriously difficult and time-consuming operation. It is, however, a task that you simply must do if you are to research your dissertation properly. Fortunately, for architecture, there are two main indices that can help you.

- *Architectural Periodicals Index (API).* This is an index to all the periodicals held in the RIBA Library, so anything you find in here can be obtained at the RIBA in London if your own school does not have it. The API is incorporated within the RIBA's online library catalogue, which gives information on over four million books, journals, articles, drawings, archives, photographs and other architectural objects held by the British Architectural Library at the RIBA. Many institutions now offer online access to this catalogue through their own online library system, or you can gain access it to directly at http://riba.sirsidynix.net.uk/uhtbin/webcat or via the RIBA's website at www.architecture.com. This online resource is fully searchable by keyword, author, title, subject, name of architect, name of building, and/or journal, and results can be printed, saved to disk or emailed. It contains:
  - Index to over 2,000 of the world's most respected architectural periodicals, including over 600 which are currently published. These periodicals cover all aspects of architecture and a range of subjects in related fields, including: architectural history, theory and criticism; building construction, technology and law; environmental planning and green building; interior design; landscape architecture; planning; and building studies.
  - Catalogue of over 150,000 books and 20,000 pamphlets.
  - Catalogue of the holdings of the Archives Collection with approximately 1.5 million items divided into over 800 individual manuscript collections. This collection holds items dating from the seventeenth century to the present day and includes: architects' personal papers, correspondence, notebooks and diaries; architects' job files, contracts, specifications and accounts; press cuttings; literary papers of architectural writers; records of architectural societies; notes and drafts of lectures, articles and books; pamphlets, brochures and information leaflets; and the RIBA's own administrative archive.
  - Catalogue of over 20,000 biographical files. Each file is unique and can contain items such as nomination papers for RIBA membership, obituaries, brochures, newspaper articles, letters or other papers relating to a specific architect or firm.
  - Catalogue of the RIBA's collection of drawings, currently numbering over one million items.
  - Catalogue of RIBA Library Photographs Collection which currently holds over 1.5 million images covering pre-history to the present, with a worldwide coverage, as well as the archive of the Architectural Press (publishers of the *Architectural Review* and *Architects' Journal*) and the work of acknowledged photographers such as Eric de Maré and Tony Ray-Jones, and the archives of twentieth-century photographers including John Maltby, John Donat and Henk Snoek.

- *The Avery Index.* This is an index to all the periodicals held by the Avery Library at the University of Columbia in New York, so, like the RIBA's online catalogue, not everything listed in here will be obtainable in your own school library. Its main advantage is that it goes a lot further back in history than does the API, indeed into the nineteenth century. Online access to the API is not available through normal free internet connection, but many institutions now offer online access to this catalogue through their own online library system. In addition, the Avery (and other architecture-related databases) can also be accessed off-campus via the 'Athens' or 'ProQuest' access management systems – ask your university librarian for details. Similar web-based access is also available in the US and other countries worldwide. As with the RIBA online catalogue, the Avery can be searched in a number of advanced ways, including by abstract, author, title, subject and artist/architect, as well as other filters for language, peer-reviewed articles, date ranges, book and exhibition reviews, interviews, journal articles and obituaries. The inclusion of illustrations, drawings, models, photographs, plans and sections can also be specified in searches. Results can be printed, saved to disk or emailed, and citations can also be generated.

  In total the Avery index currently has over 700,000 records, and so provides a comprehensive listing of journal articles published worldwide on architecture and design, archaeology, city planning, interior design, landscape architecture, and historic preservation. A complete list of the periodicals indexed is available online at www.csa.com/factsheets/supplements/avery.php. Date coverage is from the 1930s to the present, with selective coverage back to 1741, and the database is updated on a weekly basis.

Between them, these two catalogues should give you everything you need for anything produced from within the discipline of architecture, and consulting them carefully is an important part of an architectural dissertation study. Keep careful note of article references you get from the RIBA and the Avery – you don't want to have to repeat the task unnecessarily.

The API and Avery indices are not the only places to look for this kind of information: other useful sources for information and which are particularly good for periodical and journal articles in the field of architecture and closely related subjects include the following (note: many of these will require you to log-on via your university's own online library resource, or the relevant internet portal (many of which are accessible via 'Athens' or other access management system – ask your university librarian for details)):

- *Art and Architecture Complete.* Includes full-text coverage of 380 periodicals and more than 220 books, and indexes 780 academic journals, magazines and trade publications. The database also has a collection of 63,000 images. It covers a wide variety of subjects, including architecture and architectural history, art and art history, interior design and landscape design.
- *Art Bibliographies Modern.* Provides full abstracts of journal articles, books, essays, exhibition catalogs, PhD dissertations and exhibition reviews on all forms of modern and contemporary art, with more than 13,000 new entries added each year. Full coverage begins in 1974 when the first volume was digitized, but entries date back to the late 1960s. www.csa.com/factsheets/artbm-set-c.php.
- *Art, Design and Architecture Collection.* Includes access to ARTbibliographies Modern (ABM), a specialist bibliography on modern and contemporary art including full abstracts and indexing from the late 1960s onwards; Art & Humanities Full Text; Avery Index to Architectural Periodicals; Design and Applied Arts Index (DAAI), a database for all aspects of design and crafts covering journal articles, exhibition reviews and news items from 1973 to present; and International Bibliography of Art (IBA), covering scholarly literature on Western Art. www.proquest.co.uk.
- *Art Full Text.* Researchers can track the careers of artists and review their materials and methods, and find books by and about artists, as well as interviews, profiles and much more. Indexing of art reproductions helps users find virtually any work of interest— including works by emerging artists. www.ebscohost.com/academic/art-full-text.
- *Art Index.* Database with indexing of over 600 periodicals, more than 13,000 art dissertations and almost 200,000 art reproductions. Includes a database-specific thesaurus and covers fine, decorative and commercial art, as well as folk art, photography, film and architecture. www.ebscohost.com/academic/art-index.
- *Art Index Retrospective.* For the period 1929–84, and includes indexing of nearly 600 publications, many of which are peer reviewed, and citations of over 25,000 book reviews. Coverage includes fine, decorative and commercial arts. www.ebscohost.com/academic/art-index-retrospective.
- *Arts & Humanities Citation Index.* Covers over 1,300 arts, philosophy and humanities journals. Goes back to 1975 and is updated weekly. Abstracts are available from 1994 onwards. www.webofknowledge.com.
- *ICONDA.* Bibliographic database of the International Council for Building Research, Studies and Documentation (CIB). Covers worldwide technical literature on all fields of building construction, civil and construction engineering, and architecture

and town planning. Sources include periodicals, books, research reports, conference proceedings, business reports, theses and non-conventional literature normally outside the public domain. Coverage dates back to 1976. Over 400 periodicals are regularly scanned. www.ovid.com.

- *JSTOR.* Online system for archiving academic journals, founded in 1995. Provides full-text searches of digitized back issues of several hundred well-known journals. 'Books at JSTOR', launched in 2012, adds current and backlist books from several academic, scholarly and university presses. www.jstor.org.
- *Scopus/SciVerse Scopus.* World's largest abstract and citation database of peer-reviewed literature. Covers scientific, technical, medical and social sciences, including arts and humanities. Contains 47 million records from over 19,500 titles and 5,000 publishers worldwide, plus over 4.9 million conference papers. www.scopus.com.
- *Urbadoc.* Contains over 700,000 records of the literature on European urban and social research, policy and practice. www.urbadoc.com.
- *Web of Knowledge/Web of Science.* Provides access to Thomson Reuters services, including citation databases and information on cross-disciplinary research, and specialized subfields. Includes the Arts & Humanities Citation Index, Social Sciences Citation Index, Science Citation Index Expanded and Conference Proceedings Citation Index. www.webofknowledge.com.
- *Wilson Art Abstracts.* Provides indexing and abstracting of over 600 periodicals dating back to 1984, including 280 peer-reviewed journals as well as indexing and abstracting of over 13,000 art dissertations, and indexing of almost 200,000 art reproductions. Topics covered include art history and criticism, architecture and architectural history, archaeology, antiques, museum studies, graphic arts, industrial design, landscape architecture, interior design, folk art, painting, photography, pottery, sculpture, decorative arts, costume design, television and video, motion pictures, advertising art, non-western art and textiles. www.ebscohost.com/academic/art-abstracts.

Many journals and periodicals are now themselves online, often allowing you to not only search for but also download articles on your subject. For example, in 2014 the UCL library offered the following journals under the category of 'Architecture' with either full or partial online access:

> *3ZU; Access By Design; Ángulo Recto: Revista De Estudios Sobre La Ciudad Como Espacio Plural; Annales Des Ponts Et Chaussées; APT Bulletin; Apuntes; Arhitektura Raziskave;*

Archimaera; Architect; Architectural Design; Architectural Digest; Architectural Engineering and Design Management; Architectural Glass Concepts; Architectural Heritage; Architectural History; Architectural Lighting; Architectural Record; Architectural Review; Architectural Science Review; Architecture; Architecture + Design; Architektur Aktuell; Architektúra A Urbanizmus; L'Architettura; Archnet-IJAR; ARQ: Architectural Research Quarterly; Arquitectura Y Urbanismo; Assemblage; Baumeister; Bautechnik; Beton Und Stahlbetonbau; Builders Merchants Journal; Builder; Building; Building and Environment; Building Design; Building Design & Construction; Building Research and Information; Building Science; Buildings; Buildings & Landscapes; Bulletin – Association for Preservation Technology; Bulletin of Earthquake Engineering; Burgen und Schlösser; California Builder & Engineer; Canadian Architect; City & Time; Civil Engineering; Civil Engineering; the Classicist; Colorado Construction Weekly; Concrete; Concrete Products; Construction; Construction & Building Materials; Construction Bulletin; Construction Contractor; Construction Digest; Construction Digest; Construction Equipment; Construction Innovation; Construction Law Journal; Construction News; Construction Review; Constructioneer; Consulting-Specifying Engineer; Contemporary Stone & Tile Design; Crit; Cuadernos De Arquitectura Y Urbanismo; Custom Builder; Custom Home; DC Papers; De Arquitectura; Design Issues; Design Quarterly; Design Studies; Dimensions; the Dixie Contractor; Electronic Journal of Information Technology in Construction; Engineering Construction and Architectural Management; English Heritage Historical Review; ENR; Environment and Planning B, Planning and Design; Environmental Design + Construction; Fabrications; Facilities; Forum for Modern Language Studies; Future Anterior; Gestão & Tecnologia De Projetos; Glass Age; Grey Room; Haecceity Papers; Hardware Age Home Improvement Market; Home Accents Today; Home Cultures; Hospitality Design; HD; House Beautiful; ID; The International Design Magazine; Inland Architect; Interior Design; International Construction; International Journal of Lighting Research and Technology; Issues in Architecture Art and Design; Journal of Architectural and Planning Research; Journal of Architectural Education; Journal of Architectural Education; Journal of Architectural Engineering; Journal of Architecture; Journal of Asian Architecture and Building Engineering; Journal of Building Appraisal; Journal of Computing in Civil Engineering; Journal of Construction Engineering and Management; Journal of Constructional Steel Research; Journal of Earthquake Engineering; Journal of Environmental Planning and Management; Journal of Housing and the Built Environment; Journal of Housing for the Elderly; Journal of Structural Engineering; Journal of the American

Society of Architectural Historians; Journal of the Royal Asiatic Society; Journal of the Society of Architectural Historians; Journal of Urban Design; Journal of Urban Planning and Development; Landscape and Urban Planning; Lighting Research and Technology; Louisiana Contractor; Macramé: Trame E Ritagli Dell'urbanistica; Mechanics of Composite Materials and Structures; Megaron; Mid-Atlantic Construction; Midwest Construction; Midwest Contractor; Mimarlık Fakültesi Dergisi; News – Society of Architectural Historians. Southern California Chapter; Newsletter of the Association for Preservation Technology; Nexus Network Journal; Note Di Matematica; Perspecta; Perspectives in Vernacular Architecture; Places; Planning; Planning Outlook; Planning Theory & Practice; Plumbing & Mechanical; Positions; Proceedings of the ICE – Structures and Buildings; Proceedings of the ICE – Urban Design and Planning; Professional Builder; Professional Remodeler; Prosales; Prostor; Quaderni Della Ri-Vista; Remote Sensing Reviews; Renaissance Studies; Research in Engineering Design; Residential Architect; Revista Proyecto, Progreso, Arquitectura; Ri-Vista. Ricerche Per La Progettazione Del Paesaggio; Scientific American Building Monthly; Shock and Vibration; Soil Mechanics and Foundation Engineering; South Central Construction; Southwest Contractor; Der Stahlbau; The Structural Design of Tall and Special Buildings; The Structural Design of Tall Buildings; The Structural Engineer; Structural Survey; The Structurist; TD&T; Texas Construction; The Town Planning Review; Urban Design International; Vernacular Architecture; Werk, Bauen + Wohnen; Western Builder; What's New in Building; and Ýtü Dergisi/A.

Similarly, in 2013 the Columbia University Libraries listed as ejournals the following titles within 'Architecture':

3ZU; Access By Design; ACSA; Albertiana; American Architect; American Architect and Building News; Ángulo Recto; Annali Di Architettura; Annals D'arquitectura; Annuario Della R. Scuola Di Architettura in Roma; Annuario Della R. Scuola Superiore Di Architettura Di Firenze; Annuario Dell'associazione Artistica Fra I Cultori Di Architettura; AOA (Santiago); Apuntes; Archidea; Architect Designed Houses; Architect; Architects' Journal; Architectural Design; Architectural Digest; Architectural Engineering and Design Management; Architectural Glass Concepts; Architectural Heritage; Architectural History; Architectural Lighting; Architectural Record; Architectural Review; Architectural Science Review; Architectural Theory Review; Architecture; Architecture Australia; Architecture + Design; Architecture of Israel; Architektur.Aktuell; Architektúra A Urbanizmus; Architettura; Architettura Italiana; Architronic; Archivos De Arquitectura Antillana; Archnet-IJAR; Arhitektura,

Raziskave; ARQ; Arquitectura Y Urbanismo; Arts + Architecture; Arts & Crafts Homes and the Revival; Assemblage; AUS; A/Z; Baumeister; Better Homes and Gardens; Building; Building & Facilities Management; Building Design; Buildings & Landscapes; Burgen Und Schlösser; Canadian Architect; Canadian Interiors; Change Over Time; Charette; Cimaise; City & Time; Classic American Homes; Classicist; Common Bond; Competitions; Conservation Bulletin; Contemporary Stone & Tile Design; Continuité; Crit; C.R.P.R.; Cuadernos De Arquitectura; Cuadernos De La Alhambra; Cuadernos De Proyectos Arquitectónicos; Custom Builder; Custom Home; Daidalos; De arquitectura; Design Book Review; Design Cost & Data; Design Quarterly; Design Studies; Detail; Dimensions; Disegnare; DOCOMOMO Journal; Dwell; Early Homes; EGA; Eisenbahn; Ekistics; Environment and Planning. B, Planning & Design; Espaces Et Sociétés; European Architectural History Network Newsletter; Evolo; Fabrications; Facilities; Facilities Design & Management; Field; Form; Future Anterior; Gallerie Nazionali Italiane; Gestão & Tecnologia De Projetos; Giornale Degli Architetti; Glass Age; Green Places; Greensource; Grey Room; Historic Traveler; Home; Home Cultures; Hospitality Design; House & Garden; House Beautiful; Hua Zhong Jian Zhu; I Quaderni Del CNBA; Ideal Home and Garden; Inland Architect; International Journal of Architectural Computing; International Journal of Islamic Architecture; Interventions/Adaptive Reuse; Inventar Der Neueren Schweizer Architektur; Irish Arts Review Yearbook; Issues In Architecture, Art and Design; İTÜ Dergisi/A; Jianzhu Xuebao; Journal of Architectural and Planning Research; Journal of Architectural Education; Journal of Architectural Engineering; Journal of Architecture; Journal of Asian Architecture and Building Engineering; Journal of Environmental Planning and Management; Journal of Planning Education and Research; Journal of the American Planning Association; Journal of the American Society of Architectural Historians; Journal of the Society of Architectural Historians; Journal of Urban Design; Journal of Urban Planning and Development; Landscape Journal; Landscape Management; Landscape Research; Lexicon; Lighting Dimensions; Livraisons D'histoire De L'architecture; Macramè; Marg; Megaron; Memoria De Proyectos; Metropolis; Mimar; Mimarlık Fakültesi Dergisi; Mitteilungen Schweizerischer Ingenieure Und Architekten; Monu; Musiva & Sectilia; New Zealand Design Review; News – Society of Architectural Historians; Newsletter (Society of Architectural Historians of Great Britain); Newsletter of the Association for Preservation Technology; Nexus Network Journal; Old-House Interiors; Old-House Journal; Opus Incertum; Perspecta; Perspectives in Vernacular Architecture; Places; Planning; Positions; Preservation   Advocate;   Preservation   Briefs;   Preservationist;

Proceedings of the Institution of Civil Engineers; Procès-Verbaux Des Séances, Rapports De La Section Technique; Profile; Progressive Architecture; Prostor; Quaderni Della Ri-Vista; Report – Planning Advisory Service; Residential Architect; Restaurant/ Hotel Design International; Review – Society of Architectural Historians; Revista De Arquitectura; Revista De Urbanismo; Revista Proyecto, Progreso, Arquitectura; Ri-Vista; RIBA Journal; Roofing Contractor; SAH News; Schweizerische Baukunst; Shi Jie Jian Zhu; Structural Design of Tall Buildings; Swimming Pool/Spa Age; TCI; Theatre & Dance; TD&T; Thresholds; Timber Frame Homes; Time-Based Architecture International; Town Planning Review; Trama: Arquitectura Y Diseño Desde Ecuador; UME; Urban Design International; Urbanisme; Vernacular Architecture; Vernacular Architecture Newsletter; Werk; Werk-Archithese; Werk, Bauen + Wohnen; Wohnen; Xin Jian Zhu; Zeitschrift Über Das Gesamte Bauwesen.

To access these journals, you will need to visit either your university's own online library resource, or the relevant internet portal (many of which are accessible via 'Athens' or other access management system – ask your university librarian for details). Note, however, that while all the academic and more text-oriented research journals are available online, some of the more design-oriented architecture magazines are not yet available in this way, and for these you may well have to consult printed copies at a library or professional institute.

Special Collections

Your university may well have one or more special collections, often related to the city you are in and the people who have lived there. If you are not sure about the existence of these, once again, ask the librarian and/or your supervisor.

Online Resources

Many universities have invested greatly in online databases and other forms of electronic information. These can range from architecture-related data to various kinds to major national newspapers and magazines. For example, in architecture itself you might consider the following kinds of source, some of which can be accessed directly, and some of which require access via your institution's electronic library resources, or via 'Athens' or other access management system:

- *AATA Online.* Abstracts of literature related to the preservation and conservation of material cultural heritage, including works of art, material culture, and archaeological and architectural sites and materials. www.aata.getty.edu/Home.

- *Abacus USA Construction Index*. Directory of 1,500 websites, online documents, case studies and newsletters for US construction professionals, including architects, engineers and surveyors. Mainly US-based. Can be browsed or searched. Internet subject gateway. www.construction-index.com.
- *Architecture.com*. Web portal on the built environment, maintained by the RIBA. www.architecture.com.
- *Architecture: Basic Resources for Research*. Web page with a range of advice, references and links on many different aspects of architecture. Produced by the Avery Architectural & Fine Arts Library at Columbia University. www.library.columbia.edu/indiv/avery/guides/architecture.html#databases.
- *Architecture and Building*. Web page with a range of advice, references and links on many different aspects of architecture. Produced by the Architecture Studies Library at the University of Nevada. www.library.unlv.edu/arch/rsrce/webresources/.
- *Art, Design and Architecture Collection*. Includes the specialist indexes ARTbibliographies Modern (covering modern and contemporary art), Design and Applied Arts Index (aspects of design and crafts) and the International Bibliography of Art (covering scholarship on Western art history) etc. www.proquest.co.uk.
- *Art Images for College Teaching*. Royalty-free image exchange resource for the educational community. www.quod.lib.umich.edu/a/aict.
- *Art On File*. Images on architecture, parks, public art, sustainable design and sculpture parks, aimed at educators. www.artonfile.com.
- *ARTstor*. Searchable database of over one million digital images and associated catalogue data. Includes architecture, painting, sculpture, photography, decorative arts and design. Also includes images from the Columbia Image Bank: History of Art and Architecture. www.artstor.org.
- *Barbour Compendium*. Database of technical and product information for construction and health and safety experts, comprising product catalogues, regulatory documents, and directory information for manufacturers. www.barbourproductsearch.info.
- *Bibliography of the History of Art (BHA)*. Citations and abstracts for articles on Western, European and American art history periodicals and other publications. Coverage ranges from 1973 to the present. www.library.getty.edu/bha.
- *Bridgeman Education*. Visual resource offering over 410,000 images sourced directly from museums, galleries, private collections and contemporary artists all copyright cleared for educational use. www.bridgemaneducation.com.
- *Building Research Establishment*. A research, consultancy and testing company for the built environment. www.bre.co.uk.

- *CIRIA (Construction Industry Research and Information Association)*. Independent UK company owned by other companies, universities, government departments and other public sector agencies, organizations and regulators from the construction and related industries. www.ciria.org.
- *Cities and Buildings Database*. Collection of over 5,000 images of buildings and cities drawn from across time and throughout the world. www.washington.edu/ark2/.
- *Construction and Building Abstracts*. Index of literature on civil engineering and building. Includes abstracts. www.cbaweb. co.uk.
- *DAAI: Design and Applied Arts Index*. Source of abstracts and bibliographic records for articles, news items and reviews published in design and applied arts periodicals from 1973 onwards. www. proquest.co.uk.
- *Digimap*. Online digital mapping and data extraction facilities using Ordnance Survey data of Great Britain. www.digimap.edina. ac.uk.
- *Digimap – Historic Digimap*. Online access to UK historic Ordnance Survey maps from Landmark Information Group. www.digimap. edina.ac.uk.
- *Emporis Research*. Database of information and images on the building industry, providing worldwide coverage of current and historical building projects. www.research.emporis.com.
- *English Heritage*. UK government's statutory advisor on the English historic environment and buildings. www.english-heritage. org.uk.
- *Getty Images*. Stock photo agency, supplying images for business and consumers with an archive of 80 million still images and illustrations and more than 50,000 hours of stock film footage. Largely aimed at creative professionals, the media and corporate markets. www.gettyimages.com.
- *Google Image Search*. Search for images on the web. www.images. google.com.
- *Google Scholar*. Service from the Google search-engine providers, which searches articles from academic publishers, professional societies and pre-print archives. www.scholar.google.co.uk.
- *Great Buildings Collection*. Gateway to information on a thousand buildings and hundreds of leading architects. Also good for images. www.greatbuildings.com.
- *Historic American Buildings Survey (HABS), Historic American Engineering Record (HAER) and Historic American Landscape Survey (HAL)*. Digitized images on architecture, engineering and design. www.memory.loc.gov/ammem/collections/habs_haer/.
- *ICONDA*. Index of literature on all aspects of planning and building. www.ovidsp.tx.ovid.com.

- *Images of England.* Photographic record of England's listed buildings, produced by English Heritage. www.imagesofengland.org.uk.
- *Intute.* Index to internet resources selected, indexed and described by subject and information specialists. Focus on resources for teaching, learning and research. www.intute.ac.uk.
- *JISC MediaHub.* Multimedia platform offering digital image, video and audio collections accessible from a single interface. Free at the point of use. Includes cross-searching across all collections and ability to source content from a wide range of content-providers through a thumbnail and metadata search portal. www.jiscmediahub.ac.uk.
- *NYPL Digital Gallery.* Provides free and open access to over 800,000 images digitized from The New York Public Library, including illuminated manuscripts, historical maps, vintage posters, rare prints, photographs and more. www.digitalgallery.nypl.org.
- *Prints & Photographs Online Catalog, Library of Congress.* Contains catalogue records and digital images, including photographs, fine and popular prints and drawings, posters and architectural and engineering drawings. While international in scope, the collections are particularly focused on the USA. www.loc.gov/pictures/.
- *Oxford Art Online.* Full-text encyclopedia on architects, architectural history, architectural styles and movements. www.oxfordartonline.com.
- *Pidgeon Digital.* Collection of illustrated talks by architects and related designers, to which new talks are being added regularly. www.pidgeondigital.com.
- *Research Guides.* Web page with a range of advice, references and links on many different aspects of architecture. Produced by the Environmental Design Library at UC Berkeley. www.lib.berkeley.edu/ENVI/research_guides.html#architecture.
- *RIBApix.* Database of more than 35,000 architectural images taken from the photograph and drawing collections of the RIBA. Low resolution images are free to download. www.ribapix.com.
- *Sapling (Architecture, Planning and Landscape Information Gateway).* Gateway to websites on topics related to architecture, planning and landscape. UK-based, but including international resources. www.sapling.info.
- *SAHARA.* Digital images, created from submissions by members of the Society of Architectural Historians in the USA. www.sah.org/publications-and-research/sahara.
- *SPIRO.* Visual online public access to the images of the Architecture Visual Resources Library (AVRL) at the University of California Berkeley, with over 250,000 slides and 20,000 photographs. Open internet access. www.mip.berkeley.edu/spiro/.

- *ULI Development Case Studies*. Over 300 detailed case studies of completed projects ranging from low-income housing to mixed-use downtown developments to commercial and industrial projects development process. Covers projects from 1985 to the present. www.casestudies.uli.org.
- *VADS*. Portfolio of visual art collections comprising over 100,000 images that are freely available and copyright cleared for use in learning, teaching and research in the UK. www.vads.ac.uk.

Outside of the subject of architecture, you might also consider online sources such as the following. Most will require access via your institution's electronic library resources, or via 'Athens' or other access management system:

- *America: History and Life*. Database of literature covering the history and culture of the United States and Canada, from prehistory to the present. Selective indexing for over 1,700 journals from 1955 to present. Also provides full-text coverage of more than 230 journals and nearly 100 books. Includes citations and links to book and media reviews. www.ebscohost.com/academic/america-history-and-life-with-full-text.
- *ARCHON/Archives Online*. Includes contact details for record repositories in the United Kingdom and also for institutions elsewhere in the world which have substantial collections of manuscripts noted under the indexes to the National Register of Archives. www.nationalarchives.gov.uk/archon/.
- *Books in Print*. Authoritative source of bibliographic information with powerful search, discovery and collection development tools. www.booksinprint.com.
- *Centre for Research Libraries*. Collects newspapers, journals, documents, archives, and other traditional and digital resources from a global network of sources. www.crl.edu.
- *Columbia University*. Very impressive listing of linkages to university and other libraries and archives. The latter, an enormous archives listing, ranges from the NASA Historical Archive and the United States Holocaust Museum to the American Institute of Architects and the Smithsonian Institution Archives of American Art. www.columbia.edu/cu/lweb/eresources/catalogs/index.html and www.library.columbia.edu/eguides.html.
- *COPAC*. Unified access to the catalogues of some of the largest university research libraries in the UK and Ireland. www.copac.ac.uk.
- *Dictionary of National Biography*. National UK record of those who have shaped British history and culture, worldwide, from the ancient world to the present. www.oxforddnb.com.

- *Geobase.* Multidisciplinary database supplying bibliographic information and abstracts for development studies, Earth sciences, ecology, geomechanics, human geography and oceanography. Covers 2,000 international journals, including peer-reviewed and trade publications. Contains over 1.4 million records from 1980 to present. www.ovid.com.
- *Historical Abstracts.* Covers the history of the world (excluding the United States and Canada) focusing on the fifteenth century forward, including world history, military history, women's history and history of education. Provides indexing of more than 3,100 academic historical journals in over 40 languages back to 1955. www.ebscohost.com/academic/historical-abstracts.
- *Index to 19th Century American Art Periodicals (AAI).* Indexes 42 art journals published in the US during the nineteenth century. Covers articles, art notes, stories, illustrations, poems and advertisements, with information on artists and illustrators, painting, sculpture, drawing, photography, architecture and design. www. ebscohost.com/academic/index-to-19th-century-american-art.
- *Institute of Historical Research.* Provides linkages to history resources globally. www.history.ac.uk/digital/resources.
- *National Register of Archives.* The official archive and publisher for the UK government, and for England and Wales. www.nra. nationalarchives.gov.uk/nra/.
- *ProQuest Dissertations & Theses (PQDT).* World's most comprehensive collection of dissertations and theses, official digital dissertations archive for the Library of Congress and database of record for graduate research. Includes three million searchable citations to dissertation and theses from around the world from 1743 to the present day together with over one million full-text dissertations available for download. Offers full text for dissertations added since 1997 and strong retrospective full-text coverage for older works. www.proquest.co.uk/en-UK/catalogs/ databases/detail/pqdt.shtml.
- *Rutgers University Library Guide.* Provides a large range of linkages for both history and other disciplinary sources worldwide. www.libguides.rutgers.edu/home.
- *Social Sciences Citation Index.* Covers more than 2,470 journals encompassing 50 social science disciplines, as well as over 3,500 notable scientific and technical journals. Range of coverage is from the year 1956 to the present day. www.webofknowledge. com.

As you can tell from all the sources listed above, there is a vast range of information online, and you should ask your university librarian to advise you on what is available either at or via your own institution.

Other Libraries and Archives

You will not, of course, find everything you need in your own architecture library or via your university's online system. Although many books and articles may be ordered on inter-library loan, at some point you will want to move off-campus and get stuck into some serious digging around. This is where the real fun starts, and if at first it seems a little intimidating, then don't worry. Most people feel unsure of themselves when they first go to a new archive, or arrange an interview – but once you get into it, it soon becomes much easier than you might have thought.

There is an enormous variety of other libraries and archives which you might want to consult, and it is impossible to list all of them here. The best place to find the archives relevant to your research is often the footnotes and bibliography of the books related to your subject. Relevant libraries and archives can be relatively easily located using the internet, and many resources also now allow you to search their catalogues online, so at least you can see what they have before setting off for a visit. Some of the most useful include the following.

National Architectural Libraries

Many countries have one or more libraries with international standard collections of architectural material and where you can find journals, books and other publications on architecture from all around the world. If you need to make a very detailed inquiry into architectural theory or history, particularly for older subjects, you may well need to visit this kind of library. The best architectural libraries include:

- In the USA, the *Avery Library* at Columbia University in New York. www.library.columbia.edu/indiv/avery.html.
- In the UK, the *British Architectural Library* at the RIBA in London. www.architecture.com. Also has very good drawing and photograph collections.

National Copyright Libraries

A 'copyright' library should, in theory, have a copy of absolutely every book or journal published in the country's own language and on all subjects, not just architecture (although in practice some of the more obscure architecture publications are easier to find at more specialist collections such as those at the RIBA or Avery). Copyright libraries include:

- *British Library.* In London and Boston Spa and with a separate newspaper and magazine collection in London. www.bl.uk
- *Bodleian Library.* Oxford. www.bodleian.ox.ac.uk

- *Library and Archives Canada (L.A.C.).* Ottawa. www.bac-lac.gc.ca
- *Library of Congress.* Washington. www.loc.gov
- *National Library of Australia.* Canberra. www.nla.gov.au
- *National Library of Scotland.* Edinburgh. www.nls.uk
- *National Library of Wales.* Aberystwyth. www.llgc.org.uk

Most European national libraries can be located through the European Library (www.theeuropeanlibrary.org). A full worldwide listing of national libraries is available at www.wikipedia.org/wiki/List_of_national_and_state_libraries, while www.worldcat.org connects the collections and services of more than 10,000 libraries worldwide, covering over 1.5 billion items.

Research Libraries, Special Collections and Archives

These can offer a bewildering range of specialist information, from architecture, films and design to agriculture, biographical archives and cult interests. The best way to find these is through the internet, and a search through some of the following sites should help you to locate what you need. A few of the collections that you can access through the internet are also fully online, so you may not even have to leave your desk in order to access them.

City, Public and Local Libraries

These are often particularly good for dissertation topics which are based on your local city. They can usually provide highly detailed information on such topics as city development and growth, topographical maps and photographs, street life, local industry and commerce, transport, population figures and archaeological data. Local history groups can usually also be contacted through local libraries.

City Government Offices

Like local libraries, the various offices of the city government can often provide data that would be completely irretrievable through any other source. The actual organization of this material varies greatly from city to city and country to country, but of particular use are those offices which deal with planning in particular and with public works in general. Whatever the municipal system of your own city, you should be able to obtain information on such matters as planning applications, city plans, zoning and any civic building, as well as official statistics, local laws, city demographics etc.

Overseas Archives

Access to these is often difficult and, as noted above, will probably need prior verbal or written contact, with letters of recommendation. You will need to understand bureaucratic procedures, which may vary from country to country. In some archives, source material may not be made available if it is in use at the same time by another researcher. You should always check in advance so that you do not have a wasted journey.

Personal Archives

Personal papers and other documents may be in the possession of relatives and/or have access controlled by them. You may have to be very careful how you handle these, particularly if they are not in good condition, as you do not want to be held responsible for any deterioration in their condition. It is useful to check how they have been stored before you visit and inspect personal archives. You may also need to check whether you need to wear gloves to handle them or keep them out of bright light. Damage to personal papers leads not only to a loss of research knowledge but also of personal memory for the owner, so it is important to be very careful.

The Internet

As already noted above, an increasing amount of material is readily available on the internet. Apart from the archives and libraries identified above, a whole raft of other people are now putting material onto their internet sites. These include companies and other institutions, government bodies and special-interest groups.

Websites and Links

Some architects also have their own internet sites. So if you want to interview an architect, or need more details about a particular project, before contacting them directly you should make sure that the information you need is not freely available on the internet.

An excellent set of architecture-related links is hosted by the University of Nevada, Las Vegas, and can be found at www.library.unlv. edu/arch/rsrce/webresources. This set of links is organised under the following headings:

- *Reference Tools.* Accessibility/universal design; bibliographies; biographical/directory information; dictionaries, encyclopedias, thesauri; education-related; indexes to print material; information databases and image banks; internet sites: lists and architecture search engines; library catalogues; miscellaneous; product and manufacturer information; and technical information.
- *Resources.* Accessibility/universal design; architects and designers – libraries; architectural anthropology; architectural archives; architectural firms; architectural services; architecture and music; associations (selected list); blogs; booksellers and

publishers; building industry information; building types/styles; buildings; campus planning; competitions; databases; computing bibliographies, links, organizations, software, tutorials/use tips; consultants; contractors and builders; cyberspace; design: interior, industrial, graphic; digital projects; discussion groups, lists, newsgroups; education-related, accredited school links, alphabetical list of selected professional programs, continuing education, directories, ecological/environmental/sustainable design, educational initiatives, learning materials, online video collections, theses; electronic publications; facility and project management; GIS (geographic information systems); government publications, sites; green design/sustainable resources, energy efficiency; historic preservation; history; houses and house plans; housing; HVAC; image collections; indexes to print material; internet sites: lists and architecture search engines; jobs; landscape architecture, plants; Las Vegas & Clark County, Nevada; libraries, guides to library materials, librarians, library catalogues, websites; lighting; maps; news; places; planning; product and manufacturer information, furnishings, green products, housing applications, landscape lighting, miscellaneous; real estate; research, centres and groups, databases, papers and case studies, tools; safety; signs; standards and codes; themed architecture; tiles; urban environment, neighbourhoods; virtual galleries; women.

Another great set of links is provided by the Environmental Design Library at UC Berkeley, and is organized under the following headings:

- *General Research.* Book Review Sources for Environmental Design; Browser's Guide to Architecture; Buildings & Places; Citation Styles, Plagiarism & Style Manuals; Critical Evaluation of Resources; Designing a Research Strategy; How to Find a UCB Thesis or Dissertation; Image Sources for the Built Environment; Job Hunting; Library Research Using Primary Sources; Scholarly, Trade and Popular Journals: How to Identify Them; UC Berkeley Buildings & Campus Research Guide; Videos – Environmental Design Videotapes in the Media Resources Center; Other Useful Guides.
- *Architecture.* ADA & Universal Design; American Architecture; American Cultural Landscapes; Arch 170: History of Arch & Urbanism; Architecture Resources Online; Basic Reference Sources; Biographical Information; Book Reviews; Browser's Guide to Architecture: NAs; Building & Landscape Types; Building Codes & Regulatory Resources; Building Science; Building Science History; Climatic Design; Construction Resources; Daylighting & Lighting Design; Design Drawing; Design Methods & Design Research; Designing a Research Strategy; Finding Information on

Buildings & Places; Green Design Resources; Heating; Ventilation & Air Conditioning; Historic Preservation; History of Architecture; History of Asian Architecture; Landscape Architecture and Urbanism; Image Sources; Indexes & Abstracts; Job Hunting; Library Design; Local Information: American Cultures; Periodical & Newspaper Indexes; Professional Practice; Sacred Space; San Francisco Bay Area Architects & Architecture; Social & Cultural Factors in Environmental Design; Solar Design; Sundials; Teaching Architecture; Theses & Dissertations; Thesis & Dissertation Research; UC Berkeley Buildings & Campus Research Guide; Urban Design; Vernacular Architecture; Videos.

- *City & Regional Planning.* American Communities; Basic Research Resources; Biography; California Planning; Community Economic Development; Finding Local Information; General Plans; Handbooks & Professional Practice; Historic Preservation; History of Asian Architecture; Landscape Architecture, and Urbanism; History of City Planning; Housing Research; Indexes & Abstracts; International Planning; Preparing for Thesis Research; Social & Cultural Factors in Environmental Design; Sprawl & the New Urbanism; Statistics & Data: International; Statistics & Data: US; Transportation Planning; Urban Design.
- *Landscape Architecture & Environmental Planning.* Beatrix Farrand: A Bibliography of Her Life & Work; Biography; Building & Landscape Types; California Landscape Architecture; Construction; Environmental Planning; Finding Local Information – American Cultures; Historic Preservation; History and Literature of Landscape Architecture; History of Asian Architecture, Landscape Architecture, and Urbanism; Image Sources for the Built Environment; Indexes & Abstracts: Environmental Planning; Indexes & Abstracts: Landscape Architecture; LA 101 – Fundamentals of Landscape Design; LA 170 – History and Literature of Landscape Architecture; LA 171 – The American Designed Landscape Since 1850; Landscape Architecture Online; Landscape Architecture Professional Practice; Preparing for Thesis Research; Reference Sources; Social & Cultural Factors in Environmental Design.
- *Urban Design.* Book Review Sources; Building & Landscape Types; Design Methods & Design Research; Finding General Plans; Finding Information on Buildings & Places; Finding Local Information; History of City Planning; Preparing for Thesis Research; Social & Cultural Factors in Environmental Design; Sprawl & the New Urbanism; Urban Design.
- *Visual Studies.* Art Indexes; Art Portals; Biographical Sources; Organizations, Art-Related; Photography.

The Boston University Library offers a web-based guide to research in architecture at www.bu.edu/library/guides/architect.html. This covers general architecture sites, image sources, special topics such as film and architecture, bibliographic guides, indices for periodicals and dissertations, library catalogues and other useful information.

Although more planning- than architecture-oriented, also worth looking at is Cyburbia, www.cyburbia.org, a portal site for urban planners and others interested in cities and the built environment. It contains a selective directory of internet resources relevant to planning and urbanism. Cyburbia also includes information about mailing lists and newsgroups, and hosts an active bulletin board and image-hosting gallery.

Searching

When conducting searches on the internet, as with library catalogues, it is best to use a number of different key words and search engines as results can be extremely variable. Make sure you use the advanced search features of search engines such as Google, bing, Yahoo, Ask and AOL Search. If you see any useful links, make an immediate note of the URL address or add a bookmark – it is very easy to move on and to forget what you have seen, even from just a few minutes before.

Information

Exactly what information you will obtain obviously depends greatly on the subject you are investigating and the sources available to you. As with libraries, you may find a number of useful books, articles and statements. Unlike libraries, however, you may also find illustrations, document archives and other materials which can be directly downloaded for inspection at a later date. Contacts (names, email addresses, postal addresses) and links to other sites are also often obtainable.

Some internet sites, especially those on special-interest topics, also offer various forms of online discussion groups where you can pose specific questions which you may want to ask. Before doing so, however, make sure that you have checked out all the recent discussions. On the internet it is considered bad protocol to repeat oft-stated requests and questions when that information is already available.

Note-taking

When you have found something useful, you can do the same kind of note-taking that you might do in a library or paper-based archive. On the internet you also have another choice, which is to simply download or cut-and-paste the whole of a page into another program on your computer. This can be very useful, but beware that the same kind of rules apply here as to photocopying – just because you have a copy of something does not mean that you have read it, still less thought about it. So try to be reasonably selective with your collecting procedures.

Recording Sources

As with all research, you have to be very careful on the internet to make sure that you carefully note down the source from which you gathered your information. This is particularly true of the internet, because the ability to download or copy over whole pages means that you will then have a complete, digital transcription of the source, ready to be used in your dissertation. Although this may seem to be a huge advantage (such as for extended quotations), it also means that unless you are extremely fastidious in your working methods it is very easy indeed to end up unintentionally plagiarizing a source. There are therefore two things that you need to note for any piece of information gained from the internet.

1   *URL.* First, you need to know the URL – web address, usually begin-
    ning with www – of the internet site concerned. Ideally, this should
    be from the exact page rather than the general site address, such
    as 'www.hughpearman.com/2010/02.html' and not just 'www.
    hughpearman.com'. In order to do this, it is often easiest to copy
    and paste the URL, along with the information related to it, into a
    word-processing or similar program on your computer. (If you do
    this, ensure that you save the word-processing document at regular
    intervals as internet access can often cause computers to crash.)
2   *Date.* The other thing you need to know is the date at which
    you accessed the website; for example 'www.hughpearman.
    com/2010/02.html (accessed 6 June 2012)'.

Besides the information and guidance given above, there are also several other things to bear in mind when researching on the internet. If you are going to do a great deal of internet-based research for an extended dissertation, you might consider consulting a specialist guide such as Claire Hewson, *Internet Research Methods: a Practical Guide for the Social and Behavioural Sciences* (2012), Niall O'Dochartaigh, *Internet Research Skills* (2012) and Nigel Ford, *The Essential Guide to Using the Web for Research* (2011). However, for most architecture students following a few simple rules will suffice. Ruth Kamen, formerly Director of the RIBA British Architecture Library, recommends the following two main areas to watch out for:

1   *Reliability*
    •   With what authority has the website been written? Is the author,
        publisher or sponsor clearly identified? Was this resource
        found from another resource that is considered reliable? Do
        other reliable resources link to it?
    •   What is the content and scope of the website? What is the point
        of view? Is it biased? Is it a spoof? Does the information appear

to be accurate and/or complete? Can you verify it in other sources? Are there references to additional resources?

- Is the website current? Is information up to date? Are there dates on the page to indicate when the page was written, when it was first published on the web, and/or when it was last revised? If not, can you discover this by, for example, viewing page information or page source?

2   *Evaluation*

- Be an internet detective, and consider whether the URL contains a clue. For example, in www.sah.org 'sah' refers to the Society of Architectural Historians in the USA.
- Look at the domain suffix, which can you tell whether the website's producer is educational, non-profit, commercial, etc. For example, .ac=academic, .co=commercial, .com=commercial, .edu=educational, .gov=governmental, .net=Internet Service Provider, .org=non-profit making organisation.
- Which country does the website come from? For example, .de=Germany, dk=Denmark, fr=France, nl=Netherlands, uk=United Kingdom, .com=USA or international.
- Who published the page? In general, the publisher is the agency or person operating the server computer from which the document is issued. The server is usually named in the first portion of the URL, between http:// and the first /, as with UCL for http://www.ucl.ac.uk/library/uselib.shtml.
- Is the website someone's personal site? To discover this, read the URL carefully and look to see if the server is a commercial ISP or other provider of web page hosting (like aol.com). And look for a personal name (e.g. iborden or borden) following a tilde (~) or the word 'users' or 'people'.
- Consider who is responsible for the website and who wrote it. For example, click on 'home' or 'homepage' or perhaps on a logo. Truncate back along the URL (also a good trick if you get a 'page not found' message). Look for 'about us' or 'biography.' Click on 'email' or 'contact'. Or view the page source.

References

1 Henry Russell Hitchcock, *Architecture: Nineteenth and Twentieth Centuries* (Harmondsworth: Penguin, 1958).

2 Colin Rowe, *The Mathematics of the Ideal Villa and Other Essays* (Cambridge, Mass.: MIT, 1977).

3 Erwin Panofsky, *Gothic Architecture and Scholasticism* (London: Thames & Hudson, 1957).

4 Robert Venturi, Denise Scott Brown and Stephen Izenour, *Learning from Las Vegas* (Cambridge, Mass.: MIT, 1972).

5 Nikolaus Pevsner, *Pioneers of the Modern Movement: from William Morris to Walter Gropius* (London: Faber, 1936).

6 Charles Jencks, *The Architecture of the Jumping Universe: A Polemic. How Complexity Science is Changing Architecture and Culture* (London: Academy, 1995).

7 Heinrich Wölfflin, *Renaissance and Baroque* (London: Fontana, 1964).

8 Mark Girouard, *Life in the English Country House: a Social and Architectural History* (New Haven: Yale University Press, 1978); and Spiro Kostof, *A History of Architecture: Settings and Rituals* (Oxford: Oxford University Press, 1985).

9 Anthony Vidler, *Claude-Nicolas Ledoux* (Cambridge, Mass.: MIT Press, 1990).

10 See, for example, Manfredo Tafuri, *Architecture and Utopia* (Cambridge, Mass.: MIT, 1976).

11 See, for example, Jane Rendell, Barbara Penner and Iain Borden (eds), *Gender, Space, Architecture: an Interdisciplinary Introduction* (London: Routledge, 2000); Dolores Hayden, *Redesigning the American Dream: the Future of Housing, Work, and Family Life* (New York. W.W. Norton, 1984); Diane Agrest, Patricia Conway and Leslie Kanes Weisman (eds), *The Sex of Architecture* (New York: Harry N. Abrams, 1996); and Deborah Coleman, Elizabeth Danze and Carol Henderson (eds), *Architecture and Feminism* (New York: Princeton Architectural Press, 1996).

12 Mary Lutyens, *Edwin Lutyens* (London: Murray, 1980).

13 Reyner Banham, *Theory and Design in the First Machine Age* (London: Architectural Press, 1960).

14 Sigfried Giedion, *Space, Time and Architecture: the Growth of a New Tradition* (Cambridge, Mass.: Harvard University Press, 1941).

15 Mark Gottdiener, *Postmodern Semiotics: Material Culture and the Forms of Postmodern Life* (Oxford: Blackwell, 1995).

16 Jennifer Bloomer, *Architecture and the Text: the (S)crypts of Joyce and Piranesi* (New Haven: Yale University Press, 1993).

17 Anthony Vidler, *The Architectural Uncanny: Essays in the Modern Unhomely* (Cambridge, Mass.: MIT Press, 1992); and Diana Fuss and Joel Sanders, 'Berggasse 19: Inside Freud's Office', Joel Sanders (ed.), *Stud: Architectures of Masculinity* (New York: Princeton Architectural Press, 1996), pp. 112–39.

18 Juhani Pallasmaa, *The Eyes of the Skin: Architecture and the Senses,* (Chichester: John Wiley, third edition, 2012); and Jorge Otero-Pailos, *Architecture's Historical Turn: Phenomenology and the Rise of the Postmodern* (Minneapolis: University of Minnesota Press, 2010).

19 Ross King, *Emancipating Space: Geography, Architecture and Urban Design* (New York: Guilford, 1996).

20 Zeynep Çelik, *Urban Forms and Colonial Confrontations: Algiers Under French Rule* (Berkeley: University of California Press, 1997); and Abidin Kusno, *Behind the Post-Colonial: Architecture, Urban Space and Political Cultures in Indonesia* (London and New York: Routledge, 2000).

21 Iain Borden and Jane Rendell (eds), *InterSections: Architectural Histories and Critical Theories* (London: Routledge, 2000).

22 Alice Coleman, *Utopia on Trial: Vision and Reality in Planned Housing* (London: Hilary Shipman, 1985).

23 Anthony King, *The Bungalow: the Production of a Global Culture* (Oxford: Oxford University Press, 1995).

24 Kim Dovey, *Framing Places: Mediating Power in Built Form* (London: Routledge, 1999); and Thomas A. Markus, *Buildings and Power: Freedom and Control in the Origin of Building Types* (London: Routledge, 1993).

25 Michael Sorkin, *Exquisite Corpse:* Writing on Buildings (London: Verso, 1991).
26 Paul Shepheard, *What is Architecture? An Essay on Landscapes, Buildings, and Machines* (Cambridge, Mass.: MIT, 1994).
27 Jun'ichiro Tanizaki, *In Praise of Shadows* (New Haven: Leete's, 1977).
28 Jane Rendell, *Site-Writing: the Architecture of Art Criticism* (London: IB Tauris, 2010).

4 Writing

There are many ways to skin a rabbit. Writing is no different, and authors adopt a wide range of techniques, procedures and tricks in order to produce and structure their material. The advice in this chapter therefore should not be taken as a set of rules that you should follow exactly. That said, much of what is contained here summarizes much of what might be considered to be 'best practice' in dissertation writing. As with the other chapters in this book, if you follow the procedures outlined here, then you should be able to produce work of a high standard.

A large number of books offer general advice on writing and referencing, which you might also like to consult. Some of the most popular include:

> Judith Butcher, Caroline Drake and Maureen Leach, *Butcher's Copy-editing: the Cambridge Handbook for Editors, Copy-editors and Proofreaders* (Cambridge: Cambridge University Press, third edition, 2006).
> *The Chicago Manual of Style* (Chicago: University of Chicago Press, sixteenth edition, 2010).
> Roy Peter Clark, *Writing Tools: 50 Essential Strategies for Every Writer* (London: Little Brown Book Group, 2008).
> *New Oxford Style Manual* (Oxford: Oxford University Press, 2010).
> The Economist, *The Economist Style Guide* (London: Economist Books, tenth edition, 2012).
> Ernest Gowers, *The Complete Plain Words* (London: Penguin, third revised edition, 1987).
> Martin Manser and Stephen Curtis, *The Penguin Writer's Manual* (London: Penguin, 2002).

MLA Handbook for Writers of Research Papers (New York: Modern Language Association of America, seventh edition, 2009).

Glanville Price and Brian Richardson (eds), *MHRA Style Guide: a Handbook for Authors, Editors, and Writers of Theses* (London: Modern Humanities Research Association, 2008).

William Strunk and E.B. White, *The Elements of Style* (London: Collier Macmillan, fourth edition, 2000).

Andrea Sutcliffe (ed.), *New York Public Library Writer's Guide to Style and Usage* (HarperResource, 1994).

Kate Turabian, *A Manual for Writers of Term Papers, Theses and Dissertations: Chicago Style for Students and Researchers* (Chicago: University Of Chicago Press, seventh edition, 2007).

Nicholas Walliman, *Your Undergraduate Dissertation: the Essential Guide for Success* (London: Sage, 2007).

Kevin Wilson and Jennifer Wauson, *The AMA Handbook of Business Writing* (New York: AMACOM, 2010).

Structuring a Dissertation

The most basic rule in structuring any coursework – an essay as well as a dissertation – is a triad:

```
1   SAY WHAT YOU ARE GOING TO SAY
2   SAY IT
3   SAY THAT YOU HAVE SAID IT
```

In other words, you should first introduce your subject in order to let the reader know what it is you are trying to explore. Second, you need to conduct your exposition. Third, you should retrace in summary form the ground which you have previously covered. In practice, this means adopting the following structure:

1   Introduction
2   Main argument, divided into a number of sections or chapters
3   Conclusion.

Each of these parts of a dissertation performs a specific role. It is important that you understand what these roles are, and how they are carried out.

Introduction (Say What You Are Going To Say)

The introduction to your dissertation is exactly that: an introduction for the reader which explains the main content, arguments and structure of what they are about to read. As such, the introduction both orientates the reader by letting them know what lies ahead and whets their appetite by providing a few clues as to what is going to be discussed.

Architectural students often get quite worried about the introduction to their dissertation, but in fact there is no reason for this as the introduction can be simply divided into five main components. The introduction should cover:

1   *Objects of study*. Here you should briefly summarize the subject, indicating the main objects of study. This can be a simple statement identifying the main architects, buildings, texts, other cultural media, etc. that the dissertation investigates.
2   *Interpretive ideas*. Here you should introduce the main theoretical and other intellectual ideas you are bringing to bear on the subject. What are the main themes you investigate? Are there any particular sets of ideas which you use to do this?
3   *Academic context*. In order that the reader has some idea of the originality of your own work, you should briefly identify other work already completed by other historians and theorists, and note how your own work is different. In short, what work has already been done on this subject, and what new ground are you covering?
4   *Methodology*. Here you should briefly summarize the procedure you will be adopting. Is this a piece of history, theory or personal writing? Is it, for example, a piece of politicized history or a social science investigation?
5   *Dissertation structure*. This is simply a description of each section in turn – as has been done for the introduction to this book under the heading 'The Guidebook'.

You do not need to write a very lengthy introduction to your dissertation, and this should comprise no more than 20 per cent of the total wordage. For example, for a dissertation of 10,000 words in total, the introduction should be no more than 2,000 words of that total and often shorter. If you then also allow 300–400 words for each of the five sub-sections and write each one in turn, you will quickly find that the introduction is completed without too much pain or heartache.

Main Argument (Say It)

This is where the most important part of the dissertation is located – the investigation of architecture according to the questions and ideas which you pose of it. In order to achieve this target as clearly and successfully as possible, you should deploy the following five tactics.

1   *Sub-division*. Divide the main body of the dissertation into approximately three to seven chapters or sections. Each of these sections should deal with a distinct aspect of the dissertation in

turn. Deciding exactly what these sections are, and the sequence in which they run, is one of the single most important acts when writing a dissertation.

2   *Section focus.* Each section should be carefully focused on its selected topic. In other words, stick to the point. Try to keep various asides, discursions and any other extra information to a minimum. Your dissertation will be most successful if you select your particular theme for each section and doggedly pursue it.

3   *Section size.* Keep each section to approximately the same size. Assuming once again that the dissertation is 10,000 words in total, and you have used approximately 2,500 words for the introduction and the conclusion, then clearly you have about 7,500 words for the main argument. You then subdivide this again to produce, say, five sections of 1,500 words each. Alternatively, if you are dealing with a larger dissertation, the same process still holds – take the total number of words available to you, excluding introduction and conclusion, and divide that figure up into the appropriate number of sections on which you are working.

4   *Section linking.* Link each section with the next. It is often helpful to the reader if they are guided through the dissertation. To do this, you can provide linking paragraphs at the end and/or beginning of each section, very quickly summarizing where your investigation has got to and where it is going next.

5   *Section writing.* Work out exactly what you want to put in each section and then write each in turn. Although working on a computer sometimes makes it tempting to adopt the scatter-gun approach to writing, doing a bit here and a bit there, most people find it easier to work section by section through their dissertation. This not only lets you keep your own mental health in order, as you have to cope with only one issue or question at a time, it also allows you to keep a careful eye on how well you are progressing. (For more advice on writing, see below.)

Conclusion (Say That You Have Said It)

As with the introduction, many students get somewhat worried about the conclusion to their dissertation. However, there are really only two things that you need to do here.

1   *Summary statement.* You simply need to remind the reader of your argument and interpretations, drawing out the most salient points. Remember that although you will have written, redrafted and reread your dissertation many times, the reader will have been through it only once and will thus be much less familiar with your material. A simple recapitulation in the conclusion is of great help to a reader in recalling what they have just read.

2 *Speculation.* The conclusion is also the place where you might speculate upon the value of your investigations for architecture in general and perhaps outline any work that might be done in the future. Sometimes, particularly with dissertations that deal with contemporary topics, you can introduce a piece of 'late-breaking news' here, providing another twist or turn to the events that you have been covering (such as the developer has merged with a large one, the architect has won a new competition, a new theory has recently emerged).

The conclusion is often slightly shorter than the introduction, and as a general rule should be approximately 5–10 per cent of the total dissertation length.

Working Methods

One of the most difficult things to do when working on a dissertation (and indeed to give advice about) is actually doing the writing. Nearly everyone you might speak to about this will have a slightly different way of going about it, and in the end you must do what suits you best. However, once again, there a number of very useful tricks and techniques which you may find helpful in smoothing your passage through the writing process.

Reviewing Notes

In order to write your dissertation, it is obviously extremely useful if you have an intimate knowledge of the material which you have gathered together during your research. This may sound obvious, but many people spend a lot of their writing time just going through their notes and files searching for something which they half-remember having written down. Conversely, knowing exactly what is in your notes and where to find the relevant information will immensely speed up your writing and also improve your argument.

You should therefore review and read your notes thoroughly before writing, and review them at frequent stages. Some people find it helpful to carefully arrange their notes: numbering pages, organizing them into rough groups, filing them into discrete data folders and so on. Others even go so far as to prepare a rough index of their notes for all the main subjects that they wish to include in their dissertation – if you can bear to do this, it may well save you a lot of time later on, particularly if you have collected a large quantity of research material.

Writing

If you followed the previous advice about researching a dissertation (see Chapter 3), then by this stage of your dissertation project you should already have a number of notes and interpretive thoughts written down, in which case it is now time to arrange and expand them. If you have not done this, don't panic. Tackle each of your dissertation sections in turn, and think exactly what it is you want to say. Sometimes it can be of great help simply to get anything at all down on paper, and then to consider whether that really is what you wanted to say. Editing down your initial text can really help focus your thoughts. Talking to other people can also help, especially, of course, to your supervisor.

In general, most people write and think better without distractions. Turn the radio/iPod/iTunes off, turn off your mobile phone, resist the sudden temptation to do all your clothes washing, go on Facebook, put the cat out and so on.

Arranging Thoughts

A successful dissertation is not just a collection of information and ideas but a series of these things arranged into a coherent whole. In order to produce this kind of dissertation, when writing you continually have to make decisions about what you want to say next. So in the same way that each of your dissertation sections addresses an issue and leads on to the next section, within each section you should again try to arrange your thoughts clearly and methodically. In practice, this means that each paragraph should contain a distinct thought, and should then lead on to the next.

At the same time as writing each section and each paragraph (or even sentence) within it, you should at all times try to keep in mind the overall plan and structure of your dissertation. Ask yourself, what is the last thing I wrote, what do I need to say next, and where does this lead me in terms of my overall argument? The aim is, after all, not to write just anything but something which contributes to your dissertation as a whole.

Referring to the Subject

Ensure that you always refer to your subject. It is very easy in a dissertation, particularly when you have done a large amount of research, to try to include every architectural fact that you have uncovered and every idea that you have had about it. However, no matter how selective and accurate you have been in your research and note-taking, writing a dissertation is much like editing a film: a large percentage of it ends up on the cutting-room floor.

Above all, while you may, of course, want to make some parallel comparisons or contextual references, you should as much as possible try to refer directly to the subject you are investigating. Similarly, try to deploy only those ideas and arguments which are relevant to your interpretation. Adding in a load of other stuff will not impress the reader, and will only serve to cloud their understanding of what you are trying to say.

One trick to help you do this is to write about a specific illustration or quotation which you have in front of you as you write and which you include in the dissertation. That way, you can only write about something known to both you and the reader.

Assessing Work

It is a good idea to reread what you have written at regular intervals, especially after a day or so. Often you will find that something could be said more clearly, or that you have missed out an important thought. Ask yourself whether the text still makes sense to you. Could the ideas be presented more clearly? Could someone who knows little about the subject still understand it?

After rereading their work a number of times, authors often find that they cannot concentrate on their own words, which are beginning to look the same. If you find this happening, you can change the way that your text appears in much the same way that artists and designers often look at their work in a mirror in order to get a fresh perspective on it. For writers, if you have been working solely on a computer screen, you can print out the text, or if you already have a print-out, do so again but with a different font – both of these tactics will make the words seem very 'different' from how they read previously and will help you to get a new take on their sense.

Once again, your supervisor is the best person to provide a good assessment of how your work is progressing. Show her or him a sample of your work, even if only a small excerpt of the whole, as this will enable them to comprehend clearly how you are working and the kinds of thing you are trying to say.

Dissertation Size

It is very easy when writing a dissertation to massively overshoot the total number of words allowed to you. In order to avoid the need for lengthy and time-consuming editing down at a later date, you must keep a careful eye on the wordage you have written. Nearly all word-processing and related computer programs provide a word count facility, so there is no reason why this should be difficult to do. You also need to know whether the number of words you are allowed includes footnotes, bibliography, appendices, etc. For example, the 100,000-word allowance for a text-based doctoral dissertation at UCL *includes* main text, footnotes and references, but *excludes* the bibliography and appendices, while different masters courses at the same institution vary greatly in terms of what is included and what is excluded, as well as in terms of the total word allowance.

Grammar and Spelling

Although it is only the final dissertation and not the first draft that you will probably be assessed on, anything you can do to improve the standard of grammar and spelling in your manuscript will serve you well in the future. Try to correct grammar and spelling as you go along, or at the end of each day. Above all, try to resist the temptation to leave all this to the end – a badly constructed draft text will only serve to hinder your thought-processes, make it very difficult for anyone else to respond to your work in progress, hide the real word count, and in the end will just store up additional work for later on down the line. If grammar is not your strong point, and the suggestions proposed by the grammar check on your computer do not all make sense to you, find a friend or relative who is willing to go through a section of your text. He or she can annotate the errors and also explain why these are grammatically wrong.

Illustrations

Illustrations usually form a very important and frequently essential part of an architectural dissertation. Architecture is, after all, very much a visual entity and consequently some form of illustrative material often plays an integral role in any discussion of it.

However, just as you take great care to choose your words and arguments, so you should pay equal attention to the illustrations which contribute to your dissertation. Things to consider include the following:

- *Type of illustration.* What is the best kind of illustration to use at any particular moment in your dissertation? A plan, section or elevation? An interior or exterior view? A conceptual sketch or diagram? A map or site-plan? A photograph with people, giving a sense of social use and the time at which the photograph was taken? Each of these conveys a different kind of information, and you should therefore match the right illustration with the appropriate text and argument. For a longer discussion of the use of images within architectural writing, see Iain Borden, 'Imaging Architecture: Dialectical Imagery and Temporality in Architectural History', *Journal of Architecture*, v.12 n.1 (2007), pp. 57–77.
- *Atmosphere.* Illustrations have an atmospheric 'mood' as well as a technical quality. Thus a dramatic black and white photograph with heavy contrasts and red-filtered sky, showing, for example, a public square with civic buildings and lots of people, will have a very different effect from a hard-lined architect's plan of the same urban space. Your choice of what kind of illustration to include may depend on, apart from your argument, the kind of study you are undertaking: if you are writing a more interpretive account, the

black and white photograph may be more appropriate, but if you are doing a social science study, then the architect's plan may be better.

- *Usefulness.* Although many illustrations are, of course, very useful indeed, architecture students can sometimes put too many illustrations into their text. This is doubly ineffective, as not only do the extra illustrations draw attention away from those which really are adding something to the argument, but the reader of your dissertation may be cynical enough to think that you are trying to cover up for a lack of work and thought in your text. Each time you place an illustration into your dissertation, ask yourself whether it is really needed. What information does it show? Would it matter if I left it out?
- *Textual comment.* One test of whether an illustration is really useful to your dissertation is whether you refer to it in the main text. In general, you should try to refer to all illustrations, and use them to drive the main argument.

Referencing

An important part of any architectural dissertation is the referencing system – footnotes, references and bibliography – adopted in order to inform the reader as to where your information and main ideas have been derived from.

- *Footnotes/Endnotes.* Footnotes and endnotes are extra pieces of information that provide additional clarification or comment to that which is contained in the main body of the text. In general, footnotes should be kept to a minimum.
- *References.* References are shorter pieces of information which state the source for the facts or ideas concerned. In particular, references should be given for all quotations, specific pieces of information and for ideas that you have found in other texts.

There are two main systems for dealing with footnotes and references.

Harvard

In the Harvard system, as it often called, you simply place any references in the main body of the text. For example,

> Spiller argues that the influence of new biological and mechanical systems on architecture means that we must now re-assess architectural space (Spiller, 1998).

Here, a quick cross-referencing with the bibliography would provide the full details for the Spiller publication listed for the year 1998. If there is more than one publication by that author, these can be listed as 1998a, 1998b and so on.

A slightly more detailed version of the Harvard system is to include the exact page number(s) for the publication concerned. For example:

> Spiller is particularly concerned to address the surface qualities of architecture and how these might be represented in drawings (Spiller, 1998, 85–94).

The advantage of the Harvard system is that it makes references to particular authors very clear within the main body of the text. Its disadvantage, however, is that these same references can easily disrupt the flow of the main text, particularly when used in a historical or critical dissertation where a great deal of different sources are used (thus requiring many references) and/or where the writing style otherwise tends to be quite fluid. Furthermore, the reader, of course, has to look at the bibliography to find the full reference, while any footnote material still has to be dealt with in the usual manner, using superscript footnote markers (see below).

For these reasons, the Harvard system tends to be favoured predominantly in science and social science disciplines. The kind of architectural discourse which focuses on critical, cultural, historical or theoretical interpretations of the built environment, however, tends to avoid it.

Humanities

The more common way of including footnotes and references in architecture is therefore the humanities system. Here a superscript marker in the main body of the text refers the reader to extra textual material containing either footnotes or references. For example, both footnote and reference are dealt with in the following sentences:

> Spiller argues that the influence of new biological and mechanical systems on architecture means that we must now re-assess architectural space.[1] His argument ranges from alchemy and secrecy to cyborgian mutation and genocide.[2]

1 Neil Spiller, *Digital Dreams: Architecture and the New Alchemic Technologies* (London: Ellipsis, 1998), pp. 1–13.
2 Spiller is thus more concerned with the possible impact of these technologies on the architectural imagination than with their objective, technical effects.

These footnotes and references would, of course, usually be placed elsewhere in the dissertation, at the foot of the page, at the end of the current section, or at the end of the whole dissertation – any one of these is usually acceptable.

When giving the reference information for a source, note that along with the usual publications details you should also cite the exact pages to which you are referring (in the case above, pages 1–13 inclusive). Note also that the use of the prefix 'pp.' denotes multiple pages, while 'p.' is used to refer to one page only. Another convention is to abbreviate page numbers so that 42–44 becomes 42–4 (similarly, 101–192 would become 101–92 and 241–249 would become 241–9, while 59–61 or 98–104 would stay in this form).

The first use of a work in the footnotes/references should always be given in full, such as:

1 Philip Tabor, 'Striking Home: the Telematic Assault on Identity', Jonathan Hill (ed.), *Occupying Architecture: Between the Architect and the User* (London: Routledge, 1998), pp. 217–28.

2 Adrian Forty, *Concrete and Culture* (London: Reaktion Books, 2012), pp. 23–5.

This, as with all other forms of full reference, should follow the system you have adopted in your bibliography (see below). Subsequent references can then be given in abbreviated form, such as:

3 Tabor, 'Striking Home', p. 223.

4 Forty, *Concrete and Culture* p. 38.

You can also use two other forms of abbreviation. The first of these is *ibid.*, short for *ibidem*, or Latin for 'the same place'. Here you could have a series of references, all for the same source, which ran:

1 Jane Rendell, *Site-Writing: The Architecture of Art Criticism* (London: IB Tauris, 2010), pp. 61–2.

2 *Ibid.*, p. 60.

3 *Ibid.*, p. 62.

Alternatively, you may use *op. cit.*, short for *opere citato*, which is Latin for 'in the work cited'. Here you can refer back to previous references, such as:

1 Iain Borden, *Drive: Journeys through Film, Cities and Landscapes* (London: Reaktion Books), pp. 222–9.

2 Patricio del Real and Helen Gyger (eds.), *Latin American Modern Architectures* (London: Routledge, 2012), pp. 56–73.

3 Borden, *op. cit.*, p. 95.

However, while *ibid.* and *op. cit.* are much loved by academic publishers, you would do well to avoid these abbreviations. This is for the simple reason that both *ibid.* and *op. cit.* depend greatly on there being a full, prior reference to which they can accurately refer. It is all too easy when writing a dissertation to remove the full reference in the draft or final production stages, thus leaving any subsequent *ibid.* and *op. cit.* references floating without substance. At least with the abbreviated form of reference (i.e. of the form, Borden, *Drive*, p. 95) you and the reader still have some clue as to what the full reference might be.

You may wish to invest in a specialist piece of reference software – such as Easy Bib, EndNote, Mendeley, Papers, Reference Manager, RefWorks or Sente – to support this aspect of your dissertation. Another good alternative is Zotero, which works both from within web browsers and as a stand-alone application, and is currently free to download and use (www.zotero.org). Not only will these applications help you to collect and order your references, they will also help you to format and insert them into your final dissertation in a semi-automatic manner.

Bibliographies

Bibliographies are an important element of any dissertation, itemizing all the sources and major influences for the work in hand. Your supervisor and examiner will normally pay close attention to the bibliography, checking it both to see what it contains and for its formatting and attention to detail. If your bibliography is full of mistakes or otherwise incorrectly produced, this can drastically undermine the confidence that the reader will have in the rest of the dissertation.

Content

The bibliography to a dissertation should contain two kinds of information:

- *References from main text.* This includes all books, journal articles, websites, etc. that are included in your footnotes and references, and any other sources mentioned in the main body of the dissertation.
- *Other sources.* This includes any other books, articles, archives, etc. that you have consulted but which otherwise do not appear in your footnotes and references. This does not mean that you should include every book or article you have ever read or heard about (and your dissertation assessor will probably be very cynical of bibliographies padded out with irrelevant or unlikely sources), just those which have been of use to you in this dissertation.

Arrangement

It is sometimes a good idea to subdivide your bibliography into different sections. For example, if your dissertation was an investigation into the Situationist idea of psychogeography as expressed in the work of architect Constant Niewenhuys and the painter Asger Jorn, you might want to have distinct subsections on Situationists in general, Constant and Jorn.

Format

There are many different ways to format a bibliography, and it would be possible to fill up this whole book with all the various systems, rules, conventions, etc. However, in general, you need to provide all the information that you can possibly think of:

- *Books*. For whole books, you should include author(s) and editor(s), title of book, place of publication, publisher, revised edition (if appropriate) and date. The names of translators, where appropriate, are also often included.
- *Book essays and chapters*. For essays and chapters in books, you should include author, title of essay, together with the place of publication, that is, editor(s), title of book, place of publication, publisher, revised edition (if appropriate), date and page range.
- *Journal articles*. For articles in journals, you should include author, title of article, together with the place of publication, that is, title of journal, volume and issue number, date and page range.
- *Websites*. For websites you should include name and full URL of the website, and the date on which you accessed it.

Exactly how you provide this information is largely up to you. The most important thing is that you are absolutely consistent in your methods. This means not only making sure that you include all the necessary information in each bibliographic entry, but that you also pay very close attention to your use of commas, brackets, periods etc. as well as to the use of italics and quotation marks.

Note that chapters, articles, dissertations and unpublished material etc. are all put in quotation marks. This is because they are not published in themselves, but are only parts of published works, or are unpublished at all. Conversely, all book titles, journal titles, films, government reports and similar materials are set in italics, as these are published documents.

You may see older dissertations and government reports with book titles set not as italics but as underlined text. This is because nearly all typewriters had no facility for italic font faces, so underlining was used instead. Similarly, typed manuscripts used underlining to clearly indicate to the typesetter what needed to be placed into italic. These old, historic reasons for using underlining rather than italics are, however, by now more or less redundant – italic font faces can easily be selected on any computer program, and a file version can be given to the typesetter if required at a later date. So use italics, not underlining.

An example of a typical humanities bibliographic system is as follows:

- *Authored books.* Nigel Coates, *Ecstacity: Guide to Ecstacity* (London: Laurence King, 2003).
- *Multi-authored books.* Bill Hillier and Julienne Hanson, *The Social Logic of Space* (Cambridge: Cambridge University Press, 1984).
- *Edited books.* Andrea Kahn (ed.), *Drawing/Building/Text: Essays in Architectural Theory* (New York: Princeton Architectural Press, 1991).
- *Multi-edited books.* Duncan McCorquodale, Katerina Rüedi and Sarah Wigglesworth (eds), *Desiring Practices: Architecture, Gender and the Interdisciplinary* (London: Black Dog, 1996).
- *Chapters in edited books.* Carol Burns, 'On Site: Architectural Preoccupations', in Andrea Kahn (ed.), *Drawing/Building/Text: Essays in Architectural Theory* (New York: Princeton Architectural Press, 1991), pp. 147–67.
- *Chapters in multi-edited books.* Henry Urbach, 'Closets, Clothes, disClosure', in Duncan McCorquodale, Katerina Rüedi and Sarah Wigglesworth (eds), *Desiring Practices: Architecture, Gender and the Interdisciplinary* (London: Black Dog, 1996), pp. 246–63.
- *Journal/magazine articles.* Anthony Vidler, 'Bodies in Space/ Subjects in the City: Psychopathologies of Modern Urbanism', *Differences*, v. 5 n. 3 (Fall 1993), pp. 31–51.
- *Published interviews.* You should treat this as if it were a book chapter or journal article as appropriate. For example:
  - 'Space, Knowledge and Power', interview with Michel Foucault, Paul Rabinow (ed.), *The Foucault Reader* (New York: Pantheon Books, 1984), pp. 239–56.
  - 'An Interview with Fredric Jameson', *Diacritics*, v.3 n.12 (1982), pp. 72–91.
- *Self-conducted interviews.* Here you just need to give the participants, place and date of the interview:
  - Interview between author and Zaha Hadid (London, 9 November 2012).
- *Dissertations/Theses.* These should be treated like a conventional book, but as the work is not published the title is not set in italics but is placed in quotation marks:
  - Edward Dimendberg, 'Film Noir and the Spaces of Modernity' (New York: New York University, unpublished PhD thesis, 1992).
- *Archives.* Each archive has its own reference system, so you must provide not only the archive name but also enough information for someone else to locate the material you have found. For example:
  - Ebenezer Howard, speech at the opening of Homesgarth, *Papers of Sir Ebenezer Howard*, Hertfordshire County Record Office, Hertford, folio 3.
- *Websites.* Give title and web address of the site, and date accessed. For example:

- ○ 'Burford's Hall of Fame', www.vvcom/~gilmore/head/ (accessed 11 April 1995).
- *Social media.* For Facebook, Twitter, etc., give details of the web address or Twitter feed, and the date accessed or viewed. For example:
  - ○ 'WOHA Exhibits: Roger Williams University, Rhode Island, USA', www.facebook.com/woha.architects (accessed 28 November 2012).
  - ○ @tomdyckhoff, Twitter message (viewed 27 November 2012).
- *Broadcasts.* Give programme title, channel/station and date: 'Heaven, Hell and Suburbia' (BBC2, 17 April 2005).
- *Films/videos.* Give film title, studio, director and year: *Playtime* (Specta-Films, dir. Jacques Tati, 1967).

Plagiarism

Plagiarism is becoming an increasingly important issue for architecture schools and universities, who search hard for those who are plagiarizing work. Hundreds of internet sites and university guidelines have sections devoted to this practice – see, for example, www.wikipedia. org/wiki/Plagiarism, or the *MLA Handbook for Writers of Research Papers* (2009). As deliberate plagiarism is a form of cheating and fraud, penalties for proven cases are, rightly, quite severe, and often include fines and/or retaking of an academic year, substantial downgrading of the degree award, and even expulsion from the institution concerned.

The problem for anyone undertaking a dissertation is that it is actually quite easy to unintentionally plagiarize someone else's work. To prevent this, you need to know what plagiarism is, and take steps to avoid it.

What is Plagiarism?

Plagiarism is frequently defined (for example, on Wikipedia) as 'the "wrongful appropriation", "close imitation" or "purloining and publication" of another person's "language, thoughts, ideas, or expressions", and the representation of them as one's own work'. In practice, this means that if you include distinctive phrases, sentences or paragraphs from other authors, you must put this text into quotation marks, and acknowledge the source with a reference. If you do not follow this procedure, it is very likely that your work will be viewed by the examiners as an act of *plagiarism* – using someone else's ideas and words directly, while presenting them as if they were your own.

Dissertations are usually read by at least your own supervisor, and are often second-marked by another member of the faculty staff. Most dissertations in the UK are also read by an external examiner, regardless of the level of study. In the USA, masters dissertations may have an external reviewer. In addition, many academics and universities now use bespoke plagiarism-detection software such as Glatt Plagiarism Screening, iThenticate, Turnitin and WriteCheck – see www.plagiarism. com, www.ithenticate.com, www.plagiarism.org, www.turnitin.com and www.writecheck.com for details. It is therefore extremely likely that any plagiarism contained in your dissertation could and would be spotted by at least one of these assessors.

Prevention

To prevent your work from containing plagiarised elements, there are a number of easy steps that you can take.

- *Research.* As described in Chapter 3, you should at all times keep a careful note of the sources from which you have made your notes, collected information, etc.
- *Quotations.* Enclose in quotation marks every extract which you have reproduced as a quotation from a book, periodical or other source.
- *Other data.* Provide a reference for all other specific pieces of data or key ideas that you have derived from other sources.
- *General writing.* All other information should be rewritten in your own words. However, in general, it is not enough to (a) simply change the wording of an extract and to claim it as your own, or (b) simply mention the author or title in a bibliography or elsewhere. If you rewrite someone else's ideas in your own words you should still provide a reference to this source next to the sentence or paragraph concerned.

You are, of course, expected to read books and articles and to quote them with appropriate acknowledgements. But you are also expected to ensure that your dissertation is not just a collage of other people's words and ideas – you need to have digested your sources sufficiently to be able, *in your own words*, to summarize their contents and to draw conclusions from them. See www.webster.commnet.edu/mla/plagiarism.shtml which provides several useful worked examples of this in practice.

One way to help avoiding deliberate or accidental plagiarism is to write with all books, articles (and even your notes from them) out of sight. So refer to your research files, think about what you want to say about the specific issue you are concerned with, and then remove the research file from sight before writing a paragraph, page or section of your dissertation.

Many of the plagiarism software systems mentioned above also include a system whereby students can first check their essays, dissertations and theses before submitting them for formal assessment. Check with your own institution to see what they offer by way of subscription to these kinds of service.

Submitting a Draft

Apart from the final dissertation, the draft of your dissertation is the single most important document that you will produce in your dissertation studies. This is the moment at which you and your supervisor can see for the first time the totality of the research and the argument that you are putting forward, and can assess it accordingly. It is also the moment at which advice from your supervisor can make a radical difference to the success of the final dissertation, by suggesting changes of emphasis, detail, argument and so forth. If you prepare a good draft and give it to your supervisor with plenty of time in which they can respond, you can make a massive improvement to the final result.

Contents

Generally, your draft should contain all the textual parts of the dissertation – the introduction, main sections and conclusion. All essential illustrations, appendices and bibliographic information should also be provided. Footnotes and references in drafts are often not fully polished, but bear in mind that your supervisor will need to be able to see the sources from where you have obtained your information and ideas.

Quantity

As stated above, the draft should normally be presented as a complete document. Some supervisors, especially in the case of longer dissertations, will also ask to see drafts of each section or chapter of the thesis as you write them.

Format

Some supervisors prefer to be given drafts as hard copy. Others will accept email, pdf and digital files, or even website versions. Check with your supervisor in advance which format they require.

Questions

Along with the draft itself, it is often a good idea to provide your supervisor with a list of questions that you yourself are not sure about. Is the second chapter correct in emphasis? Does the argument in the third section make sense? Does the conclusion say appropriate things? Are there too many illustrations? etc.

Timing

Bear in mind that your supervisor will need adequate time in which to read your draft and give feedback. Discuss this with your supervisor carefully. When is a good time to submit? When can you expect feedback? Remember that the more time your supervisor has, the better the feedback you can expect and the better your final dissertation can become.

Word-Processing

Gone are the days when architectural students might use hand-writing or a manual typewriter to produce their dissertation drafts, and of course everyone today uses a computer to word-process or otherwise create their work. This book is not the place to discuss hardware and software capabilities in detail, but make sure that you follow the usual basic rules.

Spelling and Grammar

You should use the spell checker and grammar functions on your software, but it is also important to proofread the hard copy carefully. It is amazing the number of errors that are either missed by the software (such as, for example, typing 'from' rather than 'form', or 'tot he' rather than 'to the') or by the eye (repeated words, such as 'the the', are particularly difficult to spot on the screen).

Word Counts

Use the word count regularly in order to keep a check on length. You should do this both for the total length of the dissertation and for the size of each section or chapter.

Fonts

When you come to print out your draft, make sure you use a decent, readable font – not fonts designed for use on the screen, like Monaco, Geneva or Chicago. Serif fonts (those which have details or embellishments at the ends of some of the strokes) like Bookman, Palatino or Times are generally easier to read in longish documents such as dissertations than are sans serif fonts (those which do not have serif embellishments) such as Avant Garde, Arial, Helvetica, News Gothic or Verdana. Personally, I now use Courier, a typewriter-like serif font for my own article drafts, as it is one of the easiest to read – although it is not very space-efficient and therefore is less suitable for longer documents. The print-out should be in 10- or 12-point text, double- or even triple-spaced for easy reading.

Saving

Save your work regularly, and at least once an hour. Many word-processing programs can be set to do this automatically or to prompt you to do at, say, 15-minute intervals. In fact, it is very easy to get in to the habit of saving more or less constantly, and this will help minimize the incredible sense of frustration and annoyance when the computer crashes and work is lost.

It is also a good idea to do a 'save as' at regular intervals, such as once a week. This is useful for two reasons. First, if you make a wrong turn in your dissertation at some point, it is then relatively easy to go back to a previous version of your work. Second, files sometimes get corrupted, and if you copy that corrupted file onto your back-up (see below), then you will have no usable version. If you have done a recent 'save as', however, there is a good chance that you will still have a relatively up-to-date version available. You will almost certainly have lost some work, but at least not everything.

Back-ups

MAKE REGULAR BACK-UPS OF YOUR WORK. Every year, every dissertation programme in every single architecture school has at least one person who loses their entire dissertation because they kept it all on a disk (hard-disk, USB-drive or whatever) without making a copy, and at the last, crucial moment the disk did what all disks eventually do, which is either to get lost or stolen, or to crash horribly without any chance of repair. Even more frequently, one or more of the files on the disk can easily become corrupted through a virus, weird computer gremlins or just plain old bad luck. Either way, if this happens to you then you will have lost all of your work. You have been warned. Do not let this person be you.

> If you are reading this and have not already made a back-up of your work, stop immediately, put the book down, go to the computer and do a back-up – do this now, and repeat the process at least once a day.

To be really safe, it is also a good idea to have an off-site back-up, which will help reduce the risk of damage if you should be so unlucky as to suffer a burglary or a fire. For example, you can keep one back-up at home and another copy at your studio in the architecture school. Other people increasingly use a kind of continuous back-up system, uploading their data to a cloud-based server on an hour-by-hour basis – see Chapter 3 for suggestions for this kind of service.

Alternative Dissertations

So far, in this guide we have discussed dissertations mostly as textual documents which have been written in an academic writing style with footnotes etc., which may be augmented with images, and which are produced as artefacts printed on paper. For most architectural students, this will no doubt be the case. Indeed, many architecture schools also require that dissertations take this kind of format.

However, in some architecture schools, for some students under-taking particular kinds of research project, it may also be both possible and desirable to deviate from this model of what a dissertation might be. So instead of a text plus images, the dissertation might be produced as a video, multimedia file, performance event, website, App-based program, etc. The potential here is enormous, for there are, of course, a near-infinite number of ways of producing an expressive and theoretical document. That said, there are a number of things that you might consider.

Format and Design

Architectural documents, of course, have very often had considerable attention paid to the way in which they are formatted and designed. However, in recent years the relation between form and content has become even more intense, with documents such as *S, M, L, XL,* designed in conjunction with Bruce Mau, or *Strangely Familiar,* designed in conjunction with Studio Myerscough, or websites and blogsites such as www.bldgblog.blogspot.com, which allows for all manner of different thoughts and images to be included.[1] If you take a look at these and other, similar publications you will see that the way in which the design works is not just as an aesthetic gloss but as an integral part of the content of the book – something which helps communicate as well as make more attractive. For example, in the *Strangely Familiar* publication images are used as identifiers, concepts and diagrams, and in series, singly, temporally and dialectically. In *S, M, L, XL,* information is presented as body text, list, table, graph, banner text, layers and numerous other devices. In the case of *Strangely Familiar,* the graphics relate to the manifold experience of architecture, while in *S, M, L, XL* they are related to the interdisciplinary way in which Rem Koolhaas and the OMA office undertake the design process. So such devices can be far more than just another 'style' of presentation, and instead represent a different way of thinking about what architecture is and might be.

Writing

The way in which people write is often described as their writing 'style', suggesting that writing about architecture is just a matter of choice of language and tone. In fact writing is much more complex and funda-mental in nature, such that *how* people write can largely determine what it is that they wish to say. For example, the kinds of analytical writing about Le Corbusier's villas by, say, Stanislaus von Moos, and which concentrate on notions of design method, are very different in character from, say, John Berger's prose musing on one of Le Corbusier's villas and which, although much shorter, conveys a great deal about personal memories and meanings for its occupant.[2]

Similarly, employing different structuring devices and varying the manner of writing within a dissertation can also convey different effects. Long passages can be interspersed with shorter ones, or with quotations, graphic elements and poems. The dissertation can be circular in structure, with no obvious beginning or end, or it may be bound in an unusual manner.

Other Formats

The most radical form of alternative dissertation is often one which changes the format of the dissertation altogether. Possibilities here are, of course, legion, but some of the most common in architectural schools include those produced as video presentations, websites, television or radio-style documentaries, or films. Others have included poetry, performance events, installation artworks, sculptures, animations and App-based works. Such formats often allow something very different to be said about architecture from what is possible with a textual document; for example, sound, body movement, change over time and personal emotion are all often much more easily conveyed than they can be in a non-textual way.

Further Considerations

If you wish to undertake an alternative form of dissertation, there are a number of things which you simply must consider even before starting work.

- *Regulations.* Will your architecture school allow this kind of submission? If so, are there any precedents (who has actually completed an alternative dissertation)?
- *Supervision.* Who is willing to supervise you in this project? Do they have the necessary skills and experience?
- *Hardware and software.* Do you have intensive access to the kind of equipment you are going to need? This is particularly true for dissertation projects involving computers, programming, film and video work.
- *Risk.* Experience shows that many alternative dissertations fall into the 'high-risk' category discussed in Chapter 2. This is because they

frequently require a high degree of technical as well as intellectual capability, as well as the fact that the architecture school itself may not be used to dealing with this kind of project.

If you have considered all the above, and understand what you are getting into, then by all means go ahead. This kind of dissertation can be extremely rewarding. In doing so you should bear in mind the following issues.

Form/Content Relation

A dissertation, no matter what format it adopts, is not usually assessed primarily for the technical skill used in putting it together. As with architectural design, where a fabulous drawing of a poor building does not usually attract good marks, so in the dissertation it is the ideas, argument and coherence with which you articulate these thoughts that matters – not the graphic design or film-editing skills. What this means is that, for an alternative format of dissertation, you must avoid one of the biggest kinds of trap: namely of concentrating on the medium or form of the project at the expense of the content or ideas expressed within it. Instead, you should work simultaneously with form and content, and continually ask yourself the questions as to how the ideas you are working with are being articulated through your chosen medium. What are these ideas? How are they manifested? How precisely can they be understood? Do you need more than one kind of medium (e.g. a web-based animation and a textual document) to complete the task? It is usually better to choose a format whose rules you already understand well so that you can concentrate on forming the content and not on inventing new rules for the format. If you combine more than one format, this advice is even more important. Do not spend most of the time you have available to you by inventing new formats.

Relation to Design Work

One of the problems that students sometimes face with an alternative format dissertation is how to distinguish it from their design work. Bear in mind that the dissertation is normally considered to be a different arena in which to explore architecture that is separate from the design studio. When undertaking this kind of work you should constantly ask yourself whether you are in fact learning and communicating anything different from your portfolio and studio-based projects.

Examinability

Although you may become technically very adept, bear in mind that your supervisor and examiners may not have the same kinds of skill capability as yourself. If you have prepared, for example, an augmented reality or computer-based presentation, how will they view it? What hardware requirements must be satisfied? Will they know how to operate the equipment or software? Bear in mind also that many architecture schools send away dissertations for review by an external examiner, so you may need to consider how transportable and readable your dissertation must be in order for it to be properly examined. Finally, you should make it clear (in whatever format is most appropriate) exactly how your assessor is to understand and 'read' the medium you have used, and why its use is important: what issues it allows you to highlight that a conventional dissertation cannot, how it changes the audience for your dissertation, and why it is appropriate for a piece of work in an academic setting. A clear understanding of the methodology of your alternative dissertation is even more important than that of a conventional one, because your reader will be encountering it for the first time.

Archiving

Some architecture schools require students to place a copy of their dissertation in the school's library or other permanent archive. If you have undertaken, for example, an installation or performance-based dissertation, how will this requirement be satisfied? One possible solution may be, for example, to submit a paper-based record of your dissertation project (rather than the dissertation itself) for archiving purposes.

References

1 Rem Koolhaas and Bruce Mau, *S, M, L, XL: Office for Metropolitan Architecture*, Jennifer Sigler (ed.) (New York: Monacelli, 1995); and Iain Borden, Joe Kerr, Alicia Pivaro and Jane Rendell (eds), with Studio Myerscough (designers), *Strangely Familiar: Narratives of Architecture in the City* (London: Routledge, 1996).

2 Stanislaus von Moos, *Le Corbusier: Elements of a Synthesis* (Cambridge, Mass.: MIT, 1979); and John Berger, *Photocopies* (London: Bloomsbury, 1997), pp. 52–8.

5 Presenting

The presentation of the final dissertation is obviously an integral part of the assignment. After all the hard work selecting, researching, developing and writing your dissertation, this is the final stage necessary to ensure that you present your efforts in the best possible manner.

It is surprising, however, how many dissertations are let down at this stage by relatively small errors which detract from what would otherwise be a much better product. Architecture students can occasionally be somewhat slap-dash with their dissertation in a way that they would never countenance for their design work as drawings, models or renderings.

General Presentation

In most cases, dissertations are not intended as exercises in graphic or typographic design, so considerable efforts in this direction will not usually gain extra marks from the examiners (although a different set of criteria may apply to the kinds of alternative dissertation discussed in Chapter 4). Nonetheless, all dissertations, of whatever format, should meet certain standards. You should consider the following.

Multiple Copies

You probably will have to submit more than one copy of your dissertation, so if your architecture school asks for three copies of your dissertation, give them that number. Many schools return one copy to you. In many institutions, one of the submitted copies can be a 'best version' or 'top copy' containing, for example, full-colour or laser-copied illustrations, while the others can be of a slightly lower reproduction standard. If this is the case, you may want to check in advance that the superior version is the one which will be returned to you. No matter how many copies your architecture school asks for, and whether one is going to be returned to you or not, it is always a good idea to make an additional best version for yourself. Although your school should look very carefully after dissertations submitted to it, there is always a chance that your dissertation may be mislaid during the examination process.

Digital Copies

Many institutions also now ask for the submission of a digital copy of student dissertations, either online or by disk. Different conditions also often apply, such as file type (are only pdf files acceptable?) and file size (is there a limit of, for example, 100mb?). Make sure that you follow these requirements carefully.

Print Output

A clear text will enable the reader to work more easily through the text, and so better comprehend what you have said. To achieve a high print standard, use text laid out using a word-processor or desktop-processor software, ideally printed on a high-standard laser or letter-quality device. Inkjet printers are usually acceptable, but old dot-matrix printers should be avoided. Many institutions also ask you to print on one side of the paper only.

Paper

Print on a good-quality paper, at least 105 gsm rather than 90 gsm, which will prevent too much 'show through' from one page to another. Do not use very thick paper, however, as this will unnecessarily bulk out the dissertation.

Size and Shape

In general, most dissertations use an A4 portrait or US letter layout. Some institutions may insist on only one size. You are well advised to adopt this format unless you have a particular reason to do otherwise. If you do use a different paper size and shape, particularly anything larger than A4, bear in mind that this must be transportable and legible.

Binding

Many architecture schools require submitted dissertations to be properly bound at a professional binders, with specific conventions as to colour, lettering, dating, etc. Other schools simply ask for spiral or another suitable binding system. Whichever system your school requests, make sure that you follow the rules precisely – most PhD theses, for example, will simply not be accepted unless they exactly follow university requirements.

You should also allow plenty of time for binding to be done – it can easily take a whole day to take your final manuscript to the copy shop, make copies and bind the result. If you are using a professional binder, choose one well in advance, and preferably one who is based locally. Professional binders often need two to three days in which to turn a job around, and possibly even more during busy examination periods.

Title and Title Page

Many architectural students give their dissertations a graphic front cover, often with one large illustration relating to the dissertation subject. If you do this, make sure your name and the year of submission is also included on the front cover and/or on the spine. Immediately inside, the first page should then include the same information, together with the title and subtitle of your dissertation. As with your original proposal, this title should be meaningful, indicating the subject matter as well as the kind of interpretation you have undertaken.

Contents Page

Include a contents page with a listing of all chapter or section headings, together with page numbers.

Acknowledgements

You may wish to include an acknowledgements page, where you can thank teachers, friends, family, archive staff, etc. who have helped you in your work. If you have completed a PhD, then this list will probably be quite extensive, less so for a shorter undergraduate dissertation. Whatever the kind of dissertation, try to keep the acknowledgements relatively short, as lengthy and overly effusive acknowledgements may be seen by examiners as being somewhat indulgent.

List of Illustrations

It is good practice to include a list of all the illustrations used in the dissertation, together with their figure number (see below) and the source from which they have been obtained.

Font

As for the draft, use a 10- or 12-point serif font for the main text of your dissertation, such as Bookman, Palatino or Times for the main body of the text. Sans serif fonts such as Avant Garde, Arial, Helvetica or News

Gothic can also often be used. Unless your submission is deliberately intended to be primarily read on a screen, do not use screen fonts such as Monaco, Geneva or Chicago.

Paragraph Formatting

Arrange the main body of the text with lines that are double-spaced, and with no more than 20 words per line (although 13–15 words is more usual). These conventions help the reader to locate the beginning of the next line more easily without getting 'lost' on the page.

Dissertations should normally be set with the text left-justified and right-ragged (meaning that the left-hand edges are all flush together, while the lines vary in length creating an uneven right-hand side). You can set your software to produce fully justified text (flush on both left and right sides) but be aware that convention dictates that this is usually done only for published documents such as books and journal articles.

Resist the temptation to use right-justified and left-ragged text, or, worse still, centred text. These formats, if used at all, should be deployed extremely sparingly for header quotations, chapter or section titles, etc.

Section and Chapter Headings

These are usually set in bold, sometimes also with capitals and in a larger font size than that used for the main text (e.g. 14- or 18-point). Double check that the headings correspond to the numbering and titling given on your contents page.

Subheadings

Clearly distinguish subsections in your main text with subheadings. These can be set in bold or italic, and in the same font size as that used for the main text.

Quotations

Separate quotations (i.e. those which are not run into the main body of the text) are usually inset slightly in from the left edge by about 1 cm, and are also often single-spaced. You do not need quotation marks for quotations formatted in this manner. Resist the temptation to set quotations in italics, as this style can get rather tiring after a few pages.

Amendments to Quotations

Often you will need to slightly modify a quotation in order that it suits the grammar of your own prose, or for other purposes. For example, you may wish to start a quotation at a point which is mid-sentence in the original. This is usually dealt with by adding a capital letter within square brackets. Thus the sentence 'It is possible to say without equivocation that today in Australia a new form of ecological architecture, dependent on both natural resources and political commitment, is emerging' may be quoted as:

> [T]oday in Australia a new form of ecological architecture, dependent on both natural resources and political commitment, is emerging.

Conversely, but using the same rule of putting amendments in square brackets, the original sentence of, for example, 'No-one is more focused on bodily architecture than Kas Oosterhuis' could be inserted directly into your main text (i.e. not used as a stand-alone quotation, but embedded in the main flow of your own writing) as '[n]o-one is more focused on bodily architecture than Kas Oosterhuis'.

The same rule of using square brackets to identify your own actions also applies to omissions within quotations. For example, if you wish to miss out part of a quotation, you can add an 'ellipsis' – a series of periods and spaces – to indicate this omission. There are various ways of doing this, but one of the most accurate is to use an ellipsis in square brackets, thus indicating that this is your own act, and not that of the original author. Thus, the quotation about Australia above could be further edited as:

> [T]oday in Australia a new form of ecological architecture [...] is emerging.

Finally, you may wish to emphasize some word in the quotation that the original author had not emphasized. The way to do this is to note your act in square brackets. Thus, the original sentence 'Architecture is a purely imaginative activity' may be reproduced as 'Architecture is a purely *imaginative* activity' [emphasis added].

Note that because this is a frequent practice on the part of academic writers, when the emphasis has not been added but is indeed in the original, the dissertation writer may acknowledge this fact. For example:

> Nothing is more central to *pleasurable architecture* than gender, sexuality and bodily matters. [emphasis in original]

Footnotes, Endnotes and References

This material can be placed at the bottom of the page (footnotes), at the end of the relevant section or chapter (endnotes), or collected together at the end of the dissertation. The font is usually the same type and size as the main text, but can be smaller (say 9-point) and use a different font face (if a serif font is used for the main text, a sans serif one might be used for footnotes). Footnotes and referencing can be either continuous and run in one range from beginning to end of the dissertation, or can be reset at 1 for each new chapter or section. Formatting should otherwise follow the instructions given in Chapter 4, where you can also find introductory advice on using citation and reference managers.

Page Numbers

Page numbers (sometimes referred to as 'folios') should be included on every text page, and are normally placed centrally at the base of the page, or in the top right-hand corner. It is often not essential to number pages with only illustrations on them, although different schools may have different rules about this.

Bibliography

The font type and size for the bibliography is normally the same as that used for the main text of the dissertation. As for footnotes and references, formatting should otherwise follow the instructions given in Chapter 4. Some reference and citation managers, such as Zotero, can also help to generate and format bibliographies.

Appendices

An appendix is a useful place to put any extra data, tables, interview transcripts or other material which is original to your dissertation but which is too detailed or too obtrusive to include within the main body of the text. Sometimes a DVD, CDR or other data disk may also be included here, in which case ensure that it is securely attached and will not fall out. An appendix is not the place to put any extra thoughts, interpretations or any other information which is essential for the reader to understand your investigation. For example, an architectural dissertation might use an appendix as a place in which to put a complete list of buildings by an architect and which are otherwise unrecorded, a set of illustrations that have not previously been published, or such things as additional statistical analysis of, for example, different construction methods used in a large house-building programme. The font type and size for an appendix is normally the same as that used for the main text of the dissertation.

Index

An index is not usually required for a dissertation.

Illustrations

Which illustrations to include in your dissertation is considered in Chapter 4. When it comes to presenting your final submission, however, there are several other factors to consider.

Quality

Make sure that the illustrations you include are of a good quality. For an architectural dissertation, you will frequently need to depict a high degree of detail, so a laser copy, print or high-definition scan will frequently be required. Note also that quality degradation will also set in rapidly if you make copies of another copy. The higher quality the original, the better you can prevent this image quality from falling with subsequent copies. Images downloaded from the internet are often not of good enough quality for these purposes, so if you are using images which you have obtained in this way, check in advance how they look when printed out, particularly if you are trying to use them at a large reproduction size.

Colour

Colour copies often look good, but they can sometimes be expensive to create and may not always add anything to your argument. Indeed, many people prefer the look of black and white illustrations. However, in order to get a high-quality black and white reproduction you have to use a colour copier or printer in order to get a good definition grey-scale reproduction. If you are not sure about this, the trick here is to experiment with some differing processes for one or two different kinds of image. You can then pick the process which gives you the best quality/cost compromise.

Size

You may need to include images which are larger than your dissertation, in which case you will need to fold these into the binding, or into a pocket at the back, or other such technique. Or you may wish to request to be allowed to submit a landscape-format or oversize dissertation that can more easily cope with your illustrative material.

Positioning

In general, it is a good idea to position illustrations next to or near to the text to which they refer. Usually, it is considered adequate to place illustrations on separate pages, inserted between text pages at appropriate intervals. Alternatively, you can place them on the same page as your text, in which case be sure that your desktop-processing and/or word-processor skills are good enough to do this effectively and neatly. You should normally avoid placing all illustrations together in one part of the dissertation, although in some cases there may be a particular reason why you might want to do this; for example, when comparing the evolution of a particular building type or detail over time. If you need to refer to an illustration on several occasions, you do not have to reproduce it more than once – just refer back to the previous usage.

Figure Numbering

Give all your illustrations a unique figure number. As with footnotes, this numbering can either run in one continuous range from beginning to end, or can be divided up into sections. In the latter case, it is conventional to use 1.1, 1.2, etc. for illustrations in section 1, then 2.1, 2.2 for illustrations in section 2, and so forth. These figures can then be referred to at the appropriate juncture in the main body of the text.

Captions

Illustrations are usually given a caption, identifying the subject and sometimes making an interpretive comment. The source of each illustration can also be given next to the caption, or this information can be given for all illustrations on the 'List of Illustrations' page (see above).

Copyright

One issue that many architecture students are becoming increasingly concerned about with regards to illustrations is the thorny issue of copyright. Although this is indeed quite a complex area for commercial publications, the good news here is that unless you are copying a large part of someone else's book (say, a chapter or more of an image-based publication), and/or you are going to actually publish your research, you do not normally have to worry about copyright. In short, unless you have been expressly forbidden from doing so by a particular archive or source, you should not have to worry about copyright for use in an unpublished dissertation that has been undertaken for education purposes. If you are in any doubt, however, you should check with the source concerned.

Computer Software

Some of the basic rules of word-processing are explained in Chapter 4. For your final dissertation submission, you may well find that the same word-processing software – particularly an advanced one such as Apache OpenOffice, Apple Mac Pages, Corel WordPerfect, Google Docs, Microsoft Word/Office etc. – will be more than adequate.

You may, however, wish to investigate the potential of desktop publishing software – such as Adobe InDesign, Corel Ventura, Microsoft Publisher, Quark XPress, Scribus, Serif PagePlus, Xara Designer Pro etc. – which give much greater control over text and image manipulation. Although often quite difficult to learn, once mastered these pieces of software can be particularly useful for doing things such as integrating images closely with text, rotating or resizing images, deploying graphic elements, or other such advanced techniques. Beware, however, that these kinds of program may also have considerable drawbacks, such as their capacity to include footnotes. In general, you should probably use these programs only for the very final version of your dissertation, when you are quite sure that any changes you make will be minor in the extreme, and/or if you are already skilled at using them.

Assessment Criteria

As with all work submitted as part of a university degree, it is a good idea if you know the grounds on which that work is going to be assessed. Indeed, many universities now require departments to make these assessment criteria (as they are often called) known to students. Assessment criteria, of course, vary greatly from one architecture school to another, and are frequently quite general in character in order to allow the broadest possible range of work to be included within the architectural education process.

An architectural dissertation is no different, and you should always check your own school's assessment criteria for dissertations. To give you some indication of what might apply, the following is a typical set of assessment criteria for an architectural dissertation programme.

- *High Pass*, that is, an A grade, or first-class degree in the UK, or commendation standard piece of work. Dissertations assessed at this standard would generally be expected to show very good critical understanding of the topic – very good knowledge of the objects of study, and of the various intellectual, theoretical and interpretative ideas used to understand, analyse and assess them. An originality of research evidence – using primary and other student-discovered materials – would almost certainly be required.
- *Pass*, that is, a B grade, or second-class degree in the UK, or other good, average standard piece of work. Dissertations assessed at this standard would generally be expected to show an understanding of the subject matter, to use a range of different evidence and materials, and to demonstrate some ability to question the issues involved.
- *Low Pass*, that is, a C grade, or third-class degree in the UK, or other low standard piece of work. Dissertations assessed at this standard would generally be expected to show a basic understanding of the subject matter, and to have no fundamental errors, but probably would lack any evidence of awareness of the problems of interpretation or questioning of the subject. In many US institutions a C grade may well be a failing grade, and the advice above will refer to a low B pass.
- *Fail*, that is, a D grade, or non-honours degree in the UK, or a C grade in some US institutions, or other substandard piece of work. Dissertations assessed at this standard would generally offer only

a little or a confused understanding of the subject matter. Such dissertations might also contain basic errors of fact or argument. Dissertations which plagiarize or otherwise simply reproduce information from other sources, without the student making any sense of it to herself/himself, would also normally be assessed as being at fail standard. Clear and intentional plagiarism may also have far more serious implications, as already stated above.

Oral Examinations

Apart from submitting the dissertation itself, some dissertation programmes may also require you to undertake an oral examination in the subject – sometimes referred to as a defence, or a viva. This is common for PhD and MPhil dissertations, but less so for masters, diploma or first degree programmes.

If you are required to undertake an oral examination, you should bear the following points in mind.

Purpose

In general, the purpose of any oral examination is not to test your powers of recall down to the last detail of your dissertation, but to see if you are in command of the material through your powers of spoken expression as well as through the written word.

Examiners

You should find out in advance who the people are who are going to conduct the examination. Other information you might seek out is the interests and expertise of these people, and whether you have any say in their selection.

Examination Process

Finding out a few practical details in advance can also help you relax. Where will the examination take place? Will anyone other than yourself and the examiners be present? How long is it likely to last? How and when will you be informed of the result?

Questions and Answers

In preparing for an oral examination, you should carefully consider the kinds of questions that you might be asked. These are likely to range from the strategic (why, for example, did you choose the work of Marc Augé in order to interpret both airports and art galleries?), the methodological (how, for example, did you select the interviewees from within SOM's offices?) to the particular (was there, for example, any possibility that the American planner-architect Clarence Stein would have read the influential book *Der Städtebau* by the Austrian Camillo Sitte?).

Try to prepare your answers to these questions not as ready-made, off-the-pat responses but as the kinds of things that you would want to talk about. The more discursive and thoughtful you can be in answering, the better.

Remember also that you are not expected to know absolutely everything about your subject, just to be aware of what it is that you have done, and what it is that you have not done. So if necessary do not be afraid to show that you understand the limitations of your dissertation, or of your own knowledge. Realizing what work needs to be done next, and communicating as much, can be a very effective way of convincing your examiners that you really do understand the research process.

Attitude

The examiners are not there to catch you out, but to engage you in an intellectual debate. So try to be as relaxed and positive as possible in what you say. Take your time, and speak as slowly or quickly as you would in any conversation with your peers. If you get the chance, you can turn the examination into a kind of general discussion, and even put propositions to your examiners.

6 Afterwards

Once you have completed your dissertation, and undertaken your oral examination if appropriate, there is little more you can do other than to wait for the result. If you have followed this guidebook carefully, and you have put in some hard work and diligent thinking, then you should have done very well, and may be now thinking of ways of pursuing this kind of research further. If not, then you may be thinking of how you can redress the situation. Either way, some advice on what to do after the dissertation follows. Also included here is some advice about what to do if something has gone badly wrong during the research process, or if you have been faced with other, unavoidable difficulties.

Further Research and Study

Depending on the kind of degree you have just undertaken, there are a number of different courses which you might consider taking in order to further your studies and development in the area of architectural history, theory and writing. To find out about these, you can consult the various listings of courses which will be available in your campus careers office. Many universities also give details of their courses on the internet.

In general, however, there are a number of distinct different kinds of programme which you might consider.

Specialist First Degrees

Many art history courses offer a substantial architectural component, although you should always double-check exactly what is on offer, as this can vary greatly from year to year. These types of course will complement your existing degree with greater insight into the history of art and architecture in general, and will often raise questions of methodology and interpretation. They normally take three to four years of full-time study to complete.

Diploma/Masters Conversions

Many architecture courses at diploma level, such as those in the UK, often offer an extra period of study by which to obtain a master's degree. This typically involves a three month full-time or nine months part-time study, usually in the form of a short dissertation. These types of course are very useful for pursuing a particular interest in some more detail, and will give you an MA or equivalent qualification after your name, but will not provide the kind of specialist training offered by most dedicated masters or even some first-degree programmes.

Master's Degrees (MA, MArch, MSc, etc.)

Typically these types of course offer a period of seminar or lecture-based instruction, followed by an in-depth dissertation of substantial intellectual rigour. They are ideal for those wishing to pursue a higher research degree (see below), to enter academia, to pursue architectural journalism of arts and architectural policy, or for those who simply wish to have an extensive grounding in the possibilities of historical, critical and theoretical discussions of architecture. Most master's degrees take between one and two years (usually 12 months in the UK, often longer in the USA) for full-time study, or a part-time equivalent.

Although there are a number of history and theory master's degree courses on offer, they can be hard to locate. For the USA and Canada, where the choice is wider, see the list under Student Resources on The Society of Architectural Historians' website (www.sah.org). In the UK, there are various specialist architectural history and theory master's on offer, including the master's in architectural history and theory at the Bartlett School of Architecture, UCL (www.bartlett.ucl.ac.uk/architecture/programmes/postgraduate/ma-architectural-history). For these and other countries, you can also consult the guides to graduate course, which should be available in your university careers office.

Higher Research Degrees (MPhil/PhD)

Although sometimes including a period of seminar- or lecture-based instruction, these degrees focus in particular on the completion of a substantial 40,000–100,000-word thesis, consisting of largely original research and interpretation. In the UK, good PhD programmes should include an element of taught seminars on methodology and research skill, such as, for example, the modules on 'Critical Methodologies of

Architectural History' and 'Research and Dissemination of Architectural History' at the Bartlett School of Architecture, UCL. Thereafter, the focus is on the individual student's research, typically allowing them to complete their PhD in three to four years. In US universities, the period of seminar or lecture-based instruction varies – if you hold a UK degree recognized as equivalent to a US master's degree it is generally two years or, if you do not, then it is often three to four years. In the USA, this period usually concludes with an examination in your major and minor fields. On successful completion of these exams you move into the candidacy phase, and write and defend your dissertation proposal. The total period of study is therefore usually much longer than in a European university, and often reaches six years or more in total.

If you are thinking of starting this kind of dissertation study, check carefully with the institutions that interest you, as the institution, the discipline and the dissertation topic may all play a role in this process. In particular, as well as identifying a suitable supervisor, find out what the overall research environment is like. How many other PhD students are there? What methodology and training programmes are available? When can PhD students present work in progress to their peers? What funding is available for you to attend conferences? How many other academics, besides your supervisor, are working in the same general area? When checking where you might wish to apply, it may also help to know that many doctoral programmes dealing with architecture are in schools of art history. Again, for North America, see the list on the Society of Architectural Historians' website (www.sah.org).

Higher research degrees are particularly suitable for those wanting to enter academia and/or those wishing to focus in great depth on a particular research topic. Such degrees often take from two to three years to complete for an MPhil, or anywhere from three to ten years for a PhD. Part-time study is also often possible. Many US institutions offer fee remission or scholarships to attract research students with an already strong academic record, which in the case of overseas applicants can significantly reduce the cost of study. UK institutions attract awards from the Arts and Humanities Research Council, British Council and other funding bodies. Do not forget to enquire about these while you are researching which institution is most suitable for you.

Non-degree Courses and Study

It is, of course, not essential to take a degree at a university in order to continue studying architectural history and theory. Many universities, colleges and other educational institutions offer less formal courses in the subject, while you can also pursue your own course of study by simply reading whatever you want, and discussing it with like-minded friends and colleagues.

Publications

Publishing Your Work

If your dissertation has been particularly well received, and/or you feel that you have been able to make an original contribution to architectural thinking, then you may want to see if you can publish your work and make it available to a wider audience. There are a number of possible ways of doing this, but beware that in all cases you will often have to make some considerable changes to your dissertation in order to suit the requirements of your intended place of publication and its readership.

Competitions

Perhaps the easiest way to further publicize your work is to enter your dissertation into one of the many competitions available to student dissertations. For example, most of the examples included in this handbook have been submitted to the competition for student dissertations held annually by the RIBA in London. Many other countries and institutions have similar competitions, some with significant funding attached, and you should ask your supervisor and other teachers for their advice on this matter.

Publishers

Publishers are generally only interested in publishing doctoral dissertations, but in some instances a master's dissertation may be sufficiently original to develop into a publication. If you think this might be the case, discuss it with your tutor and any other teachers at your institution who have publication experience. If they agree with your view, they may be able to suggest the best publishers for you to contact. Alternately, you may wish to contact a publisher whose books come closest to your subject area – your bibliography should be a good source. If the initial informal contact with the publisher is encouraging, you will probably need to write a book proposal. If so, you should ask for the guidelines from the publisher. It may take a long time – as much as two years – for a book to develop from proposal to full manuscript, often with no guarantee of publication at the end of the process. You should be prepared for a lot of revisions and additional research for little or no financial remuneration.

Academic Journals

Many architectural journals will consider publishing articles based on dissertations – and some examples of dissertations published in this way are included in the following section of this book. The best way to do this is to look in your institution's architecture library and select, say, three or four journals which seem most likely to be interested in your work. Again, your supervisor and other teachers can also give you advice here. You can then follow the chosen journals' instructions as to length, formatting, etc. (and make sure you follow these closely) and send it off for consideration. Many journals operate a referee system, where each submission is considered by one or more independent academic advisors, so you may have to wait a while before receiving a response.

However, before going to all the trouble and effort of turning your dissertation into article form, which can take much longer than you might think, you may want first of all to approach the journal's editor on a more informal basis, just to see if they would be willing, in principle, to consider your work. You can then avoid wasting your time by making an inappropriate submission.

Professional Magazines

The various monthly or weekly architectural magazines may also be interested in running a feature on your dissertation, particularly if it deals with an architect or architectural issue in current debate. Again, an informal approach to the features editor is always a good first step in this direction.

Student Publications

Publications and other events, such as conferences and symposia, organized by students (usually graduates) are another way of furthering your work, and can often involve very useful intense discussions. They are also often much quicker in turnaround times than other academic journals, and much less beholden to market forces than professional magazines, so your chances of seeing your work published and discussed in the near future is much more likely.

Internet

Depending on your dissertation subject, a relevant interest group or site-leader may be interested in including your work on their internet site. Alternatively, you can, of course, easily set up your own personal web page or blog, and post up the dissertation yourself. Either way, you can reach potentially enormous numbers of people very quickly, and at minimal cost.

Copyright and Privacy

If you are intending to use your dissertation for publication purposes, you should also be aware that there may be copyright and privacy issues that were not important when doing the original dissertations, but which are very important indeed when publishing in the public domain (and this includes websites, blogs and other digital channels of communication). These are likely to fall into one or more of three areas.

Illustrations

If you have used any illustrations other than those taken by yourself, then you must seek permission from the owner of the original source before you can reproduce it in the public realm. So for any painting or artwork in a gallery, any map or diagram in an archive, any photograph taken by another photographer, any illustration taken out of another book or other publication, their source must be consulted and their permission sought in writing. This may apply even if you have taken the photograph yourself, particularly if you have taken it out of a book, of an artwork or film, or in the interior of a building. (Note, however, that if you have taken a photograph of a building, and particularly of the exterior of a building, you will not usually need to seek permission.)

In the USA, most images belong in the public domain if they are more than 50 years old – otherwise you must get permission to publish them, or you will have to publish without illustrations. In the USA it is also customary to publish your PhD dissertation with UMI (University Microfilms Inc.), in which case you must get permission to use all other illustrations, or alternatively publish the dissertation without illustrations.

Furthermore, many sources or copyright owners may charge you a fee to reproduce an illustration. Charges vary, but can be anything from a few pounds or dollars, to two-, three- or even four-figure numbers.

The other problem is the quality of the images that you have. Photocopies or scans of images, while good enough for a dissertation, are not normally of an acceptable standard for publication, and you may need to obtain higher-quality images for inclusion in any published version of your dissertation.

Privacy

If you have interviewed or obtained other private information from an individual in the course of your dissertation research, you must seek their permission before you can publish it elsewhere. Just because someone was willing to speak to you as part of your educational research does not mean that the same person will be as keen to see their private views or details placed into the public realm. Many will be happy to oblige, but check first – this is very important, particularly in the USA, where you might be barred from publication or sued if prior permission is not obtained.

Commercial Sensitivity

In a similar manner, if you have obtained information of a commercial nature directly from an organization, such as the economic turnover of an architectural practice or construction company, then you need to check first that you can reproduce this information in the public realm.

Money from Publishing

One final point about publishing your work. Most academic texts – journals, magazines and books alike – are printed in very small production runs, and do not generate substantial income for the publisher. As a result, authors often receive only a very small fee, or a small percentage of the royalties. If you are intending to publish your work, you should therefore bear in mind that you are very unlikely to make much profit, if at all, from your efforts.

Troubleshooting

As in any educational programme, sometimes something can go wrong during an architectural dissertation project, often for a reason beyond anyone's control. This section identifies some of the most common problems and some of the possible responses that may be open to you. But be aware that this part of the handbook, perhaps more than any other, requires you to check with the specific regulations and options of your own institution. In any case, the general rule with all the circumstances listed below is to talk to your supervisor and/or other tutors as soon as you think that something might be wrong. Keeping the issue bottled up inside you will not help matters, so the earlier you discuss the problem, often the easier it will be to sort something out.

Wrong Subject

Sometimes students realize, and often at a stage when they are quite well advanced with their project, that they have chosen the wrong subject. This can be for a number of reasons, from the intellectual, to the personal, to the pragmatic. Either way, the best thing to do here is to discuss the matter with your supervisor at the earliest possible opportunity. It may well be that you do not need to completely alter the topic of your dissertation, and that a relatively simple reorientation of the project may be all that is necessary. Alternatively, you and your supervisor may be able to come up with a new but related topic that will be comparatively easy to develop.

Dyslexia and Personal Problems

As with any academic subject, many architecture students suffer from dyslexia. The exact nature of dyslexia and its cause are a matter of some debate and dispute, and it is enough to say here simply that it can produce in sufferers a degree of difficulty in reading, writing and general information processing.

If you know that you suffer from dyslexia, or even if you just think that this might be the case, you should talk to your tutors – most architecture schools have one member of the faculty who has been specifically nominated to deal with this problem. He or she can then take you through your institution's procedures for dyslexia, and explain to you the possible responses. These may include giving extra allowance or marks for coursework, or time extensions to submissions and examinations. Some universities also have schemes whereby dyslexia sufferers are provided with special computers and/or software to help them in their writing assignments.

The same applies to any other personal problems that you may be faced with over the course of your architectural studies. If, for example, you have particular difficulties concerning your health, family, personal relationships, finances, accommodation and so forth, you should discuss this in confidence with your tutors. They can direct you to possible sources of help, as well as making sure that any serious problems are accounted for during the examination process.

Lost Dissertation

Sometimes students lose their entire dissertation, or all the work done so far, before the final submission. Normally this is because they have suffered a computer crash and not made a back-up, although sometimes it is because they lost the only hard copy and had no computer version. If this happens to you, and it is a computer problem, try to speak to an advanced computer expert, who can often recover files that a normal person could not. If this does not work, and your dissertation really has been lost, you have no option than to repeat the work. Your supervisor can advise you as to the procedures for doing this, and any time extensions, resubmission procedures, etc. that may be open to you.

Missed Deadline

If you accidentally miss the deadline for the final submission, you should inform your supervisor and/or programme leader immediately, and often something can be worked out. Do not just stay silent and hope that things will be sorted out later.

Retakes

An architectural dissertation is rather like a driving test: not everyone passes first time. This can happen for a number of reasons, not all of which are necessarily the students' own fault. As an independently researched and written document, there are many things which might go astray with your dissertation (although following this guidebook should help to prevent the vast majority of these).

If you do happen to fail your dissertation, you should talk to your supervisor at the earliest possible date and discuss what was wrong with your submission. In many cases, you may only have to make relatively minor alterations in order to raise the dissertation to a pass standard for resubmitted work. Alternatively, you may be better advised to start afresh on a wholly new topic.

It is also worth checking with your supervisor exactly what opportunities for resubmission are allowed under your institution's regulations. If you are allowed only one resubmission, then it is obviously important in the extreme that you pass the next time around, particularly if you also need this pass standard in order to satisfy the requirements for professional architectural accreditation. In such circumstances you would want to make the dissertation resubmission the very top priority of your current list of tasks to complete.

Appealing Against Results

If you have failed your dissertation, or you feel that you have received an unjustly low mark, you may wish to appeal against the result. Here you should check first of all with your institution's regulations for allowing such an appeal. Many, for example, have quite complex marking systems involving two internal markers and an external examiner for all assessed material, and will therefore not allow any appeal simply on the grounds that these people might have somehow got it wrong.

However, if you believe, and have some evidence to support your belief, that, for example, your tutors were prejudiced against you, that marking and examination procedures were not followed correctly, that you received wholly inadequate supervision, or that extenuating circumstances should have been taken into account when assessing your work, you may indeed want to launch an appeal. Although emotion can obviously run high in these kinds of cases, try to put forward your case as rationally and as briefly as possible, while including all relevant detail and supporting evidence. An appeal explained in this manner, rather than one full of vitriol and heated opinion, is much more likely to be considered and to be accepted.

7 Dissertation Examples

Joseph Godlewski

Alien and Distant: Rem Koolhaas on Film in Lagos, Nigeria

Abstract

This article seeks to evaluate Rem Koolhaas's investigations of the sub-Saharan megapolis of Lagos, Nigeria. The literature on Lagos produced by Koolhaas and the Harvard Project on the City has been both lauded and criticized by several sources. Less attention, however, has been paid to two documentary films chronicling their Lagos "research studio." The central component of this article is a close reading of these two films. It concludes that the research studio is a potentially effective method for learning about cities, though what Koolhaas produces is a seductive but ultimately myopic account of Lagos's urban dynamics.

Rem Koolhaas is a slippery character. Principal architect of the world-renowned Office of Metropolitan Architecture (OMA), urban theorist, Harvard professor, and author of the influential texts *Delirious New York* (1978) and *S,M,L,XL* (1995), among others, his work is not easy to dismiss. That he has managed to transcend the tight boundaries of architectural academia to make his way in the larger field of pop cultural discourse makes it all the more necessary to engage with that which he produces. His theoretical polemics, like his buildings, have the ability to awe, inspire and challenge boundaries, yet at the same time to frustrate, perplex and inundate one with irony, cynicism and contradiction. The research he produced with the Harvard Project on the City (HPC) regarding the sub-Saharan megapolis of Lagos, Nigeria, is no exception. This article seeks to evaluate Koolhaas's work on Lagos, in particular two documentary films chronicling his and the HPC's "research studio" there.

The literature produced by Koolhaas and his team on Lagos has been widely discussed, but less attention has been paid to the films, directed by Dutch filmmaker Bregtje van der Haak. This article is therefore focused less on Lagos than on an architect's and a filmmaker's representation of a particular African city. What is one to make of Koolhaas's Lagosian speculation that the West African metropolis is a "paradigmatic case-study of a city at the forefront of globalizing modernity"?[1] What can be learned about the developing and developed world from this work?

I argue here that the films clearly demonstrate the problems and contradictions evident in Koolhaas's written work on Lagos. His inwardly focused imaginings of the city's processes of "self-organization" cause him to overlook the more convincing economic and political forces shaping it. Similar to art critic and curator Okui Enwezor's assessment, this article makes the case that unlike the bulk of Koolhaas's impressive oeuvre, "the Lagos research tends to resist [his] complete mastery."[2] Though my analysis is largely critical, my intention is to examine the films and their implications and to suggest alternative ways forward for architectural criticism.

Discursive Production: Evidence

The work produced in the HPC Lagos research studio was conducted between 1998 and 2001, and was initially intended to be a collaborative design effort between the HPC and the University of Lagos (UNILAG).[3] But it remained a Koolhaas-Harvard effort, and subsequently formed the basis for articles in two books, *Mutations* (2001) and *Under Siege: Four African Cities – Freetown, Johannesburg, Kinshasa, Lagos* (2002).

Mutations features an essay on Lagos and a section devoted to "Urban Africa" in its "photographic dossier." After a few pages of fragmentary thoughts and images, Koolhaas speculates that the survival strategy of Lagos "might be better understood as a form of collective research, conducted by a team of eight-to-twenty-five million."[4] Visually bold, the 720-page book features large color photos, over-sized fonts, and provocative, though characteristically short, essays on architecture and urbanism. *Mutations* is one of several products forged by the synergy of Koolhaas and Harvard's Graduate School of Design.

The second result of the Harvard study is a short essay entitled "Fragments of a Lecture on Lagos," taken from a conference and workshop held in Lagos in 2002. The essay, along with other contributions from the conference, is part of the publication *Under Siege: Four African Cities – Freetown, Johannesburg, Kinshasa, Lagos*. In the essay, Koolhaas contended that the "work is not inspired by the need to discover ever more exotic, violent, extreme urban thrills." However, that initial critical impulse is undermined by statements regarding how degraded sites of urban conditions, "smoldering, as if it were a gigantic rubbish dump," are "actually intense emancipatory zones."[5] Speaking of the reaction to the lecture at the conference, parts of which make it into the documentary films, Enwezor mentioned Koolhaas's "enviable capacity of being able to generate wild admiration and opprobrium at the same time."[6]

There is one additional work from the Lagos research – the forthcoming book *Lagos: How it Works*. However, in contrast to the machine-like efficiency of Koolhaas's voluminous publishing career, it seems to be in a perpetual state of delay, and unfortunately will not serve as part of my analysis here.

In addition to this written work the Lagos research incorporates van der Haak's two films documenting Koolhaas and his photographer Edgar Cleijne's time in Lagos. *Lagos/Koolhaas* charts the architect's tourist-like fascination as he travels around the city. The same can be said for the film *Lagos Wide & Close: An Interactive Journey into an Exploding City*, produced in 2005. Though there's been a fair amount of discussion about the written work, surprisingly little has been said about the films. My primary focus on the filmic representations is therefore intended to fill a gap in the existing literature. In general, it is intriguing that two films were produced from the Lagos project, whereas the rest of Koolhaas's oeuvre has largely been confined to the (albeit profuse) print medium. Why was it necessary to put the Lagos research on film? Why were there two films made?

Beyond their informational content, the films may also be analyzed as cinematic representations of Lagos and the iconic architect within it. Indeed, I argue that it is precisely in the films that the performative quality of Koolhaas's processes of theorization are most clearly articulated. Certainly no stranger to contradictions, it is within them that he can most audaciously act these out. Rather than seeking to understand how or why Lagos is the way it is, he instead looks at Lagos "as is." Together, Koolhaas and van der Haak blend sound and image to create, at times, unexpected cinematic tensions. And the final products have much more in common with music videos or television commercials, in that they serve to entertain rather than provide a critical understanding of the environments they ostensibly document. Moreover, it is in the films that Koolhaas can more thoroughly develop his fraught conception of "foreground" and "background," or "wide and close." This binary conceptualization of depth allows him to view Lagos as a detached observer, understanding the city's morphology as a "self-regulating system." Koolhaas is thus able to overlook the sticky complexities he confronts on the ground in favor of the seeming elegance he detects from above.

Both the documentary films are assembled from material shot during three trips to Nigeria by van der Haak. Though there is significant overlap between them, each has a unique form and distinct elements, many of which are problematic. Though the language in the films is perhaps less grandiloquent than in Koolhaas's writings on the city, the combination of audio and visual material with his theoretical performance make for a provocative filmic engagement.

The HPC was started with the explicit intention to "identify which cities were changing most quickly and understand how they were changing."[7] Though the stated aims of the project seem commendable, the way material gathered by it is presented is problematic for several reasons. By looking at the books and films, I intend to clarify these problems.

Though garnering significant acclaim from the popular press and the design community, both *Mutations* and *Under Siege: Four African Cities* have been critiqued by a range of commentators for their numerous weaknesses.[8] Geographer Matthew Gandy delivered perhaps the harshest and most precise blow in his essay "Learning from Lagos," in which he systematically picked apart Koolhaas's writings as aestheticized urban fantasies disconnected from history and politics.[9] Unlike Koolhaas, Gandy took a historical perspective, writing, "The informal economy of poverty celebrated by the Harvard team is the result of a specific set of policies pursued by Nigeria's military dictatorships over the last decades under IMF and World Bank guidance, which decimated the metropolitan economy."[10] Elsewhere, Gandy has pointed to the "African exceptionalism" such research entails, and warned of the "categories of ontological difference" it reinforces.[11]

Other academics have been less thorough regarding Koolhaas's work on Lagos, but equally dismissive. Anthropologist James Ferguson correctly paired the work with that of economist Hernando de Soto, who sees the informal economy as the result of "micro-entrepreneurs" using their inventive creativity, optimistically reconceptualizing the notion of the urban poor.[12] A different critique is advanced by art historian Jean-Loup Amselle, who has argued Koolhaas sees African cities as "reservoirs of primitivism that provide an alternative to old cities in the North."[13] In the end, the critiques see Koolhaas's research studio producing work which not only ignores historical and political concerns, but promotes an essentialist reading of the city that undermines its purported desire to invent a new vocabulary for speaking about cities. The authority afforded Koolhaas in the design community seems to dissolve when his work is held up to the lens of academic review outside the confines of the architectural discipline.

Not a stranger to film, Koolhaas made an independent film in the 1970s and wrote an unused script for sexploitation film director Russ Meyer.[14] The striking candor of Koolhaas in the interviews woven throughout the films is more revealing than the complex prose exhibited in the two Lagos publications. Perhaps most importantly, though, the films contain interviews with the city's inhabitants, who have a tendency to undercut Koolhaas's distanced narration and otherwise harmonious conceptualization of the city.

Lagos/Koolhaas (2002)

In short, *Lagos/Koolhaas* is a film about first contact. Produced in 2002, it is told as a story of architectural discovery, an "encounter" between Koolhaas and something, he says, "I didn't know anything about: Africa." It opens with a split screen featuring a close-up of Koolhaas's eyes hovering above the slums of Lagos, with the sounds of a city in the background (fig.1).

The visual display of this binaric opposition sets the stage for the later development of the plot. Koolhaas's eyes are those of masculine Western modernity, whereas Lagos, tellingly situated under his gaze, stands in for Third World urban dysfunction, disconnected from "normal" civilization. The film is a tale of this confrontation. Much like the travel writing critiqued in Mary Louise Pratt's *Imperial Eyes: Travel Writing and Transculturation*, the site of the film is this "contact zone" or space of encounter. Koolhaas's detached tone throughout the film emphasizes the "anti-conquest" strategies of representation that Pratt noted in the writings of bourgeois travelers in the eighteenth and nineteenth centuries. In these accounts, there was a consistent attempt

Figure 1 Binaric opposition: the architect and the city. Image from *Lagos/Koolhaas* courtesy of Icarus Films.

to distance the writer from the violence and subjugation of earlier missions of conquest. The alibi in these narratives was that the writer was always just "collecting data" or surveying the land.[15] There's a similar distanciation in Koolhaas's words.

The opening sequence concludes with a helicopter perspective over the city center, accompanied by an interview between the film's director and the architect. Van der Haak asks, "Why Lagos, Nigeria?" To which Koolhaas replies:

> When I started the Harvard Project on the City, I wanted to understand how cities were changing and which cities were changing most quickly. At that point it became really interesting to look at the city that was almost disconnected from the global system. So, it became incredibly exciting to learn to capture what was so alien, so distant.

The film compiles footage from interviews with Koolhaas and the director, scenes from Koolhaas's appearances on a local television show, interviews with inhabitants of the city, and clips from a lecture Koolhaas gave in Lagos in 2002 as part of the *Documenta* series. It is loosely organized around a simplified narrative of the world-renowned architect visiting a city that at first seemed dysfunctional and chaotic, but improves during the short period of time that he's there. By the end of the film, Koolhaas has learned to appreciate the city as a "self-organizing system." He concludes by remarking that Lagos is an "extreme form of modernization, not some kind of African model." And he returns to his earlier thinking about the inexorable socio-technical forces of modernization expounded in *Delirious New York* – Manhattanism exported to an African context. The open-ended fantasy world of Coney Island is superimposed onto Lagos's informal marketplace.

Being interviewed on the Lagos talk show *New Dawn at Ten*, Koolhaas rather dryly explains how he "wanted to be the first to understand how [Lagos] works."[16] Again ignoring the fact that several Nigerian scholars have in fact already attempted to "understand how Lagos works," he goes on to remark:

> Lagos is a city of huge contrasts. It has elements of a modern city – skyscrapers, roads – but also a strong presence of the informal. We are fascinated by the self-organizing entities of Lagos, like the Alaba International Electronics Market. . . . Because of the deficiencies in the public sector, there are enormous initiatives taken by private organizations.[17]

Here Koolhaas rather seamlessly shifts from the traditional talking points of an architect to those of a neoliberal populist such as C.K. Prahalad seeking to entrepreneurially empower the world's poor. Proponents of populist notions of eliminating poverty through profit see enormous potential in the vast population of marginalized laborers in the world's informal economies. They celebrate the people's economy and emphasize the incredible potential for wealth generation. Though Koolhaas's research isn't seeking to eradicate poverty, the language he uses to theorize Lagos is strikingly similar to that displayed in Prahalad's *Fortune at the Bottom of the Pyramid*. There, Prahalad wrote admiringly of initiatives offered as "a framework for the active engagement of the private sector at the BOP [Bottom of the Pyramid]."[18] Similar to Koolhaas's observation of the "deficiencies of the public sector," Prahalad wrote of ways the BOP "can transform the poverty alleviation task from one of constant struggle with subsidies and aid to entrepreneurship and the generation of wealth. When the poor at the BOP are treated as consumers, they can reap the benefits of respect, choice, and self-esteem and have an opportunity to climb out of the poverty trap."[19] And what Prahalad characterized as "profitable win-win engagements" Koolhaas similarly characterizes as "total self-help effort[s]."[20] It is this optimistic casting of the entrepreneurial self and relentless faith in market mechanisms which animate both Prahalad's and Koolhaas's work.

Similarly, it is remarkable Koolhaas doesn't mention the work of Hernando de Soto – considered the prime advocate of the informal sector's "entrepreneurial spirit." De Soto believes that it is through private property that assets can begin to take on a "parallel life as capital outside the physical world."[21] His ideas have been advocated by a range of economists and political leaders from Ronald Reagan to Bill Clinton to Nigeria's Olesegun Obasanjo, who appears as a sort of administrative hero in Koolhaas's Lagos films.[22] Koolhaas's disengaged position in regard to existing "entrepreneurial" literature can be read as either a scholarly oversight or a concerted effort to cast himself as an innovative theoretician of emergent conditions. Again, this question lies beyond the scope of this investigation. However, it is interesting to speculate whether Koolhaas is genuine in his intentions, or if the films indeed are a stage-set for a kind of ironic performance.

Koolhaas's self-proclaimed fascination with the "self-organizing" entities at the informal Alaba International Market provides one of the more memorable and contradictory scenes from *Lagos/Koolhaas*. Koolhaas claims that his work is not "inspired by the need to discover ever more exotic, violent, extreme, urban thrills."[23] However, the Alaba sequence seeks to provide an exciting representation of the power of informal markets, and it can easily be read as an ode to the "invisible hand," and evidence for William Easterly's belief that "the poor help themselves."[24]

In the film, Koolhaas comments that the research team's first discovery was that of the "self-organizing processes of Lagos: the ability of the population to take its fate into its own hands, and to survive on its own wits." Paradoxically, Koolhaas's observations fetishize economic activities, yet the subjects he studies seemingly have no means to meaningful political action. Instead, they're diminished to simple economic actors in a city conceived as a giant "teeming marketplace." He further casts this kind of activity as a bizarre never-before-seen phenomenon, further buttressing the false sense of novelty and African exceptionalism that undergirds many of his speculations. When speaking of Alaba to the television interviewer, Koolhaas comments that "those kinds of initiatives don't exist in any other situation in which I'm aware of." Urban informality certainly is not a new or localized phenomenon. This fact again calls into question whether Koolhaas is serious or simply trying to provoke his audience.

The Alaba scene depicts traders unloading unboxed electronics wrapped in plastic. Consumers carry off VCRs, stacked ten high, on their heads. A crowd gathers to take part in the excitement of the informal marketplace. Koolhaas comments that the market operates on "the sheer intelligence of the self-organizing system." And the layered sequence ultimately builds to a rapid-fire display of images triumphantly set to the music of *Carmina Burana*, accompanying the video introduction to Michael Jackson's 1992 *Dangerous Tour* displayed on a black-market television set. What is one to take away from such an ecstatic "unplanned" spectacle?

An interview with a manager of the market reveals that most of the electronics sold there are imported. He lists the countries – Japan, Singapore, Italy and Spain, among others – suggesting a vast transnational network of underground electronics trading (fig. 2). A diagram

Figure 2 The Alaba Electronics Market has gained international recognition. Image from *Lagos/Koolhaas* courtesy of Icarus Films.

in the *Mutations* essay refers to this same informal web as the "Alaba Pangea."[25] But doesn't this undermine Koolhaas's characterization of Lagos as a city "disconnected from the global system"? What exactly is Koolhaas's attitude toward planning?

In a separate interview with van der Haak, Koolhaas seems to suggest another contradiction, a counter-position to the market euphoria and scepticism about planning suggested in the HPC research, particularly that on display in the Alaba scene. He claims, "by the end of the nineties, the endless idolatry of the market had become irritating."[26] This position directly contradicts the scene at Alaba and the earlier interview in which he marvelled at the market's ability to "organize itself" and create its "own system of law and order." Van der Haak asks, "I thought that your starting point for looking at Lagos was your interest in a city that is not planned, a self-organizing network city?" Koolhaas responds at length:

> In the early nineties, I was very sceptical about the value of planning – about what it could do. Lagos was a confrontation with that scepticism. Initially, I thought: yes, this shows planning makes no sense – it's irrelevant. But now I've begun to see the subtleties in Lagos – that self-organization is inscribed upon an organized model of the city. There's a weird interdependence between the planned and unplanned. . . . If you extrapolate current trends, there are many signs that show the world is going to be a horrible place. There are many reasons to believe laissez-faire is not the answer. So planning is becoming more interesting to me. It represents a cycle from scepticism to an awareness that we have to try to assume the role of planners, perhaps in a new way.[27]

Koolhaas's response is deeply contradictory. He seems to want it both ways: planning is both relevant and irrelevant. Koolhaas restates his faith in planning, yet fetishizes everything unplanned like the Alaba Market. One might reason that this contradiction relates to an unfair characterization of Koolhaas's ideas by the film's director; however, the distaste for planning that colors much of the written work continues into the documentary films. By the end of *Lagos/Koolhaas*, Koolhaas arrives at a new, perhaps hybrid understanding of Lagos. He puts forth a new "universal" theory of modernism, speculating that the future of all cities will have "a combination of the rigid and free." He qualifies his exuberance for the market, remarking, "self-organization is inscribed upon an organized model of the city."

In his book *The Architecture of Fear*, Nigerian planner Tunde Agbola (another scholar overlooked by Koolhaas) attempted to come to terms with another side of Lagos's unfettered urban informality – violence. Unlike Koolhaas's euphoric optimism, Agbola depicted hostile city residents fending for themselves and relying on survivalist mechanisms.

Agbola wrote of "the social discord created by huge contrasts in economic well-being, that is abject poverty in close juxtaposition with great wealth."[28] Other than mentioning his mobile position in relation to the "dangerous" city, Koolhaas avoids engaging the social reality of the city he's theorizing about. The physical manifestations of this violence are conspicuously absent in the analysis he arrives at from the cockpit of a helicopter or hanging out the side of a car. In contrast, Agbola conducted a thorough survey of households to investigate how urban residents cope with urban violence. What emerges is not a pretty picture:

> The general appearance of most buildings in the low to medium density areas of Lagos is like that of fortress/strongholds. . . .
> In the areas around the house, strong assertions of territoriality were made through the building of fences of various types.[29]

Though at times wearisome, the methodical fieldwork and documentation contained in Agbola's book provide evidence of an uneven urban geography constructed in response to patterns of violence. Its findings are consistent with historical antecedents, and it moves beyond a purely market-focused analysis. In short, it attempts to explain phenomenon, rather than uncritically accepting them at face value.

An alternative imagining of African urbanism can be found in the work of AbdouMaliq Simone. In contrast to the seeming pessimism of Agbola and the bizarre sanguinity of Koolhaas, Simone has developed the concept of "people as infrastructure."[30] This is a more nuanced, perhaps less dichotomizing, view of informality, one that balances a critique of structural socio-political and economic contributors to urban injustice with recognition of the improvisational creativity of the temporal social networks of African urban informality. As he has argued, "Seeing African cities only in terms of their colonial and post-colonial relationships, however, often makes them difficult to see how 'modern,' 'innovative,' and 'resourceful' they may actually be."[31] He has also stressed the "ways in which African cities are productive," and operate under "a broad range of tactical abilities aimed at maximizing economic opportunities through transversal engagements across territories and disparate arrangements of power."[32] Understanding these relationships, he has argued, is crucial in remaking Africa itself.

In contrast to Agbola's surveys or Simone's ethnographic perspective, Koolhaas's method of analysis can best be described as improvisational and impressionistic. He began his career as a journalist, and in many ways he seems to be returning to this as he develops a method for looking at Lagos. In an interview with van der Haak, Koolhaas explains, "We invented the method as we went along. . . . Of course, I have a method and a certain amount of objectivity. But in the end, I look at Lagos as a writer, and with the freedoms of a writer."[33]

Koolhaas graphically summarizes this improvement in an absurd diagram displayed during the *Documenta* lecture featured in both films (fig. 3). He goes on to explain the parabolic graph: "So for me, this is really the curve of our arrival. . . . We didn't know we were witnessing a rock-bottom moment. . . . And then what we are looking at since is a degree of improvement in Lagos's fortunes."[34] By sheer historical coincidence, Koolhaas and his Harvard research team seem to have arrived at the precise nadir of Nigerian history. As he explains during a television interview:

> Lagos is becoming more normal, more like other cities, much less dramatic. You can see it in certain areas, particularly on Victoria Island, that there is an attempt to make Lagos more like a typical city. Some of the extreme conditions have diminished; the traffic is flowing now, the airport is working. There are a number of recognizable urban conditions that are typical of other cities.

Again, Lagos is constantly referred to not by what it is, but what it is not. Though it isn't indicative of the Orientalist tendency to set the "other" apart in a timeless and exotic space, Koolhaas manages to maintain the positional superiority of the "normal" Western city by suggesting that the continuing development of Lagos is leading toward its possible future status as a "typical" city. He reasons with the

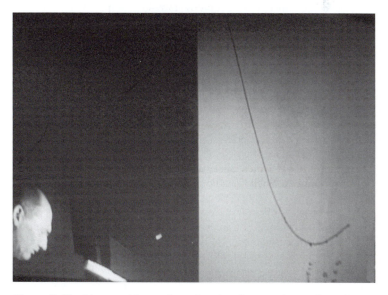

Figure 3 The history of Lagos in a singular diagram. Image from *Lagos/Koolhaas* courtesy of Icarus Films.

interviewer that "there's a definite sense of improvement." Cleijne, Koolhaas's photographer, confirms this conception of an urban trickle-down effect: "There's proof that Lagos is changing. Not everywhere; it's spreading out from Victoria Island. Victoria Island now has pavement, the drainage system has been renovated." The concentration of these technical improvements in affluent areas such as on Victoria Island, of course, repeats a familiar colonial pattern. Gandy, for one, has described at length how colonial administrators operating under a "hygienist" discourse disproportionately concentrated infrastructure improvements in wealthy enclaves "to produce a cultural dualism between modernity and 'tradition.'"[35] I point this out not to belittle the progress discerned by Koolhaas, but to situate it in a larger historical legacy – a point which the HPC consistently neglects to do.

Another striking oversight in Koolhaas's pseudo-historical approach is the discussion of the relationship between Lagos and other cities, particularly Nigeria's seat of parliamentary power – Abuja. As Lawrence Vale pointed out in *Architecture, Power and National Identity*, Nigeria elected to shift its capital north from Lagos to Abuja in 1975.[36] The politics behind this move and its effects on Lagosian conurbation cannot be understated. The selection of Abuja was not just an ambitious creation of a new capital, but implied a denial of the existing one, which was deemed unacceptable by Nigeria's military rulers of the 1970s. Indeed, Vale argued that the northern elite "deliberately increased the problems of Lagos in order to marginalize the city and make inevitable the decision to move the capital."[37] With the move there also occurred a shift in the flow of the nation's petroleum revenues from Lagos to Abuja. Without the resources to maintain its vast infrastructure, Lagos was, in effect, left to its own devices. Koolhaas's urban analysis, however, theorizes Lagos in isolation rather than as a relational product of a complex struggle for power and identity between Nigeria's "heterogeneous and fractious" population.[38]

But the HPC's sparse use of history overlooks more than the effects of Nigeria's colonial administration and the post-independence decision to move the nation's capital. A particularly uncomfortable silence occurs during a scene at a football match sponsored by the oil company Royal Dutch Shell, at which a banner looms in the distance proclaiming "Shell Cup: Football and Education Hand in Hand." Another factor triggering the "exploding city" Koolhaas set out to analyze is the massive influx of people dispossessed from their land in the Niger Delta by the ecological disaster wrought by the extraction of oil there. Indeed, David Harvey has called this process "accumulation by dispossession."[39] All of this, however, fails to be indicated in the HPC work, and it is eventually subsumed in Koolhaas's zealous pronouncement of Lagos's projected population numbers: "Every hour, more than 50 people start their new lives in the African city of Lagos" is the opening graphic in *Lagos Wide & Close*. Never mentioned by

Koolhaas is the fact that between 1975 and 2000, Nigeria earned almost $250 billion in oil revenues. Yet during that time the number of people living on less than a dollar a day more than quadrupled from 19 million to nearly 90 million, and per-capita income declined by more than 15 per cent.[40] An account of Royal Dutch Shell's role in this process of dispossession is beyond the scope of this discussion, but it has been thoroughly documented by other sources.

During the split-screen scene of the Shell-funded football match, television interviewer Funmi Iyanda talks about the necessity of making friends with a "big man" for protection in a city which lacks a "system which operates by the letter" (fig. 4). As if oblivious to these stories of lived adversity, Koolhaas instead emphasizes "learning about new ways of living . . . as a spontaneous reaction to a changing city." This disjuncture exists in both films, though is arguably more pronounced in the second, particularly in certain combinations of "interactive" viewing experience. If not to provoke the audience, why do van der Haak and Koolhaas decide to pair these images? Moments such as the one depicting the football match happen intermittently in the film, and lead one to question whether Koolhaas is actually ignorant of this relationship or if he's simply trying to provoke the viewer. Because of the sheer number of tense moments, contradictory statements, and

Figure 4 The Shell Cup. Image from *Lagos/Koolhaas* courtesy of Icarus Films.

implausible gaps in knowledge, it is difficult to imagine that at least some of these aren't intentional.

Watching *Lagos/Koolhaas* one is struck by Koolhaas's harmonic conceptualization of Lagos's urban dysfunction. Upon a closer reading of the film and Nigerian history, however, Koolhaas's conclusions about Lagos's informal organization seem even more bizarre and deliberately provocative. Inflected by a neoliberal understanding of market mechanisms and a disregard for socio-political conflict, Lagos/Koolhaas can best be understood as a film about an individual architect's experience with the city, rather than a historically situated documentary about a particular African city.

Lagos Wide & Close (2004)

The second film, *Lagos Wide & Close: An Interactive Journey into an Exploding City*, though constructed from much of the same footage as the first film, differs in fundamental ways. Largely an improvement on the first film, its most obvious additional feature is an interactive feature on the DVD which allows the viewer to choose between two camera angles: a "close" view featuring ground-level scenes of everyday Lagosians, and a "wide" view comprised mostly of aerial footage taken from the perspective of a helicopter. Michel de Certeau has made a similar distinction between the "walking city" and the "panorama-city." As he wrote, "The panorama-city is a "theoretical" (that is, visual) simulacrum, in short a picture, whose condition of possibility is an oblivion and misunderstanding of practices. . . ."[41] It can be said Koolhaas's panoramic speculations in *Lagos Wide & Close*, much like his aerial musings in *Lagos/Koolhaas* commit the same "misunderstandings of practices."

In addition to the choice of perspective, the viewer can select one of three soundtracks: Koolhaas's commentary, conversations with Lagos residents, or sounds of the city. Altogether, there are six possible combinations of audio and visual material on the DVD. Of the audio tracks, the commentary by Koolhaas is much the same as on *Lagos/Koolhaas*, though it's assembled in a different order. However, many of the conversations with inhabitants and sounds of Lagos are unique to the second film. In addition, several scenes from the first film are conspicuously absent in *Lagos Wide & Close*, including the celebratory *Carmina Burana* / Alaba Market scene, a humorous scene in a hat boutique where Koolhaas claims to find a "definite sign of improvement," and many of the interview scenes from the Lagos talk show *New Dawn on Ten*. As the booklet accompanying *Wide & Close* explains,

> *Lagos/Koolhaas* is as much a portrait of the architect and his research methods. . . . But another, more personal interpretation of the city was embedded in the 55 hours of material [director

Bregtje van der Haak] shot during her three trips to Nigeria. . . .
If Koolhaas looked at the patterns of Lagos from afar and then
zoomed in on the details, van der Haak started from within,
letting personal encounters gradually reveal clues for deciphering
the larger picture.[42]

Though the description and experimental layout are promising, *Lagos
Wide & Close* ultimately commits many of the same errors as *Lagos/
Koolhaas*.

Another difference between the first film and *Wide & Close* involves
packaging and graphic design. The packaging of *Wide & Close* is much
flashier, capturing vast urban vistas from above and emphasizing the
aesthetic dimension of Koolhaas's proclamations about the city and the
HPC's findings. In particular, the design of the DVD menu screen, as
well as the cover and information booklet, amplify Koolhaas's conception of formal patterns seen from the "wide" perspective provided by a
helicopter. And transitions between pages of the "interactive journey"
provide a morphing kaleidoscopic patterning of the city.

In critiquing the disjuncture between the urban dysfunction depicted
in *Mutations* and that book's slick graphic design, Gandy noted the
"faint resemblance . . . to a giant Mandelbrot or perhaps a Deleuzian
algorithm."[43] This disjuncture and formalist understanding of the structure of the city is even more pronounced in *Wide & Close*. In many ways,
the film can be seen as a more refined, yet programmatically separated
version of *Lagos/Koolhaas*. Despite the film's title, its design inevitably
favors the "wide" perspective exemplified by Koolhaas, rather than the
"close" perspective of the people interviewed. And because the audience is composed largely of architects and urban planners attracted by
the star power of Koolhaas, a safe assumption is that not many viewers
ultimately take in the film through the "close" camera angle or view to
the film while listening to the "sounds of the city" track.

The "innovative" interactive layout, while at first seeming to provide
a more open-ended depiction of the city, also has the tendency to
undermine the initial intention of the HPC to develop a "new conceptual
framework and vocabulary for phenomena that can no longer be
described within the traditional categories of architecture, landscape,
and urban planning."[44] By functionally separating the various layers
of information, it sometimes contradicts the detached speculations of
Koolhaas. For example, as the viewer listens to Koolhaas wax poetic
about the "definite sense of improvement," the camera shows a
fourteen-year-old boy, Ahmed, selling bagged water on the cramped
highways of the city. He earns about six cents per bag while bobbing
and weaving through cars and trucks. In general, the "close" images
undermine or provide potential misreadings of Koolhaas's heretofore
harmonious conception of a "self-organizing entity," while "wide"
images are similarly complicated by the voice of inhabitants. And the

"sounds of the city" track largely remains impressionistic, doing little to alter the conveyed meaning of the image, whether "wide" or "close."

Another disjuncture between form and content involves an interview with danfo driver Olawole Busayo. As he reveals the contested terrain of passenger transport, Koolhaas pronounces the spirited intentions of the HPC to broaden existing vocabularies to describe cities. These disjunctions operate in multiple directions with varying degrees of intensity, though they do tend to have the effect of undermining or complicating Koolhaas's conceptualizations. Whether or not these semantic conflicts were intentionally staged by van der Haak or Koolhaas is highly unlikely, though their existence is intriguing. Ultimately, any nuanced reading of *Lagos Wide & Close,* like *Lagos/Koolhaas,* is subsumed beneath the narrative of the world-class architect confronting the "alien" and "distant" urbanism of Lagos.

Findings

To summarize and underscore the problems of the HPC Lagos research, it is useful to make a list. The problems outlined above cluster around five themes which recur at particular moments in the articles and films. Before moving to a conclusion and discussion of alternative approaches, let me quickly enumerate and describe these. The list is not intended to be authoritative or comprehensive; nor are its categories distinct. But it does help elucidate the issues.

False Novelty. In part of an interview featured in the second film, *Lagos Wide & Close,* Koolhaas baldly asserts that "Nobody has really looked at the combination of very big cities, like Lagos, and real poverty."[45] This incredibly misinformed statement, supposedly explaining why he has chosen to study Lagos, is characteristic of the rest of the work. It seems to imply that no one has ever looked at Lagos seriously before. His extraterritorial excursion to Nigeria is framed as an innovative journey to an "exploding city," proceeding as though the encounter with Lagos were unprecedented. Any reference to other scholarship on Lagos, African cities, or cities in general has either been ignored or muted as if to amplify Koolhaas's wry sense of provocation, "emergence," and innovation. In fact, the work produced by the Lagos studio shares similarities with multiple bodies of work, many of which aren't new at all. Whether or not Koolhaas's lack of acknowledgement of this work is intentional or not, again, is beyond the scope of this investigation.

Such avoidance of contemporary debates in African urbanism has the effect of delinking the research from the structural constraints faced by theorists like Achille Mbembe, Sarah Nuttal, and AbdouMaliq Simone. Instead, Koolhaas remarks that he is in "extraterritorial waters," and would like to approach Lagos from a removed position, in much the same way he approached New York.[46] And elsewhere he claims, "it

was clear that nobody really knew what was happening in Africa."[47]
Koolhaas's pretence to theoretical originality when speculating on the
urban future from Lagos ultimately proves unsustainable, though, in
that he joins a growing debate about cities in the developing world.

The focus here is on the rhetorical effects of such an elision. Part of
this investigation is to contextualize the HPC's work, situating it in
a broader field of discursive production and revealing its rhetorical
congruencies. It thus aims to reduce Lagos's exceptional quality and the
pervasive sense of it as beyond comparison to "normal" cities.

Dehistoricized. Related to the Lagos Project's sense of unprecedent-
edness is its odd relation to history. Mark Jarzombek has commented
on Koolhaas's "careless and almost comical use of historical evidence,"
a characterization which can certainly be said to apply to the Lagos
work.[48] Other than an acknowledgement of a period of "modernization" in the 1970s and a sense that the current project was being conducted during a period of transition in Nigeria to democratic rule,
the city is otherwise taken prima facie. And any notion of Nigeria
having endured centuries of colonial rule is nearly absent from the
research, as are the effects of post-war "development" schemes initi-
ated by the IMF and World Bank. Further, the city is seen in isolation
from the history of other cities; as mentioned earlier, the oversight of
Abuja's relation to Lagos was a particularly serious one on the part
of Koolhaas.

As Derek Gregory has astutely argued, it's imperative to contest
these "amnesiac histories."[49] Much as Gayatri Spivak critiqued post-
structuralist and Marxist philosophers for their "sanctioned igno-
rance" of imperialism and their own role in the production of ideology,
this review of Koolhaas's research indicates how it proceeds with the
same oversight.[50] Unaware that his musings have their own implications in economic as well as intellectual history, his speculations about
Lagos's conurbation act as legitimized evidence for a particular entrepreneurial understanding of the urban poor. Again, whether or not
Koolhaas intentionally avoids history (as he does existing scholarship)
is beyond the scope of this paper. However, his lack of historical perspective subsequently makes it much easier for him to depoliticize the
urban context.

Depoliticized. Tied to the absence of history is the HPC's cursory
treatment of the city's political economy. Rather than engaging with
serious analysis of the structural constraints and economic instability
faced by the people of Lagos, Koolhaas chooses to revel in the city's
explosive population growth and its ability to "self-organize" in spite
of the presence of decaying infrastructure. Ignoring the underlying
reasons for these conditions, Koolhaas's research is ultimately about
surface appearances. Nigeria's violent geography of petro-capitalist
development, and its poverty, slum evictions, and chronic ethnic strife,

are quietly elided. Politics are drained from the analysis, and the agency of Lagos's inhabitants is narrowly conceived as their participation in the city's thriving informal economy.

In a strange syncretism, Koolhaas merges the apocalyptic vision of a city with inhabitants stripped of historical agency, epitomized by the work of Mike Davis, Robert Kaplan, or Patrick Chabal, with the neoliberal populism exemplified by William Easterly, Hernando de Soto, and C.K. Prahalad. The heroic entrepreneur is celebrated for his ability to navigate the enclave urbanism and "stinking mountains of shit" left behind in the wake of corrupt military regimes, structural adjustment programs, and trade liberalization.[51]

Describing Lagos's Alaba Electronics Market in utter fascination, Koolhaas remarks that it, "in a way, organizes itself – it has a chairman, and even its own system of law and order. Three days ago we watched a court case. There's even a small prison."[52] The "self-regulating" quality of this system is fetishized, taking precedent over all other struggles, and the city is conceived as a homeostatic organic entity.[53] Koolhaas's photographer explains, "Because of the complexity there, you think, at first, that it's not organized. But there's an informal organization that you can see more clearly from a helicopter than from the ground."[54]

The similarities to the Chicago School of Urban Sociology's conception of human ecology are striking. Burgess's "social ecological" understanding of the city's Darwinian metabolism is inscribed in his seminal concentric ring diagram.[55] Koolhaas's aerial view operates with the same organic and structural assumptions. The clarity of the diagram, however, belies the violence which engenders it.

Exoticized. One of the problems with the exceptionalist position Koolhaas takes on Lagos is that it removes from possibility the explicit comparison to "normal," ostensibly Western, cities. Ignored in much of the popular globalization literature, Africa remains a space of "absolute otherness," counterposed to the liberating flows of the networked world system as "mute, abject, and otherworldly" and beyond comparison.[56]

The HPC's take on Lagos does little to subvert this tendency. Though Koolhaas inverts the pathology prevalent in dominant modes of African urban analysis, his compensatory fetishism and romanticization of Lagos's urban ills does little to unsettle its status as a distinct urban other. In fact, it operates in much the same way.

As Edward Said famously argued, much nineteenth-century European culture "gained in strength and identity by setting itself off against the Orient as a sort of surrogate and even underground self."[57] Koolhaas proceeds as a twenty-first-century Edward Lane heroically capturing the strange urbanism of this "alien" and "distant" city. His voyeuristic position in relation to Lagos seems to have learned little from intellectual developments in postcolonial theory over the course of the second-half of the last century. Speaking of his engagement with the city, he writes:

> Our initial engagement with the city was from a mobile position. Partly out of fear, we stayed in the car. That meant, in essence, we were preoccupied with the foreground, and, at that time, Lagos had an incredibly dense foreground. . . . Lagos seemed to be a city of burning edges.[58]

One example serves to demonstrate the detached relationship Koolhaas maintains with the city and its inhabitants. One wonders who took the photograph, contained in "Fragments of a Lecture on Lagos," of Koolhaas taking a photograph while hanging out of the side of a moving car? Was it someone from the Harvard research team? Koolhaas's syncretism of this apocalyptic outlook with a celebration of Lagos's informal survival mechanisms serves dually to set it apart from the "normal" city, creating a necessary "other" by which to judge "normal" Western cities. In order to make sense of this disjunction, he devises a stratagem of "foreground" and "background," or the "wide and close." It is the "wide" or "background" view which allows him to retreat from an embedded understanding of the city's urban conditions. It allows him to more fluidly postulate the theory of Lagos as a "self-organizing entity."

Institutional Framework. Lastly, the discursive boundaries which the HPC ostensibly set out to challenge ultimately end up reconstituted. The conscious move to study a city which had largely been overlooked by urban theory is admirable. It presents a challenge to the way knowledge about cities is produced, and it interrogates the discipline of architecture's penchant for shutting itself from "informality." However, because Koolhaas is unwilling to be self-reflexive as to his position in the system of architectural production, those institutional frameworks are reinforced.

Who provides the money for the research and the production of the books and films? How are these connected to Harvard and the Office of Metropolitan Architecture? Koolhaas "employs" graduate students at an expensive private institution to produce works in a neoliberal "informal" arrangement similar to those documented in the Lagos research. The lack of meaningful comparative thought between the production of space in Lagos and the West instead has the tendency to create an essentialized other, ontologically set apart.

Conclusions and Alternative Ways Forward

So what is one to make of Koolhaas and the Harvard Project on the City's work in Lagos? As the field of African urban theory continues to burgeon, what lessons can be taken from Koolhaas's observations? As in Delirious New York, is the project simply another case of Koolhaas euphorically surfing the Großstadt, only this time off the coast of the Gulf of Guinea? So far, my assessment has been primarily critical. However, upon closer inspection the limitations of the research seem to suggest alternative approaches.

Koolhaas's initial intuition to examine Lagos as a way of countering architecture and urban theory's chronic Eurocentrism can be seen as a qualified success. If he hadn't taken on Lagos, I, a Western-educated white male, arguably wouldn't be studying it all. The celebrity status and institutional mechanisms behind Koolhaas and the HPC are seemingly able to generate interest in a diverse range of topics, Lagos notwithstanding. The resulting discourse, laudatory or critical of the project, has started to fill a gap in the literature about this city of 12 million inhabitants. It can be read as one of many contributions to the growing sense that architectural theory should address global practice rather than singular monuments in the Western world.

True to his earlier theoretical work, Koolhaas successfully "disrupts" the perceived autonomy of architecture as an internalized exercise separate from political or economic concerns. However, in the same breath, he reinforces formalist auto-generative understandings of the city when he describes it as a "self-regulating entity," thus undercutting the initial disruption. As Gandy has pointed out, this approach can best be understood as "neo-organicist," in that it repeats classic formalist urban imaginings.[59] Further, conceiving of Lagos as a "teeming market-place" sheds light on how Koolhaas's thinking about the metropolis fits with his older, more established understandings of architecture in relation to the larger processes of capitalist development and modern-ization. The similar enthusiasm for the emancipatory and open-ended possibilities of crisis moments in capitalism with that of neoliberal scholars is compelling.

In a perhaps unexpected way, Koolhaas's speculations are not much unlike Marxist geographer Mike Davis's hellish, but naturalized portrayal of a "slum ecology" and "urban involution." Davis doesn't put the optimistic spin that Koolhaas does on this condition, but the bird's-eye perspective and troublesome sense of inevitability are pervasive in both. The reader/viewer is ultimately left feeling rather disempowered. What can one do but ride "the wave"? Whether it be the "stinking mountains of shit" in Davis, or the rapturous flows of commodities in a globalized economy in Koolhaas, one can only surrender when presented with the theoretical "panorama-city" in each. Both of these views, to borrow a phrase from Sarah Nuttal and Achille Mbembe, display "a certain failure of the imagination."[60]

A possible alternative to these views is put forth by another Marxist geographer, David Harvey, and his conception of the "insurgent architect" in *Spaces of Hope*. Looking to Harvey's call for "courage of the mind" to imagine alternatives isn't just an idealistic sidestep to the harsh realities posed in Koolhaas and Davis.[61] In fact, it seeks to find an alternative which is more grounded in historico-political reality. Koolhaas's tendency to overlook spatialized power relations and his omission of the shifting forms of political collaboration, urban social movements, and spaces of contestation in the city leaves his analysis ineffectual. Instead, the city is taken prima facie.

In an essay on Koolhaas's writing on cities, William Saunders summarized the above point well when he described how Koolhaas's weakness "can be understood as resulting from his unfortunate conviction that creative freedom, which he values above all, does not need to be engaged with otherness – that it needs, in fact, to be capricious, private fantasy ex nihilo, inscribed on a tabula rasa."[62] It is remarkable, or perhaps revelatory, that Koolhaas can apply his universal theory of an urban future which is "a combination of the rigid in free" so inflexibly in such diverse contexts, spatially and temporally. Koolhaas's predisposition to generalize about cities and ignore the complexity of social practices he witnesses is ultimately quite frustrating.

In contrast, AbdouMaliq Simone's use of Henri Lefebvre's work in his article "People as Infrastructure" provides a much more convincing take on urban Africa. Acknowledging the tremendous constraints on Africa's urban residents, he is also able to indicate the intricately social space at work. Rather than receding into metaphors about "self-organization" or romanticizing the "freedom" at play in these contexts, Simone sought to highlight the heterogeneous social "linkages" and modes of organization required to make these spaces work, despite tremendous constraints. These "platform[s] for social transaction and livelihood" are by no means self-evident (indeed, they are often invisible), and require an engaged understanding of the urban socioeconomic context inaccessible from a helicopter or cursory site visits.[63]

Regarding the use of the "research studio" as an alternative approach to traditionally conceived design-proposal studios, it remains one with immense, albeit risky potential, despite the missteps of the HPC. If the research generates nothing but hyperbolized conjecture from surface readings of an existing condition, the studio's promise quickly dissipates. Flyovers in a helicopter and drive-bys in a speeding car won't cut it. Theorist Kazys Varnelis has asked an instructive question of the "design studio": "How does it help us to re-envision the world anew?"[64] It seems a critical component of any research studio, then – especially those undertaken by Western scholars in a non-Western context – that it should develop a deep understanding of the historical and cultural context from which the data is being collected. Perhaps worse than producing depthless readings of an urban context would be to unwittingly (or wittingly) replicate colonial legacies latent in the urban morphology. In this regard, the capacity for "drive-by" approaches to generate formalist, oversimplified misunderstandings of the city seems dangerously high and academically irresponsible.

The potential of the "research studio" is ultimately related to how the "research" is collected. Koolhaas and the HPC team's methods are unfortunately unconvincing. Yet they do open themselves to proposals as to how they might be improved. It's fitting that large portions of the films are devoted to interviews of Rem Koolhaas. If this relationship was inverted, and more ethnographic data were collected from residents in the city over a longer period of time, a more telling picture of how space is produced and contested could have been revealed. Put another way, the project contained too much of Koolhaas's "wide" perspective and not enough of Lagos "up close." Koolhaas's tendency to contradict himself and to make bold statements about the marked "improvement" in the urban fabric only serve to further undercut any knowledge he or the HPC may have produced.

References

1   R. Koolhaas and Harvard Project on the City, "Lagos," in S. Boeri, S. Kwinter, N. Tazi, and H.U. Obrist, eds., *Mutations* (Barcelona: Actar, 2001), p.653.

2   O. Enwezor, "Terminal Modernity: Rem Koolhaas's Discourse on Entropy," in *Considering Rem Koolhaas and the Office of Metropolitan Architecture: What is OMA?* (Rotterdam: NAi Publishers, 2003), p.119.

3   I.S. Okoye, "Architecture, History, and the Debate on Identity in Ethiopia, Ghana, Nigeria, and South Africa," *Journal of the Society of Architectural Historians*, Vol.61 No.3 (September 2002), pp.381–96. Okoye discusses the project in relation to the question of whether architecture should be considered a science or technology. Along the way he reveals a fascinating dimension of the project's original conception. He's ultimately more critical of Nigerian conceptions of architectural pedagogy than of Koolhaas. As he writes, "In the ten days or so of that [1998] visit, Koolhaas consulted with faculty at UNILAG. In June 1999, Koolhaas wrote from the U.S. university inviting the university to enter a partnership with Harvard on a new theoretical project on Lagos. The study was meant to comprehend the conurbation in new ways and to come to a series of proposals for its reconfiguration. . . . Koolhaas's 'failure' to have the Lagos project follow the cooperative lines he sought devolved from his proposal's having brought to crisis the ideology of architecture as science." p.384.

4   Koolhaas and HPC, "Lagos," p.719.

5   R. Koolhaas, "Fragments of a Lecture on Lagos," in O. Enwezor et al., *Under Siege: Four African Cities – Freetown, Johannesburg, Kinshasa, Lagos: Documenta 11, Platform 4* (Ostfildern-Ruit: Hatje Cantz, 2002), p.177.

6   Enwezor, "Terminal Modernity," p.110. Enwezor sees this dual reception as a generational issue. As he writes, the "full room was evenly divided between opposing camps of supporters (mostly enthusiastic young students) and detractors (older observers, less sanguine about his theory of Lagos)."

7   Interview with director Bregtje van der Haak, p.16. Page numbers refer to supplemental booklet accompanying DVD.

8   For examples of popular acclaim, see G. Wolf, *Wired*, 9.06 (June 2001); J. Sigler, "Interview with Rem Koolhaas," *Index*, 2000; and *Classic Archined*, "Koolhaas's Blindspot," March 30, 2001. An article written by Frederic Jameson before

the Lagos studio is equally laudatory of the Project on the City in general. F. Jameson, "Future City," *New Left Review*, May–June 2003.

9 M. Gandy, "Learning from Lagos," *New Left Review*, Vol.33 (2005). The title of this article surely references Robert Venturi's famous "research studio" and resultant book, *Learning from Las Vegas* (1972).

10 Ibid., p.42.

11 M. Gandy, "Planning, Anti-Planning and the Infrastructure Crisis Facing Metropolitan Lagos," *Urban Studies*, Vol.43 No.2 (February 2006), pp.371–96. In the article, he concludes that a "workable conception of the public realm must form an integral element in any tentative steps towards more progressive approaches to urban policy-making in the post-Abacha era and the return to civilian rule."

12 J. Ferguson, *African Studies Review*, Vol.50 No.2 (September 2007), pp.71–86. 13. J.-L. Amselle, "Primitivism and Postcolonialism in the Arts," *MLN*, Vol.118 No.4 (September, 2003), pp.974–88.

13 J.-L. Amselle, "Primitivism and Postcolonialism in the Arts," *MLN*, Vol.118 No.4 (September, 2003), pp.974–88.

14 R. Vine, "Post-delirium," *Art in America*, Vol.83 No.4 (April 1995), p.35.

15 M.L. Pratt, *Imperial Eyes: Travel Writing and Transculturation* (New York: Routledge, 1992).

16 Interview, January 24, 2001, *New Dawn at Ten*, p.8.

17 Ibid.

18 C.K. Prahalad, *The Fortune at the Bottom of the Pyramid* (Upper Saddle River, PA: Wharton School Publishing, 2004), p.xiv.

19 Ibid., p.99.

20 Ibid., p.xv.

21 H. de Soto, *The Mystery of Capital: Why Capitalism Triumphs in the West and Fails Everywhere Else* (New York: Basic Books, 2000), p.5.

22 www.ltsca.ca/documents/corporate/corp%20outline.pdf, accessed January 23, 2010.

23 Koolhaas, "Fragments of a Lecture on Lagos," p.175.

24 W. Easterly, *The White Man's Burden: Why the West's Efforts to Aid the Rest Have Done So Much Ill and So Little Good* (New York: Penguin Press, 2006), p.26.

25 Koolhaas and HPC, "Lagos," p.704.

26 Interview, Bregtje van der Haak, July 5, 2002, p.16.

27 Ibid., p.18.

28 T. Agbola, *Architecture of Fear* (Ibidan: IFPA, 1997), p.3.

29 Ibid., pp.68–69.

30 A. Simone, "People as Infrastructure: Intersecting Fragments in Johannesburg," *Public Culture*, Vol.16 No.3 (2004), pp.407–29.

31 A. Simone, *For the City Yet To Come* (Durham: Duke University, 2004), p.2.

32 Ibid., p.2.

33 Interview, Bregtje van der Haak, July 5, 2002, p. 20.

34 Imagining the audience's reception to this simplistic diagram is an amusing thought. As noted earlier, Enwezor remarked that older observers were "less sanguine" about his theory of Lagos.

35 Gandy, "Planning, Anti-Planning and the Infrastructure Crisis Facing Metropolitan Lagos," p.375.

36 L.J. Vale, *Architecture, Power, and National Identity* (New Haven: Yale University Press, 1992), p.156.

37 Ibid., p.162.

38 Ibid., p.161.

39 D. Harvey, *A Brief History of Neoliberalism* (Oxford: Oxford University Press, 2005) p.178.

40 X. Sala-i-Martin and A. Subramanian, "Addressing the Natural Resource Curse: An Illustration from Nigeria," Columbia University, Department of Economics, Discussion Paper Series 0203-15, May 2003, p.41.

41 M. de Certeau, *The Practice of Everyday Life* (Berkeley: University of California Press, 1984), p.93.

42 *Lagos Wide & Close: An Interactive Journey in an Exploding City*, directed by Bregtje van der Haak, 2005, p.2.

43 Gandy, "Learning from Lagos," p.41.

44 R. Koolhaas and HPC, "Introduction," in Boeri, Kwinter, Tazi, and Obrist, eds., *Mutations*, p.19.

45 *Lagos Wide & Close.*

46 R. Koolhaas and HPC, "Introduction," p.20.

47 Ibid., p.14.

48 M. Jarzombek, "The Disciplinary Dislocations of (Architectural) History," *Journal of the Society of Architectural Historians*, Vol.58 No.3 (September 1999), p.490.

49 D. Gregory, *The Colonial Present* (Berkeley: University of California Press, 2004), p.10.

50 G.C. Spivak, "Can The Subaltern Speak," in C. Nelson and L. Grossberg, eds., *Marxism and the Interpretation of Culture* (Urbana: University of Illinois Press, 1988), pp.270–313.

51 M. Davis, *Planet of Slums* (London: Verso, 2006), p.138.

52 Interview, Funmi Iyanda, p.9.

53 Gandy has called Koolhaas's approach "neo-organicist," because it takes its operational metaphors from the field of cybernetics rather than human biology, as did the classic organicist texts in urban discourse. Gandy, "Learning from Lagos," p.39.

54 Interview, Funmi Iyanda, p.9.

55 E.W. Burgess, "The Growth of the City: An Introduction to a Research Project," in R.E. Park, E.W. Burgess, and R.D. McKenzie, eds., *The City* (Chicago: University of Chicago, 1925).

56 A. Mbembe and S. Nuttal, "Writing the World from an African Metropolis," *Public Culture*, Vol.16 No.3 (2004), p.348.

57 E. Said, *Orientalism* (New York: Pantheon Books, 1978), p.3.

58 Koolhaas, "Fragments of a Lecture on Lagos," p.175.

59 Gandy, "Learning From Lagos," p.39n5.

60 S. Nuttal and A. Mbembe, "A Blasé Attitude: A Response to Michael Watts," *Public Culture,* Vol.17 No.1 (2005), pp.193–201.

61 D. Harvey, *Spaces of Hope* (Berkeley: University of California Press, 2000).

62 W.S. Saunders, "Koolhaas's Writing on Cities: Poetic Perception or Gnomic Fantasy," *Journal of Architectural Education*, Vol.51 No.1 (September 1997), p.61.

63 Simone, "People as Infrastructure," p.410.

64 K. Varnelis, "Is There Research in the Studio?" http://varnelis.net/articles/is_there_research_in_the_studio, accessed January, 2010.

Ocean Howell

The "Creative Class" and the Gentrifying City: Skateboarding in Philadelphia's Love Park

Abstract

This study explores the recent spatial politics of John F. Kennedy Plaza, "Love Park" – a piece of Philadelphia's mid-1960s Penn Center redevelopments. By the turn of the century Love Park had become a center of a growing international skateboard culture, appearing widely in magazines and videos, and on ESPN. In 2002 the city redesigned the park in order to deter the skateboarders, to the vocal protests of a broad-based coalition that included Edmund Bacon and over half the city council members. Through a review of city planning documents, local newspaper reportage, and personal interviews, I argue that the Love Park debates illustrate the extent to which "bohemian" or "countercultural" lifestyles are becoming institutionalized as instruments of urban development.

Introduction

This study is about consumer culture, class politics, and urban space. Specifically it is a story about skateboarding in John F. Kennedy Plaza – better known as Love Park – in center city Philadelphia. The plaza was completed in 1965 – at the height of the Great Society, in an era of public works and social welfare programs – as part of the Penn Center redevelopments. It was created in a modernist mode of development, which is to say that it was centrally planned, publicly funded, state led, and aesthetically intended to represent a broadly conceived public or citizenry. In the first two decades the plaza was a favorite lunch spot for local office workers, but also attracted users of all classes with protests and spontaneous street games. Under the strain of "reforms" to public welfare programs set into motion by the Reagan administration, however, the plaza became a makeshift home for the homeless by the late 1980s.

Around this same time the skateboarders – almost all teenage males from the surrounding working class neighborhoods and suburbs – began using the plaza. At first the skaters were treated much like the homeless by the police and the local press. But by the late 1990s, the skateboarders were widely praised by city elites like planners, local architecture critics, the editorial boards of major newspapers, and over half the city council members. In the public eye, the skateboarders were tempering the activities of the homeless population, injecting skateboard industry capital into the plaza, and generating a hip image for the city. Even so, Mayor John Street's administration had the plaza redesigned at public expense in order to deter the skateboarders. At the time of writing (2005) there is a high profile debate in the city of Philadelphia about whether the skateboarders should be allowed back into the plaza. I argue that what is at stake in this debate is not only access to Love Park, but the city of Philadelphia's transition to a new mode of urban economic development.

In order to trace the contours of this transition, I review some recent policy documents from the Philadelphia city government, alongside the influential writings of Richard Florida, a professor at Carnegie Mellon University who has weighed in on the side of the skateboarders. In Florida's framework, the best strategy to stimulate urban growth is to appeal not to employers, but to gay, bohemian, and foreign-born populations. Whether they have money or not, these members of the "creative class" will attract the employers – largely in technology-based industries – by generating an "organic" street culture.

I argue that what is obscured in the novel particularities of the Love Park case is a familiar story of urban class conflict. As with the so-called bohemian populations from San Francisco's SOMA district to New York City's SoHo district, the skateboarders have here served as both the subject and the object of class displacement. The next wave of renewal in Love Park is being carried out according to the logic of gentrification.

As Neil Smith shows, gentrification is something of a "chaotic concept" – sometimes it is state-initiated, sometimes it is led by corporate-scale capital, sometimes it is instigated by loose consortiums of individual investors with or without direct subsidies from city governments, and often it is effected by some combination thereof. Though the term is at times understood to refer only to the "upscaling" of working class residential neighborhoods, I use this term to refer to any reclaiming of urban space by people of a higher socioeconomic position than the current users.

Writing in 1996, Neil Smith said that he no longer felt that it was useful to make a strict distinction between the fine-grained gentrification of the 1990s and the large scale urban renewal of the post-war decades: both modes of development were geared toward a class remake of central cities, after all, so both must be understood in terms of a more inclusive rubric of gentrification.[1] I agree with Smith that urban renewal and gentrification both remake cities in the image of the upper classes. However, I will maintain this strict distinction, referring to urban renewal projects as *modernization*, and to piecemeal "reinvestment" and "reclamation" based development as *gentrification*. I do so for several reasons. The first is that the spatial programs of the respective modes of development are completely different: while urban renewal tended to level and then replace existing urban fabric, gentrification tends to rehabilitate existing urban fabric; urban renewal was almost always carried out with state moneys, gentrification may or may not be. The second reason is to respect the discursive contexts in which these modes of development have taken place: few people were talking about the Penn Center redevelopment in terms of "gentrification" in 1960s Philadelphia, and few people are talking about the modernization of Love Park today. The third reason, closely related to the second, is that I wish to analyze the discourses that underwrite these modes of development.

I also draw insights from recent work on the geographies of youth culture, particularly the work of Iain Borden. Borden's groundbreaking work – *Skateboarding, Space and the City: Architecture and the Body* – demonstrates how skateboarding reasserts "*use* values as opposed to exchange values" in the "left-over spaces of modernist planning."[2] "Architecture," he writes, "is intended for the production of things – either products as commodities in factories, knowledge in universities and museums, labour power in housing, information and decisions in offices, and so on. . . . Skateboarding however offers no such contribution, consuming the building while not engaging with its productive activity."[3] I argue that Borden is correct that skateboarding "performs a critique" of modernist space, but that when viewed from the framework of the gentrifying city, skateboarding can be reconfigured as productive – it produces marketable "street culture" imagery, and reclaims space. I seek to build on Borden's work by showing that, while skateboarding does perform a critique of the modernist mode of development, in Love Park it has been reconfigured as an instrument of development.

As shock troops of gentrification, young skateboarders – with no personal memory of the post-war contract between labor and capital – must be understood as a kind of individualized labor, producing surplus value by leading the reclamation of this space. Finally, I argue that the story of Love Park is also a story about the continuing privatization of citizenship. In the Love Park debates, the populace has been splintered into interest groups who must fund their own use of the space in order to gain legitimate access.

The History of Love Park

The modernization of Philadelphia began with the arrival of the City Beautiful in 1906, when Paul Cret, Horace Trumbauer, and Charles C. Zantzinger designed the Benjamin Franklin Parkway. This Haussmann-esque boulevard cut through Penn's grid from a site on the Schuylkill River – which would later house the new Museum of Art – in the northeast, to city hall at its southeast terminus. In 1917 the parkway would be converted "from an urban boulevard to a green wedge of park" by the landscape architect Jacques Greber.[4] But no architect had yet addressed the problem at the southeast terminus of the parkway: an unceremonious six-way intersection at the foot of city hall.

Edmund Bacon's 1932 master's thesis at Cornell – a Burnham-inspired Civic Center for Philadelphia – removed city hall and relieved the traffic jam with a half roundabout, surrounding a plaza. When Bacon took over as director of the Planning Commission in 1949, he had given up on the civic center, but started advocating for the plaza. It appeared first in the West Plaza-Hahnemann redevelopment area, which was later broken into two smaller redevelopment projects.[5] The plaza ended up part of the Penn Center developments, receiving both federal and local funding. Designed by Vincent Kling, the park opened in 1965, and was dedicated John F. Kennedy Plaza in 1967.

Judging from a survey of reportage on the plaza in the *Philadelphia Inquirer*, the park appears to have hosted a vibrant public life. There are descriptions of a crowded lunch hour, a lively chess scene, regular double Dutch competitions, and an annual ritual dating from at least 1974 in which the local Catholic high school girls jumped into the fountain on the last day of school.[6] The space seems to have been well used, well liked, and well integrated in terms of class:

> Even with the fountain shut off, the lunchtime crowd gathered around the empty basin at JFK Plaza. Executives from Bell Telephone across the street sunned themselves, a woman shooed a bumblebee away from her ginger ale, . . . a young man made kissing noises at pretty women who passed, and when the breeze was right, the inevitable odor of marijuana wafted by.[7]

Located across the street from city hall, the space was a favorite for staging protests. Given that Philadelphia suffered deep cuts to both public housing and programs for the mentally ill, the "Rally to stop Reaganomics," staged in the plaza in 1982, appears now to have had an ominous prescience.[8] Later in the decade the bill came due, as the *Inquirer* began reporting in 1989 that Philadelphians were "watching JFK Plaza turn into an open-air dormitory," and an "open-air mental-health clinic."[9] From there reportage on the plaza was dominated by accounts of "urine stains and patches of vomit," panhandling, and drug abuse, all conveyed with metaphors of darkness and death.[10] By 1991 the paper was publishing articles with titles like "Who Eats at JFK Plaza? Brown-Baggers, Homeless – and Rats."[11]

Around this time, the paper also started reporting on the increasing presence of what they would later call the "the skate rats."[12] Skateboarders had discovered that Love Park – with its open plan, stairs, handrails, marble benches, and granite planters – was "skateboard heaven."[13] As an industry, skateboarding was financially "in the depths of despair," during this period, but it did continue to produce magazines and videos, and to distribute them internationally.[14] Following the model of San Francisco's Justin Herman Plaza, Love Park became a darling of the skateboard media, appearing countless times in both editorial content and in advertisements for skateboards, wheels, bearings, clothing, shoes, and retail shops.

The primary users of the park during the early 1990s were homeless and skateboarders, and both were occasionally painted with the same brush in popular discourse. When a police officer described entering Love Park as follows: "It's like when you've got a room full of roaches and turn on the light," he was talking about skateboarders, though homeless, like skaters, were compared to rats often enough.[15] The *Inquirer* registered an ambivalent position on this new group. "A park for skateboarders? For those dudes in backward baseball caps who dart between cars, plow into pedestrians, and gouge the granite in public plazas? It's an idea whose time has not quite come. The dominant trend continues to be punitive, with more and more communities restricting or banning skateboarding as dangerous, destructive, even anti-social."[16] In 1995 a Common Pleas Court Judge, Richard B. Klein, complained that the "The average person has been taken off the plaza. This is a total waste of city money and frankly, gross stupidity."[17]

By the millennium, the problem intensified, as the skateboard industry grew to about $1.5 billion. There were not only four retail skateboard shops in center city Philadelphia, there were also at least a dozen professional skateboarders, skate photographers, and skate videographers who were based in the city. Love Park was everywhere – simulations of the plaza even appeared in video games that reached a market much broader than only skateboarders – making the space "a world famous icon" for youth culture.[18] (See Fig. 1.) The plaza was overflowing with skateboarders.

Figure 1 Professional skateboarder Josh Kalis appears in June 2002 advertisement for DC Shoes. Love Park appeared regularly in editorial content and in equipment advertisements in skateboard media. (Source: DC Shoes; photograph by Mike Blabac.)

In 2000 the council passed a citywide ban on skateboarding that specifically called out Love Park.[19] The ban was enforced with sweeps and often-violent police tactics, which are well documented in skateboard videos.[20] But public support for the skateboarders was mounting. On August 11, 2001, Inga Saffron, the *Inquirer* architecture critic, wrote an opinion piece titled "Don't trash thrashers": "Are skateboarders bad for JFK Plaza? No. They're the good users. Banning them won't make the poorly designed park inviting to others." "Frankly," she wrote, "I really miss the dudes."[21]

The plaza had enough notoriety in the skateboard world to attract ESPN's X-Games in 2001 and 2002. ESPN wanted to hold the event in the plaza itself, but the mayor's office offered Dilworth Plaza on the west side of city hall across the street instead, which was where the Games were ultimately held.[22] The Games generated an estimated $80 million in revenue for the city of Philadelphia, but shortly before ESPN arrived in the summer of 2002, the city fenced off Love Park to prepare for a redesign of the space.[23] ESPN did not renew its contract with the city for a third year.

Mayor Street promised to find another site where the city would build a "world class facility" for skateboarders, but in the meantime, the city had hired architects Synterra & Buell Kratzer Powell to renovate Love Park, for a price tag of $800,000. The architects installed a new drainage system and introduced planters, teak benches, and patches of grass. Saffron's review in the *Inquirer* called the work "slapdash" and "badly executed." "To block the skateboarders' path, they installed an array of sickly pink concrete planters and trash cans." The problem with this "Pepto-Bismol-tinted makeover," Saffron wrote, was "the city's priorities. Its main goal was to get rid of skateboarders; it wasn't to make LOVE Park a good urban space."[24] (See Fig. 2.) Saffron's review was only the first salvo in a barrage of negative press.

In September of 2002 "an assortment of the city's leading business and policy organizations" flew in Richard Florida – a Columbia urban planning Ph.D. and bestselling author – to speak to an audience of three hundred and fifty on the subject of urban economic development. Commenting on the remake of Love Park, Florida said "Skate parks are very important to young people, an intrinsic part of their creative culture, part of their identity. We should be expanding skate parks. . . . To take the park away is to tell them that they are not valid. Big mistake."[25] In October Edmund Bacon showed up in the new Love Park with television crews and a skateboard. After skateboarding across the space, the ninety-two-year-old Bacon announced that "by this act of civil disobedience, I am showing my displeasure with the mayor's actions." Vincent Kling was also in attendance to protest the ban and the redesign.[26]

By 2003, skateboarding had become an issue in the mayoral election. As part of his ultimately unsuccessful campaign, Republican candidate

Figure 2 Detail of redesign of Love Park, by Synterra. Flower planters and wooden benches are strategically placed to obstruct skateboarders' approach to the original granite ledges. (Photograph by Scott Kip.)

Sam Katz skateboarded across Love Park, declaring that if he were elected, the skateboarders would be returned. It was later revealed that Street's campaign finance manager repeatedly asked him to reconsider the ban – "It will do wonders for the re-election" – calling Street's position "wrong, both operationally and politically."[27]

In response to the Street administration's policies the skateboarders created a non-profit lobbying group, called the Skateboard Advocacy Network (SAN), led by a skater named Scott Kip who worked in the woodshop at a local arts college. Enlisting the help of local activists, editors, lawyers, architects, and planners who were sympathetic, SAN began negotiating with the city for a compromise, producing what it called a "balanced solution" proposal. If some of the obstructing planters were removed, the skateboarders would agree to use only certain areas of the park, only after 3 p.m., to avoid conflict with the lunch crowd. (See Fig. 3.) The city told SAN that it would have to consider how much money it would cost to maintain the park, given the skaters' high-impact use. SAN then found a 1999 report from city controller's office stating that "In fiscal year 1998, the City spent approximately $3100 to repair damage to the park's granite pavers that was caused by skateboarders. . . . In addition, according to Fairmont

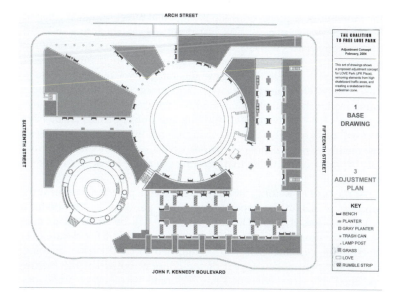

Figure 3 One of several "Adjustment Plans" offered by the Coalition to Free Love Park, an organization formed by the Skateboard Advocacy Network, along with the preservation group, the Independence Hall Association, and the advocacy group, Young Involved Philadelphia. The Coalition proposed to remove obstructions to skateboarding (planters, trash cans, and benches) from some areas of the plaza, while adding in rumble strips to the pathway parallel to John F. Kennedy Boulevard, in order to ensure a pedestrian-only zone in that part of the park.

Park officials, the City may have to spend approximately $50,000 in the near future to repair granite capping in the park damaged by skateboarders."[28] When SAN said that it could easily raise this amount, the city's managing director, Phillip Goldsmith, replied that the findings of that report were out of date and that the city would have to conduct another study. Goldsmith returned with a report estimating that if skateboarding were permitted, maintenance of the park would cost $100,000 a year.

When, in the beginning of 2004, SAN came back with a pledge for $1 million over the next ten years – if the skateboarders were allowed to return to Love Park – the Street administration was taken aback. The money came from a $100 million, California-based skateboard shoe manufacturer called DC, who sponsored several Philadelphia-based professional skateboarders. Barbara Grant, the mayor's spokeswoman, "said the skateboard advocates overstepped their bounds by negotiating the million-dollar pledge, despite the fact that Street said he'd consider their compromise plan."[29] "We just don't see skateboarding in LOVE Park," Grant said.[30] In a city that was planning to "close dozens of recreation centers [and] fire stations" because of ever-tightening budgets, the decision to reject the money generated even more unfavorable press.[31] John Dougherty, the city's Democratic Party treasurer and a union leader stated that "[t]his kind of investment in public resources represents the type of creative thinking and public-private partnership that will push our city forward . . . In the end, this means more jobs for our members, more commerce on our streets, and more vitality for our City."[32] The *Inquirer* wrote that rejecting the money was "a stunningly backward move."[33]

At the time of writing, the city has selected a parcel of land near the Museum of Art, at the opposite end of the parkway, as the site for a future skateboard park. The skateboarders will be expected to raise $4 million in private funding if it is to be built.[34] But the debate over whether the skateboarders will be returned to Love Park is ongoing. They have the public support of the editorial boards of the *Inquirer* and the *Daily News*, Vincent Kling, Edmund Bacon, local professors, over half of the city council members (eleven out of the seventeen), the executive director of the Pennsylvania Economy League, and the Independence Hall Association (a preservation group), among many other influential figures in Philadelphia. On June 6, 2004, the *Inquirer*'s Chris Satullo published an editorial titled "LOVE Park remains a test case of Philadelphia's will to thrive." Invoking the work of Richard Florida, he wrote that

> [T]he editorial page I lead has crusaded to restore skateboarding to LOVE Park, a.k.a. JFK Plaza, the awkward little square with the Robert Indiana sculpture near City Hall. This has convinced many serious sorts that the Editorial Board has lost its mind: "What is it with you guys and these obnoxious skaters? They're scruffy, rude, chip the concrete and annoy the lunchers. Why not worry about something important?" This is important. LOVE Park is a test case of whether this city can do the things that cities must do to thrive. Smart cities don't spit on serendipity. They open themselves to spirit, creativity, happy accident, and innovation — with all the messiness they entail. They don't just tuck in the coverlet and try to keep things peaceful while they die.

What has changed in theories of urban economics that so many opinion makers in Philadelphia now see "scruffy skaters" as not only an opportunity for development, but as an indicator of whether or not the city can survive?

Skateboarding on the "Boho Index," Skateboarders as "Creative Class"

To understand the terms of this debate, I turn now to the writings of Richard Florida, a consultant who has worked with cities all over the United States and Canada. Florida's 2002 book *The Rise of the Creative Class: And How It's Transforming Work, Leisure, Community and Everyday Life* is becoming standard reading on syllabi in graduate urban planning, public policy, and economic development programs. A basic premise underlying his argument is that

> The economic need for creativity has registered itself in the rise of a new class, which I call the creative class. Some *38 million* Americans, 30 percent of all employed people, belong to this class. I define the core of the creative class to include people in science and engineering, architecture and design, education, arts, music and entertainment, whose economic function is to create new ideas, new technology and/or new creative content. Around the core, the creative class also includes a broader group of *creative professionals* in business and finance, law, health care and related fields.[35]

In an increasingly consumer-based economy, Florida sees an inversion of the socioeconomic hierarchy between the professionals and the artists. The creative class is the "norm-setting class," the new "dominant class in America."[36]

What does Florida believe these new circumstances mean for urban planning and policy? For starters, it means that cities should no longer be catering to the traditional professions, trying to bring in jobs by bringing in companies by creating infrastructure and offering tax breaks. Rather, cities should be bringing in members of the "creative class" with lifestyle amenities. So the city is no longer industrial engine, or even "growth machine," but rather an "entertainment machine."[37]

This phrase was coined by Terry Nichols Clark, Professor of Sociology at the University of Chicago and the Coordinator of the Fiscal Austerity and Urban Innovation Project. Florida's ideas influenced Clark to take amenities seriously, and ultimately to devote an entire volume, *The City as an Entertainment Machine*, to the subject. In Clark's chapter, "Amenities Drive Urban Growth: A New Paradigm and Policy Linkages," he cites his research from the Fiscal Austerity and Urban Innovation Project: "We completed a national survey in 1984 and 1996 of mayors in all U.S. cities over 25,000 population. Results suggest the national importance of a pattern of leadership that we have termed the New Political Culture, which is distinctly responsive to consumption rather than just production."[38] The New Political Culture is one in which cities respond to the reality that "contemporary consumption practice extends to the consumption of space. The lifestyle concerns of social participants are increasingly important in defining the overall rationale for, and in turn driving, other urban social processes. Quality of life is not a mere by-product of production; it defines and drives much of the new processes of production."[39]

The 1968 *Annual Report of the Philadelphia Redevelopment Authority* opens with a paean to the modernizing, and modernist city: "Center City, riding the momentum created by the [urban renewal] program, was a forest of cranes and booms as new buildings popped up like spring flowers, glistening with promise of more tax returns to the city."[40] At the beginning of the new millennium, the modernist growth machine was sputtering. Writing in 2001, Florida quoted then CEO of Hewlett Packard, Carly Fiorina, addressing "a conference of governors recently: 'Keep your tax incentives and highway interchanges, [she stated,] we will go where the highly skilled people are.'"[41] The glimmer that 1960s urban leaders saw in office towers, 2000s leaders see in renovated art galleries, cafes, and plazas.

There is, in Florida's phrase, a new "Hegemony of the Street."[42] One conclusion to be drawn from this observation is that cities should no longer put so many resources into what Florida refers to as "'SOB' – the high-art triumvirate of a symphony orchestra, an opera company, and a ballet company."[43] Stadia are also off the agenda, since the "creative class" favors individual sports, where they "set their own pace and create their own rules."[44] (As the *Inquirer* opined "Think skateboarding, that is, before baseball stadiums."[45]) "[T]he creative class is drawn to organic and indigenous street-level culture. . . . Much of it is native and of-the-moment, rather than art imported from another century for audiences imported from the suburbs."[46] "To prosper in the creative Age," Florida writes, "regions have to offer a people climate that satisfies this group's social interests and lifestyle needs."[47] Seattle and San Francisco started as bohemian and gay meccas: "New York had Christopher Street and SoHo long before Silicon Alley erupted," Florida writes, "All of these places were open, diverse and culturally creative first. *Then* they became technologically creative and subsequently gave rise to new high-tech firms and industries."[48]

In his 2001 piece, "Technology and Tolerance: The Importance of Diversity to High-Technology Growth," published by the Brookings Institute, Florida set out to quantify this observation. He developed a Gay Index, a Bohemian (or "Boho") Index, a Foreign-Born Index, and a Composite Diversity Index, which is the sum of the rankings of the other three. "We compare our diversity measures to a measure of high-technology industry concentration and growth developed by the Milken Institute."[49] Florida finds striking correlations: "The leading indicator of a metropolitan area's high-technology success is a large gay population. . . . A high concentration of artists or 'bohemians' follows gays," and a high concentration of foreign-born residents also helps to predict high-tech success.[50]

When Florida weighed in on the side of the skaters during his trip to Philadelphia in 2002, presumably he understood them under the rubric of the "Bohemian Index." While the "scruffy," "rude" skateboarders may have been viewed as marginal in the early 1990s, by the 2000s they were beginning to be represented as the new model citizens and new model workers. "In culture as in business," Florida believes, "Everything Interesting Happens at the Margins."[51]

While Philadelphia has begun to cater to specialized lifestyles – with a gay-oriented tourist marketing campaign and negotiations with SAN for a new skatepark – I argue in the following section that the city has not adopted Florida's more inclusive conception of class.

New Century Neighborhoods, Exclusivity Avenues, and the Question of Class

Under Mayor Street the city has launched programs called the Neighborhood Transformation Initiative and New Century Neighborhoods. The programs set out to "advance the quality of life in neighborhoods with a coordinated and targeted code enforcement program to abate public nuisances."[52] They also aimed to "[u]se limited public resources to leverage private investment dollars to provide higher levels of maintenance, service, and amenity. Encourage rehabilitation and new development to appeal primarily to middle and upper-income households but also to maintain fair housing opportunities for low-moderate income households."[53] The $1 million offer from DC seems in line with the strategy of leveraging "private investment dollars to provide higher levels of maintenance, service, and amenity" – the conflict is about whom the amenities are for. While the *Inquirer's* Satullo, or Florida, might view the skateboarders as bohemian or creative class, the Street administration views the skateboarders as a "public nuisance" – or as Goldsmith put it "'a pimple on an elephant's hide'" – perhaps one that doesn't "appeal" to "middle and upper-income households."[54]

The City Controller's Report offers another possible insight into the city's policy toward skateboarders. In a section titled "Potential Future City Marketing Avenues," the controller writes that:

> Selling exclusivity is a way that the City can further capitalize on marketing efforts. By offering companies the right to be the exclusive providers of a product in Philadelphia, the City can multiply the value of its concessionaire-type contracts. Companies have demonstrated their desire to pay private and public entities a premium for arrangements that create official sponsors, vendors, or suppliers.[55]

Love Park is listed as one of the six "Potential Future City Exclusivity Avenues."[56] Perhaps a private company may want to open a restaurant in the now vacant visitor's center, the report suggests; and in exchange for exclusivity, the company would "provide maintenance services" in the park, which "suffers from neglect."[57] Even though they are not restaurateurs, again DC's offer seems to fit the bill; indeed the controller himself, Jonathon Saidel, urged the city to accept the offer.[58]

Of the many who supported the plan (including the *Inquirer*) and the few who opposed the plan (including *The Sentinel*), the only voice that objected to the very principle of "corporate sponsorship or support of municipal functions or properties" was the cantankerous lefty weekly, *The Daily News*.[59] While acknowledging the city's fiscal problems, the paper opined that "[t]he line between selling our citizenry and pimping them is a thin one."[60] Given the negative press, the city was largely quiet about its reasons for rejecting the offer, yet – in light of its policy reports which recommend that the city actively seek out corporate "sponsorship" – it is clear that protecting the citizenry against the corporatization of municipal property was not among them. With no other prospects for private "sponsorship" – at least none that have been made public – why give up such an offer?

Debates about this kind of public/private "partnering" seem to always employ a specific vocabulary (like "consumer" or "client" instead of "citizen") and I want to suggest that the language itself offers a clue. For example, consider one of the other Potential Future Marketing Avenues identified by the controller: "a boutique to sell used City property, including old street signs, parking meters, demo voting machines, and memorabilia from the City's defunct Civic Center."[61] Is Love Park one of the items being sold, or could it even be the boutique itself?

Many American cities are facing fiscal problems that have led them to begin treating their public space as intellectual property. Philadelphia is no exception. The controller suggests that "[t]he city can explore legally trademarking and copyrighting images and representations of much reproduced icons, or it could issue licenses to vendors to sell 'official City of Philadelphia' Liberty Bell and Independence Hall souvenirs."[62] Richard Indiana's LOVE sculpture would be a natural candidate for such an exploration. Would LOVE's further association with skateboarding dilute or preclude a future exclusivity deal?

Whatever the case, the administration's policy reports make clear that the city is proceeding from a belief that people of whatever class location "oppose the introduction" of people "perceived to have lower socio-economic characteristics than those that already exist in the community."[63] Furthermore, given that the reports also state the city needs to appeal to people of "upper-income" brackets, it is clear that the city is trying to nurture upper-class community in Love Park.[64] And as the *Inquirer* has observed: "Serious skateboarding largely attracts working-class kids."[65]

Gentrification as Equalizer

Florida's book is a call to class consciousness: "The members of the creative class today need to see that their economic function makes them the natural – indeed the only possible – leaders of twenty-first-century society. But being newly emergent, the creative class does not yet have the awareness of itself, *as a class*, that is needed."[66] Without this class consciousness, the creative class will be unable to realize its historical calling – to "pursue a collective vision of a better and more prosperous future for all."[67] But if class is understood in terms of economic status and the type of labor that one performs, then there is something counterintuitive about Florida's creative class, where a high school teacher and a neighborhood artist are of the same class as a biotech researcher and a hedge fund manager. On what basis would these people identify with one another? Is it really something so amorphous as "creativity"?

In Florida's account what holds all of these people together is that they drive urban growth. "Bohemian presence," Florida writes, "predicts . . . high-tech industry concentration."[68] But Florida has no predictions about what happens to the Bohemians once the high-tech capital has been concentrated. What holds "Bohemians" and "creative professionals" together is not class at all, but their participation in the process of gentrification. However, they each play different roles, at different stages, and they each benefit unequally.

If the city is an entertainment machine, then Adorno and Horkheimer's "culture industry" no longer serves as just ideological legitimation for the economy, but as the urban economy's main motor. And with the creative class, we see not only "culture" that elides and naturalizes class inequalities, but also *a class politics* that elides and naturalizes class inequalities. Such inequalities were not entirely lost on the skateboarders in Love Park.

"We Made This Place Alive": Skateboarders as the Shock Troops of Gentrification

I spoke with a Philadelphia planner who observed that Edmund Bacon's "understanding what skaters were doing in Love Park was like his understanding that Society Hill needed to be preserved."[69] In the 1950s, when his counterparts in other US cities were clear cutting struggling neighborhoods with Title 1 money, Bacon used this money to rehabilitate a distinguished but distressed housing stock in Philadelphia's Society Hill.[70] In this early and influential model of gentrification, Bacon showed that renewal could happen on a more fine-grained scale. There are many obvious differences between the Society Hill and Love Park stories – for one thing, the former project was carried out by old money elites, with federal subsidies, while the skaters in Love Park were banned – but both are stories of "reclamation."

In a 2002-videotaped interview in front of the fenced-off Love Park, a frustrated skateboarder named Ricky Oyola said:

> We should be able to do whatever we want here. We made this place. We made this place alive. Honestly we made this place worth anything. It was just fuckin' drug dealers, dudes chillin' up there, fightin' each other all the time, every day, you know what I mean. Like that's all it was. We came here and we gave it life. We gave it to where people could walk by and not feel scared because you got these little scrawny kids on skateboards here next to these fuckin' big time drug dealers: if these little kids aren't scared, why should I be scared? I'm a thirty-year-old man coming from work.[71]

Oyola's predicament is familiar to artists and bohemians from San Francisco's SOMA district to Manhattan's SoHo district. As the unwitting shock troops of gentrification – injecting a small capital flow into a distressed area – they eventually suffer from the same process that they precipitate.[72] The first wave of elites in 1950s Society Hill, of course, benefited enormously from their reclamation – what stories of gentrification have in common is not who the winners are, or even necessarily who the losers are, but the fact that the losers are typically erased from the story. Just as Oyola erased the homeless population in his statements, he is now being erased by the anti-skate redesigns of the plaza. While many of the skateboarders point out that they had befriended and built community with the homeless, it is certain that one of the reasons local opinion makers sided with the skateboarders was their belief that they deterred the homeless.[73] Challenging the skateboard ban, Saffron asked: "why chase out the park's main constituency, leaving it to the sort of people who use the space for long naps and personal grooming?"[74]

The *Inquirer* editor Satullo opined that "Ed Bacon celebrates how skaters' discovery of LOVE breathed *life* into his design."[75] As in Oyola's assertion that skateboarders made this place *alive*, it follows that Love was only death before the skaters arrived. This is another expression of the narrative that equates homeless populations with darkness or, worse yet, nothingness. Saffron, for example, referred to Love Park as "an urban black hole."[76] When a square full of people is described as "empty," those people are typically homeless. Before receiving federal funding, Society Hill needed to be officially diagnosed with "blight" (a plant biology term used to describe a spreading disease), and as with Love Park, Society Hill was described using terms like "barren" or "dead space." What Society Hill and Love Park have in common is a mode of describing social problems in terms of *natural* decay, when in fact those problems are better understood through an analysis of policy: red-lining and federally subsidized suburbanization in the 1950s, and the evisceration of public housing and mental health programs in the 1980s.

In the early 1990s skateboarders were, like the homeless, compared to rats and cockroaches. But as skateboarding grew to a \$1.5 billion industry in the early 2000s, bringing in millions to the city coffers, the activity rose out of the category of "quality-of-life crime" in local elite opinion.[77] A survey of the *Inquirer* from January to December 2004 shows that not only did the reportage on skateboarding increase as the stories on homelessness decreased, but also that the skaters began to serve as a syntagmatic substitution for homeless populations in political discourse. In fact many local politicians – like councilwoman Jannie Blackwell – who had fought for the homeless on the grounds that everyone was entitled to access to public goods, now fight for skateboarders, invoking the same modernist ideal of universal access.[78] As the homeless are phased out of the debates about access, the bottom rung on the social ladder is now occupied by the skateboarders, a group who everyone understands can pay the price of admission. Homelessness, then, is emptied of its political subjectivity, and is reconceived as an unfortunate fact of nature, and the homeless themselves as an "element" that ebbs and flows like the tides.

Conclusion

In the shift from the city of the Great Society to the gentrifying city comes a shift in outlook. Florida presents a sanguine view of this transition: "People have come to accept that they are on their own – that the traditional sources of security and entitlement no longer exist, or even matter. This is a sea change."[79] This sea change has been acted out in the space of Love Park. While it is not the case that all people have accepted the condition Florida describes, the statement does seem to accurately represent most of the skateboarders. Indeed they have no personal memory of there ever having been "traditional sources of security and entitlement," having been born in the 1970s and 1980s, and having come to adult consciousness in the 1990s and 2000s.

Borden's *Skateboarding, Space and the City* makes the case that the activity is a "critical exterior to architecture."[80] Skateboarding, he argues, interrogates and challenges the meanings of "the left-over spaces of modernist planning, or the spaces of decision-making (typically the urban plaza) which symbolize not through overt iconography but through the expansivity of space."[81] The book provides a history of skateboarding beginning in the 1970s, yet since the book's publication in 2001, the relationship between skateboarding and the city has been reconfigured in ways that force a re-evaluation of Borden's argument. From the 1970s to the 1990s modernist plazas like Love Park were largely abandoned by municipal governments; and at this same time, skateboarding was a marginal industry. Observing this period, it makes sense to argue, as Borden does, that skateboarding "involves great effort, but produces no commodity ready for exchange."[82] But in recent years, skateboarders have delivered Love Park to the city of Philadelphia in a new, more marketable form. In the 2000s, as the skateboard industry has grown to over a billion dollars, and as cities have begun to reinvest in their left-over modernist spaces, many opinion makers have begun to perceive some "synergies." Skateboarding may have been a wrench in the modernist "growth machine," but in Philadelphia it has been retooled as a cog in the entertainment machine.

The modernization of Philadelphia began when the parkway was cut through Penn's grid in 1906. Love Park was constructed at the parkway's terminus in front of city hall in 1965. Even through the fiscal crisis of the 1970s, the park was well used by Philadelphia citizens of all classes. With the "reforms" of the welfare state in the 1980s came a different sort of inhabitation of the park – if there was no housing or mental health services, at least there was public space. In recent years the youthful defiance of skateboarders has serendipitously reclaimed Love Park – generating revenue through media exposure and producing a marketable image for the city – all while deterring the presence of the homeless. Now the skateboarders, in turn, are being phased out to make way for the next reclamation. Love Park was an expression of the modernist city, both architecturally and socially. On the same site is now emerging the gentrifying city, where you are on your own.

Acknowledgments

In the Architecture and Geography departments at U.C. Berkeley, I would like to thank Kathleen James-Chakraborty, Allan Pred, and Paul Groth who offered insightful comments on various versions of this essay. Special thanks go to Greig Crysler who has commented on all those versions. I also thank the *JAE*'s anonymous reviewers for their excellent critiques of this piece. Finally, this essay could not have been written without information provided by Scott Kip. For all the assistance that I received, any errors of fact or interpretation remain my own.

References

1 Neil Smith, *The New Urban Frontier: Gentrification and the Revanchist City* (London: Routledge, 1996) p. 39.

2 Iain Borden, *Skateboarding, Space, and the City: Architecture and the Body* (Oxford: Berg, 2001), p. 237 and p. 188.

3 Ibid. p. 231.

4 David B. Brownlee, *Building the City Beautiful: The Benjamin Franklin Parkway and the Philadelphia Museum of Art* (Philadelphia: Philadelphia Museum of Art, 1989), p. 31.

5 See Philadelphia Redevelopment Authority, *Annual Report of the Philadelphia Redevelopment Authority* (1963), and Philadelphia Redevelopment Authority, *Annual Report of the Philadelphia Redevelopment Authority* (1964).

6 See Clark Deleon, "The Scene in Philadelphia and its Suburbs," *Philadelphia Inquirer*, February 19, 1981; Dick Pothier, "Chess Fans Find Friendly Challenge at JFK Plaza," *Philadelphia Inquirer*, August 19, 1986; Douglas J. Keating, "TV/Radio Talk: Original Writers, Crew Rehired To Revive 'Saturday Night Live,'" *Philadelphia Inquirer*, July 28, 1981; and Clark Deleon, "The Scene in Philadelphia and its Suburbs," *Philadelphia Inquirer*, June 13, 1981.

7 Clark Deleon, "The Scene in Philadelphia and its Suburbs," February 19, 1981.

8 See Editorial, "Hud's Sins Phila. Could Have Used Some Of That $2 Billion," *Philadelphia Inquirer*, July 14, 1989, as well as Russell Cooke, "Reagan Budget Cuts Prompt Phila. Rally Next Month," *Philadelphia Inquirer*, April 7, 1982.

9 See Editorial, "Hud's Sins" as well as Editorial, "The Mental-Health Puzzle Some May Think They've Come Up With an Easy Answer, But They're Wrong;" *Philadelphia Inquirer*, September 17, 1989.

10 See Editorial, "Hud's Sins"; Amy Rosenberg, "Mayor Unveils New Strategy for the Homeless Panhandling Will Be Discouraged. So Will On-Street Feeding. Instead, Long-Term Solutions Will Be the Focus," *Philadelphia Inquirer*, October 1, 1993; and Thomas Ferrick Jr. and Maida Odom, "Living on the Streets of Center City Ranks of the Homeless Soar," *Philadelphia Inquirer*, November 26, 1989.

11 Ginny Wiegand, "Who Eats at JFK Plaza? Brown-Baggers, Homeless – And Rats," *Philadelphia Inquirer*, November 5, 1991.

12 Daniel Rubin, "No 'Love' for Skateboarders Instead, A South Philadelphia Home," *Philadelphia Inquirer*, March 3, 1995.

13 See "Love Story," On Video, 411 Productions, 2004, DVD. In 1987 The *Philadelphia Inquirer* suggested that it was the homeless who gave JFK Plaza the name "Love Park" during this period. See Vernon Loeb, "Heat Changes Little for Homeless," *Philadelphia Inquirer*, June 16, 1987.

14 Karen Heller, "Chairman of the Board," *Philadelphia Inquirer*, August 2, 2000.

15 Howard Goodman, "The City's Love Park – a Gateway for Visitors – Is Home to the Homeless and Lures Skateboarders," *Philadelphia Inquirer*, August 25, 1996.

16 Marie McCullough, "Skateboarders Slowly Gain Right-of-Way – And a Few Parks \ The Sport Long Has Been Restricted or Banned as Dangerous. Some Communities, However, Are Building Places Just For It," *Philadelphia Inquirer*, April 30, 1995.

17 Daniel Rubin, "No 'Love' for Skateboarders."

18 "Love Story," On Video.

19 City Of Philadelphia, Bill NO. 000147, Title 10, Section 10-610.

20 See "Love Story," *On Video and Sight Unseen*, Transworld Skateboarding, 2001, videocassette.

21 Inga Saffron, "Don't Trash Thrashers," *Philadelphia Inquirer*, August 11, 2001.

22 "Love Story," On Video.

23 Ibid.

24 Saffron, "Disappointing developments on 15th St.," *Philadelphia Inquirer*, August 23, 2002.

25 Cover Story, "I Can Fix Your City," *Philadelphia City Paper*, September 12–18, 2002.

26   Howard Altman, "LOVE Burns Bacon," *Philadelphia City Paper*, October 31–November 6, 2002.

27   Marcia Gelbart, "Street's Musings, Worries, in E-Mails," *Philadelphia Inquirer*, March 27, 2005.

28   Jonathan A. Saidel with Brett H. Mandel, Kevin J. Babyak, and David A. Volpe, *Philadelphia: A New Urban Direction* (Philadelphia: Saint Joseph's University Press, 1999), p. 138.

29   Carla Anderson, "Cover Story: City to boarders and shoe $$: Keep walking," *Philadelphia Daily News*, June 2, 2004.

30   Ibid.

31   Editorial, "For LOVE, Money," *Philadelphia Inquirer*, June 2, 2004.

32   Anderson, "Keep walking."

33   Editorial, "For LOVE, Money."

34   Inga Saffron, "Changing Skylines," *Philadelphia Inquirer*, May 6, 2005.

35   Richard Florida, *The Rise of the Creative Class: And How It's Transforming Work, Leisure, Community and Everyday Life* (New York: Basic Books, 2002), p. 8.

36   Ibid. p. 317 and Ibid. p. xi.

37   Harvey Molotch, "The City as a Growth Machine," *American Journal of Sociology*, 82/2 (1976): pp. 309–332.

38   Terry Nichols Clark with Richard Lloyd, Kenneth K. Wong, and Pushpam Jain, "Amenities Drive Urban Growth: A New Paradigm and Policy Linkages," in Terry Nichols Clark, ed., *City as Entertainment Machine* (Oxford: Elsevier, 2004), p. 302.

39   Ibid. p. 299.

40   Philadelphia Redevelopment Authority, *Annual Report of the Philadelphia Redevelopment Authority* (1968.), p. 4.

41   Richard Florida with Gary Gates, "Technology and Tolerance: The Importance of Diversity to High-Technology Growth," *The Brookings Institution, Survey Series* (Washington DC: The Brookings Institution, 2001), p. 2.

42   Florida, *The Rise of the Creative Class*, p. 182.

43   Ibid. p. 182.

44   Ibid. p. 175.

45   Chris Satullo, "LOVE Park remains a test case of Philadelphia's will to thrive," *Philadelphia Inquirer*, June 6, 2004.

46   Florida, *The Rise of the Creative Class*, p. 182.

47   Ibid. p. 295.

48   Ibid. p. 206.

49   Florida with Gates, "Technology and Tolerance," p. 3.

50   Florida with Gates, "Technology and Tolerance," p. 1.

51   Florida, *The Rise of the Creative Class*, p. 184.

52   Ibid. p. 20.

53   Ibid. p. 20.

54   Satullo, "LOVE Park remains a test case."

55   Philadelphia City Controller, *Philadelphia: A New Urban Direction*, p. 145.

56   Ibid. p. 146.

57   Ibid. p. 146.

58   Anderson, "Keep walking."

59   See Editorial, "Skateboard grant hides an agenda," *The Sentinel*, June 3, 2004 as well as Editorial, "Skate Off," *Philadelphia Daily News*, June 3, 2004.

60   Editorial, "Skate Off."

61 Saidel, p. 144.
62 Ibid. p. 145.
63 Philadelphia City Planning Commission, *New Century Neighborhoods*, p. 6.
64 Ibid. p. 20.
65 Heller, "Chairman of the Board."
66 Florida, *The Rise of the Creative Class*, p. 315.
67 Ibid. p. xii.
68 Ibid. p 42.
69 Personal interview, Greg Heller, November 5, 2004.
70 Smith, *The New Urban Frontier*.
71 "Love Story," *On Video*.
72 Smith, *The New Urban Frontier*, p. 20.
73 "Love Story," On Video.
74 Saffron, "Don't Trash Thrashers."
75 Satullo, "LOVE Park remains a test case." Emphasis added.
76 Inga Saffron, "City planner's legacy not the sweet deal WHYY sells," *Philadelphia Inquirer*, September 23, 2004
77 Saidel, p. 201.
78 Compare Rosenberg, "New Strategy for the Homeless Panhandling," May 14, 1993 and *On Video* 2004.
79 Ibid. p. 115.
80 Borden, *Skateboarding*, p. 1.
81 Ibid. p. 188.
82 Ibid. p. 1.

Mairi Johnson

Once Upon a Sign: Relationships of Architecture and Narrative in the United States Holocaust Memorial Museum

Abstract

This paper is concerned with ways in which meaning, assembled into narratives, can be injected into architecture. Rather than seeking the translation of narrative tools into new architectural devices, each section interrogates an existing architectural technique to examine the ways in which it can become the entry point for narrative into a corner of a design. The United States Holocaust Museum, as a building infused with narrative, is used as a testing ground for these hypotheses.

Architecture is real and narrative is imaginary but they race towards each other with the inevitability of opposing magnets. Their union is fleeting and ambiguous. A building will remain just a building and must be judged as such and the implied meaning will always be just a narrative that can be told without the presence of the building. But while there is no dishonour in the pure state of either of the two disciplines, their mutual trespass is a store of potential richness.

The similarities between architecture and narrative are only really analogous, although in their differences lies their mutual usefulness. When a building is charged with carrying a meaning, the architecture will fail to convey the narrative with the specificity of the original verbal form but it will add a life that the narrative could never have hoped to have achieved. This is narrative's gain – buildings enrich the world from which narratives are generated.

Our understanding of the world and ourselves is organized for communication into narratives constructed in verbal language. Verbal language is relatively easy to manipulate compared to other modes of expression and therefore it is possible to be quite precise and strong in describing our reactions to the world and what its meaning is to us. Architecture can have a similar emotive power to language and thus it seems a seductive vehicle for carrying the gravity and intricacy of our understanding. But verbal language and architecture are not interchangeable. Architecture's power is intuitive; to describe a building in words is an illusionary code but, because the desire to describe is there, born from the emotive capability of the architecture, the on-going relationship between architecture and narrative is sustained.

The assertion that configurations of forms and materials may have an inherent meaning is dangerous ground in the late twentieth century. The narrative/architecture relationship is important because narrative is concerned with the fundamental construction of meaning. Narrative is the form through which feelings, places, interactions and situations are researched and recorded and is therefore a fund on which to draw during the design process. Architecture offers an opportunity to be concrete about a theoretical idea while at the same time allowing designers to use their own intuitions, memories and experiences to create personal spatial metaphors. This shows that architecture and narrative can be united in the mind of the architect, but more here than they can ever be united in the result of the union as it is perceived in the building itself. All the attempts to fuse buildings with a specific significance fall at the same hurdle: the interpretation only exists in the mind of the designer and if the user, or subject, does not understand what is being referred to then the applied meaning dissolves leaving an architecture of pure formalism.

This paper is concerned with ways in which meaning, assembled into narratives, can be injected into architecture. Rather than seeking the translation of narrative tools into new architectural devices, each section interrogates an existing architectural technique to examine the ways in which it can become the entry point for narrative into a corner of a design that then goes on to influence the whole ensemble. The first of these is symbolism, the instance when a part of a building stands as a direct sign for a segment of meaning. The second is the use of sequences in architecture which introduces the designed relationship between time, space and movement. The third instance examines the willing suspension of disbelief: architecture that intends to create a realm that is detached from the world outside a boundary, but is still linked to that world in some way, enabling the subject to understand the significance of the difference.

The United States Holocaust Memorial Museum in Washington DC is an interesting testing ground for this study. The architect is James Ingo Freed of Cobb, Pei, Freed and Partners and it was opened to the public in April 1993. Freed has deliberately set out to make this a meaningful building that will imply an essence of the Holocaust through its architecture. Freed's means to do this is to design the building as a 'resonator'[1] that will be in phase with other memories in the minds of the building's users and amplify them. By stimulating personal memories the associations will act as metaphors to relate people to the Holocaust on a visceral level as well as intellectually, even though the only actual experience of the Holocaust that most of them will have will be that acquired during their time in the building. Freed writes:

> The problem, of course is that if you deal with the
> conceptualisation of metaphors you run the risk of the metaphor
> not being understood in the same way by others. What we have
> tried to do is to construct symbolic forms that are in some cases
> very banal, ought to be banal, and in other cases are more

abstract and open ended. People read different things into these forms but they are not empty. The idiosyncrasies create something to jog the memory. The multiple readings that occur are sometimes intentional, sometimes not. We consciously didn't want to force the one reading that we knew, and we had to have several reasons for doing each thing.[2]

The Holocaust itself is a subject of awesome gravity and Freed's intentions in dealing with it are brave and honourable, but that does not make the result beyond criticism. Bernard Tschumi asks, 'Is there such a thing as an architectural narrative? A narrative not only presupposes a sequence but also a language. As we all know, the "language" of architecture, the architecture "that speaks", is a controversial matter. Another question: If such architectural narrative corresponds to the narrative of literature, would space intersect with signs to give us a discourse?'[3] The Holocaust Memorial Museum attempts this and to some extent succeeds.

The Holocaust as a narrative in America

Holocaust survivors are 2–3% of American Jews, themselves 3–4% of the whole population in the USA, yet the Holocaust Memorial Museum is one of the most visited buildings in the country. The horrific events perpetrated by the Nazis are not of immediate personal relevance to most people but their import has been singled out for respect and commemoration.

1995 was the fiftieth anniversary of the liberation of the Nazi concentration camps by the allied soldiers. Over those fifty years the importance of the Holocaust has grown to become notably prominent in the USA, an interesting preoccupation especially considering America's relationship to the original events. Unlike Germany it is not the homeland of the perpetrators, unlike Israel it does not have a special relationship to the victims and unlike Poland it is not the site of the camps themselves. It is true that many Jews fled to the USA to escape the persecutions, but although they make up a relatively small percentage of the population they are a minority that has been extraordinarily important in the country at large, socially, politically and, crucially, in the media.

The Holocaust has not been a central part of American Jewish concern until quite recently. During the post-war decades the Holocaust was quite marginal, not only in the consciousness of American gentiles but also of Jews as they sought to make a safe home in their adopted country. The testament of survivors was soothed away by other Jews who were already well integrated and encouraged other survivors to forget the ghastly past and allow themselves to be assumed into America where anti-Semitic barriers were rapidly tumbling. When a

Holocaust memorial was proposed for New York City in the 1940s it was unanimously rejected by Jewish organizations because it would make Jews appear as 'helpless victims'.

Retrospectively, the silence can be read as Jewish repression and, in the case of immigrant survivors, as a struggle to bear the agony of memories. Gentile guilt may also have been a factor in the apparent social amnesia. At that time the term 'Holocaust' was not an accepted term for the horrific events that had occurred and Jewish persecution was just one aspect among many Nazi atrocities. After the war there was rapid political realignment between America and the countries of Europe so it was an urgent ideological task of American foreign policy to make Germany appear as positively as possible, repressing possible parallels between the Nazi and Soviet regimes.

The fear of a renewed Holocaust in the weeks immediately preceding the Six Days War in 1967 was the most specific catalyst for heightening Holocaust consciousness. It was feared that the combined Arab armies would eradicate the Jews in Israel and that the Jewish homeland would be obliterated for ever. Holocaust imagery had played little part in mobilizing support for Israel until this point, but as the Israelis perceived indifference from the rest of the world, sharp reminders of recent Jewish history began to appear.

This period also brought a significant generational shift in Jewish leadership. Those committed to the earlier, low profile, 'don't make waves' posture, were replaced by a more assertive younger generation.[4] But if the style of the emerging Holocaust discourse owed something to the radicals of the 1960s, its content was philosophically conservative. Discussion of the Holocaust has often treated it as a startling revelation of the existence of depravity in humankind, exposing the naïveté of those with utopian, or even ameliorative, social aspirations.

The 1970s saw the full recognition of the Holocaust in the American scene with the establishment of the Presidential Commission on the Holocaust by Jimmy Carter, arguably to pacify Jewish voters who felt him insufficiently supportive of Israel or to divert humanitarian attention away from Vietnam. The final report of the Presidential Commission for the Holocaust called for an institution that was at once of a 'symbolic and artistic beauty that is visually and emotionally moving in accordance with the solemn nature of the Holocaust' and which would 'present' the Holocaust to the nation.

The Holocaust Memorial Council was established in response to the Presidential Commission in 1980 by a unanimous Act of Congress and mandated to 'plan, construct and oversee the operation of a permanent living memorial to the victims of the Holocaust.' The Council was comprised of survivors, scholars, curators and designers. All these individuals had varying ideas as to how the museum should be. There were also battles with the Washington DC Fine Arts Commission, empowered to maintain a style that it felt was fitting to the city.

Freed was commissioned in November 1986 and presented his final scheme to the Council in April 1987 who approved it unanimously. In June of the same year the Fine Arts Commission also unanimously approved the design. The Holocaust Memorial Museum was destined to be a building of the establishment. It would be a node between the corporate building type and what America could digest as the Holocaust.

President Clinton dedicated the museum on April 22 1993 and it was opened to the public three days later. At the dedication he spoke of the need to 'deepen our memory and our humanity and to transmit these lessons from generation to generation' – a need revealed by a recent survey that showed that only 37% of Americans were familiar with the Holocaust.

But the centrality of the Holocaust has been chosen, not imposed. Millions of dollars have been raised for memorials and institutions across the country. The Holocaust has almost superseded religious beliefs in the self-understanding of American Jews. The rate of inter-marriage among Jews is 50%. With the long-range survival of the community in question, Jews for whom the Torah and the Covenant still retain meaning are asking if the Holocaust-centred identity is an effective response to centrifugal forces.

When you wish upon a sign – narrative meaning in architecture through symbolism

The Holocaust is beginning to assume all the attributes of myth: the epic proportion, the association with a particular place, archetypal but remote characters, the lives of ordinary people being dictated by a power beyond their control. Myth is a kind of distilled narrative, a higher order of significance which is the given background to which other narratives can refer. As the myth is perpetuated, it no longer becomes necessary to tell the whole story to allude to the original significance. The myth assumes the status of allegory which is linked to the original narrative by a symbolic language that is not necessarily verbal. The distinctions between all these terms are very slippery. Jennifer Bloomer differentiates between them by describing allegory as 'the dark background against which the bright world of the symbol might stand out.'[5]

The system of relationships between the myth and the symbol, the signified and the sign, is not absolute; it has a short sell-by date. Society forgets some myths and acquires others so that the sign/signified relationship is in constant metamorphosis. Benjamin would say that this is because of the intrinsic nature of the symbol:

> The symbol is, in fact, something that because of its nature rejects an univocal reading. Its meanings tend to escape and its characteristic is that of revealing and hiding at the same time

[. . .] It follows therefore, that the qualities of the architectural symbol are the same as those of the artistic "sign": ambiguous, disposed to accept different meanings, transparent and fixed within a pre-established code, and at the same time, able to transgress the laws of that code.[6]

Classical buildings are arrays of signs. The formal details of Greek temples can be shown to be direct representations of the sacrificial offerings with which the original wooden temples were adorned. Even as the wooden forms have fossilized to stone over the centuries, there remains a certain literalism between what the architecture represents and the form that represents it. Barthes acknowledges this, writing: 'To some degree the form (of the sign) resembles the content as if it were actually produced by it, so that the symbolic consciousness masks an unacknowledged determinism'.[7] The classical edifice that originated as the architecture of Greek temples has been subverted to mean 'building that houses power and wealth' and a temple is only one of the building types that now uses this arrangement of forms. The once relatively figurative architecture is now seen as abstract, but an abstraction which can evoke very specific responses.

It was always inevitable that the Holocaust Memorial Museum would have a certain amount of symbolic content, situated as it is in Washington DC which, as a city, stands as a built symbol of the utopian ideal of democracy. The museum does not have a frontage on to the greensward of the Mall, the symbolic garden of America, but is one block to the South, straddling between 14th Street and 15th Street. Walking around the base of the Washington monument provides a vista which encompasses the Capitol, symbol of democracy, the museums along the edge of the Mall, symbols of knowledge, people playing baseball or jogging – happy citizens enjoying the leisure afforded by a well-run country. The front entrance of the museum is just visible down 14th Street and does not immediately jar with the superficially Elysian setting.

The Holocaust Memorial Museum is externally a classical build-ing. This is not surprising considering its location at the heart of the American establishment, an establishment that still uses classicism for most of its civic buildings. Freed was not unaware of the association he was taking on: 'There was always the problem of the use of classical lan-guage in relation to the Nazi appropriation of monumental classicism. I think that I've got a critique of neoclassicism in the building. Rather than appropriation it is classicism used as a tool of critical dialogue, a tool for expressing duality.'[8]

Standing between the limestone National Bureau of Engraving and Printing on one side and the Victorian brick Auditors Building on the other, the Holocaust Memorial Museum makes an architectural link between these two by using both brick and limestone in the facades.

Figure 1 The entrance for groups of visitors on 15th Street. (© Mairi Johnson.)

> Bringing the brick in from one side and the limestone from the other reflects a condition of the Holocaust: at the one end you have the structure of the modern state, the monumental – and yet that structure embraces the most primitive urban condition at the other end – the little village. This strategy accomplished several things. It tied us to Washington, and also made the building very particular to its site, while permitting us to do things with the form of the building that we could never have done otherwise. It allowed us to argue with the Fine Arts Commission for the need to deal differently with the scale of forms. And it allowed us to form certain critiques of the monumental Washington front.[9]

The screen in front of the 14th Street entrance is symbolic of the gate as a lie – that an invited path may be a false trail. This recalls the gateway into Auschwitz that had 'Arbeit macht frei', 'Work Makes Free', written across its arch. What at first appears to be the monumental way into the building is in fact a mask: behind the screen the sky is still visible above and the door itself is much smaller and some way beyond in a steel and glass pavilion. Freed said of this move, 'the screen in the front portal is not there to force a reading, but to make evident the need for interpretation. Things call for interpretation but remain insufficient in themselves.'

The screen, comprised of rectangles incised out of a smooth wall to suggest unadorned columns and entablature, is an integral part of the classical architecture. This, together with the watch towers along one side of the buildings and other references to surveillance and industrial buildings, is presumably what Freed is referring to when he writes of a 'critique' of classicism. The result is somewhat clumsy but the architectural discourse between the building's similarities to classicism and its obvious deviances does draw attention to the fact that there is something about this building that is disturbingly different from its obedient neighbours.

The decision to make the Hall of Remembrance a symbolic structure within the overall scheme was decided before Freed was appointed architect. The Committee specified that the hall should be hexagonal in plan to symbolize the Star of David and also the six million Jews killed and that its volume would be clearly visible on the outside of the building as monument to all the people who died. The interior is comprised of a sheltered ambulatory around the edge of a large space. Broad steps lead down to the empty central area that has the eternal flame at one side, opposite the entrance. The corners of the hexagon are opened as long strip windows which Freed writes represent hope as opposed to enclosure and makes the walls into free standing plaques or tablets.

The floor of the hall is of a rusty red to symbolize the blood of the victims. Inscribed on the wall are the words, 'What have you done? Your brother's blood cries out from the ground' – Genesis 4:10. The floor reads first as shiny corporate marble, the second level meaning as blood seeping from the ground is only revealed by the explanatory quotation on the wall nearby. When I visited the museum people were reluctant to descend the steps and enter the central space. It is an uncomfortable place if the only memory of the Holocaust that you have is the one just acquired in the permanent exhibition, one feels unworthy to cross the door to the flame.

The unity and calm of the Hall are horribly marred by a clumsy wheelchair lift to bring people with special needs into the central space. It seems strange that in so considered a building such a requirement should have been forgotten but then perhaps the lift is a deliberate move to inject uneasiness, signifying that all is never as resolved as it seems. Freed writes in his article on the design of the museum, 'I go around and take things away from people in the office who are trying to resolve them. I don't want this building to look too worked over. I want it to be a little raw still. Not just in the materials but in the conceptualisation and even in the actualisation.'[10] Even so, the wheelchair lift appears to be a mistake, not a chosen aesthetic.

The roof of the Hall is made of a large domed skylight which is an allusion to the freedom of the sky. Freed heard from survivors that their first memory of the camps was of being closed in, of fences, and that the only place that was not hemmed in by barriers was the sky. Having said this, the skylight is actually very heavily structured and calls to mind a descending cage more than space and freedom, but perhaps this is another of Freed's intentionally ambiguous gestures.

There are details elsewhere that come directly from the death camps and are then abstracted by their use in the building. The camps did not produce specialized building types, existing patterns were adapted, such as the barracks at Auschwitz which were originally designed as

Figure 2 The Hall of Remembrance. (© Mairi Johnson.)

Figure 3 Wheelchair lift in the Hall of Remembrance. (© Mairi Johnson.)

military stables. The differences that fitted a building for the Holocaust are small, so finding forms that specifically evoke the Holocaust is a delicate task.

The ovens that cremated the bodies of victims were built of brick that later had to be strapped with steel as the furnaces became overused to the extent that they might explode from the build-up of internal gases. Freed saw this in the camps and adapted it as an emblem in the Memorial Museum, abstracted to the use of heavy steel on a brick wall. Nowhere in the camps is the strapping criss-crossed or detailed to meet the wall in the same way as Freed has done, but still it speaks of the Holocaust.

A handrail in the Hall of Witness is built in the form of a rail from the tracks that ferried people to their death. The handrail is not an actual rail but is visibly assembled from pieces of steel so that it is the shape of a rail but not a single casting. To take actual pieces from Germany and bring them to Washington and use them in the building itself rather than as an exhibit would be a macabre kind of kitsch, but to remake them so that they are obviously a false version is also unsatisfactory because, as in the case of the handrail, the form is still too literal and has not made the leap into architectural language. To read this form as an architecture, it is an ugly handrail; to read it as a piece of railway track, it is poorly constructed and unfunctional.

This is where the design of the building falls down. As has been discussed, symbols tend to resemble what they symbolize to some extent. This building symbolizes the Holocaust which as a concept is deeply

Figure 4 The handrail in the Hall of Witness. (© Mairi Johnson.)

horrific but which had built manifestations that were superficially unremarkable. In some instances Freed has taken something that in its literal form is fairly ordinary and abstracted it in the building as an ugly detail. This is not a great achievement. To make a building that is deliberately ugly is a disservice to the people that the building commemorates because most people visiting the building will not read the architecture with the sophistication that is required and will not see why details and spaces have taken the form that they have. All that will be left is the awkwardness. Even if it were completely legible the awkwardness would not be excusable. It is not wrong of Freed to use every available device for delivering meaning in buildings, but the architecture that results must be able to stand without its meaning and still satisfy aesthetically and practically.

Following the Yellow Brick Road – narrative sequences in architectural sequences

The use of architectural sequences is seductive because the sequence never offers a comprehensive view. The device itself is a method of obscuring, delivering only one step at a time so that the present is denied and memory and anticipation are everything. The anticipated, the imagined and also the past are always more perfect than the real present. This is the alluring power of the sequence.

An event is something out of the ordinary that heightens the properties of the everyday situation. For a narrative, the story is moved forward by events involving the characters against the background of a succession of scenes. An architectural event is the physical manifestation of a human event – even the presence of the building itself. Similar to a narrative event, an architectural event is an interruption in the ambient landscape. In the salt flats of Utah a wall is an architectural event. In the middle of the city there are many walls and so a door or window in the wall may have more significance than the wall itself. The narrative event of turning off the street into a building is marked by the architectural event of the entrance way. The building can be a backdrop for these events which over time will scar its surfaces and leave a trace, or the building can be moulded from the start to incorporate the needs of the projected events that will happen there.

The sequence of events forms the plot of the narrative. The plot can compress time in epic leaps or stretch time with elaborate detail even to the point of arresting it as the events are revealed in several places at a particular point in the fiction. To draw an analogy between narrative sequence and architectural sequence is to highlight the designed relationship of time and space in architecture. This is not simply a spatialized version of a narrative because time cannot be manipulated by architecture in the same way, but a parallel can be drawn between the idea of a narrative plot and buildings that use a controlled route as a device.

The result of using sequence as a method of accumulating meaning is little different from static symbolism except that the order of symbols is planned and the way that they are seen is choreographed so that extra significance can be derived from the order or frequency in which symbols are apprehended. There is an implied assumption that the subject is complicit with the architecture in fulfilling the potentialities of the sequence but in most cases this is wishful thinking. Buildings are not necessarily visited only once and under normal circumstances the sequence of spaces is not necessarily always gone through in the same order. Using the device of repetition can help to make the sequence more legible. This could be repetition in the plan or the section to construct 'spot the difference' situations where the significance is in what has changed. Repetition is also important in narrative tradition, particularly in its oral beginnings. The best storyteller was not the person who made up the best stories but the person who had the best way of retelling a story.

The plot of the Holocaust Memorial Museum is multi-stranded. The primary function of the building is to expose and structure the events of the Holocaust for people who have little or no connections to those events themselves. The museum building makes frequent use of architectural sequences although not everyone visiting the building will go through all the sequences. The museum contains a permanent exhibition and two special exhibition galleries with changing displays. Hand in hand with this are educational facilities for teachers and their classes, two auditoria for relevant films, lectures, symposia and musical presentations, available outside the opening hours of the museum. Education and research are carried out through the Wexner Learning Center, a computer-based learning facility, and also the Library and Archives which house collections of books, documents, photographs, oral histories, film and video. The museum opens itself to the accumulation of information and survivors and their families are encouraged to come and tell their own story and donate their own possessions to the museum's growing collection of artefacts. The administrative centre and cafeteria are in a smaller building a few steps away from the main building itself but not adjoined to it. Each person visiting the building for whatever reason will have their own relationship to the building and to the other people there, the other characters in the plot.

The plan is organized on either side of the central void of the Hall of Witness which is the main circulation space on the ground floor and from which the other public areas can be accessed. The permanent exhibition begins on the third floor and spirals down to the first floor crossing above and through the Hall of Witness on bridges at each floor during the descent. Several designed sequences wind around each other and are addressed to different users. For instance, the processional route across the Hall of Witness and up to the Hall of Remembrance is very different from the sequence of the permanent exhibition although they both end in the same place. Most visitors will enter the building at the main approach on 14th Street; here again the sequence of spaces is very deliberately manipulated. The following paragraph is summarized from Freed's own description of the entrance sequence.

The screen on 14th Street at the front of the building is a lie. It is not the entrance because the area behind it is open to the sky with the actual threshold in a glazed wall beyond. There are two entrances, one for visitors and one for parties, visitors immediately undergo a segregation left or right, not life or death. The entrance vestibule for individuals is off to the left but on penetrating these doors you find yourself in a little pavilion with the passage through off axis again. We disorientate you, shifting and centring you three times, to separate you emotionally as well as visually from Washington. From the entrance area you step out into the Hall of Witness onto a raw steel deck in one corner of the great space. There is a feeling of self-consciousness as you realise that you can be seen from the mounting vantage points above the hall and that in relation to the hall floor you are on a stage. This structure orientates you to the elevators or lets you descend to the temporary visits or move across the hall and up the stairs. There is a slot along the edge of the hall and the grid shifts. This is perhaps banal but it is important for two reasons. One is that it allows light downstairs, the other is that it separates the experience of going into and out of the museums from the experience of the content of the building. The skylight over the Hall of Witness cuts diagonally across the hall because that is the path of travel. We did this to disengage you, to move you diagonally across the space. If you think of it, it becomes apparent that such a skylight would be twisted – twisted by the geometry, but also by the force of the logic that sends you diagonally across, the tension of the diagonal splitting the space in two.

A scholar heading for the library will pass into the entrance pavilion but immediately turn left through a small door that leads to the elevators that go straight to the fifth floor, avoiding the crowds, the permanent exhibition and the check points.

In architectural sequences the movement between sites of symbolic significance is as worthy of consideration as the nodes of signs themselves. Movement can be dealt with in two ways: firstly as a symbolically neutral interlude between the contemplation of one array of signs and the next. This freeing of movement from symbolic baggage allows movement to develop its own independent characteristics in contrast to the stasis of the halting points. Secondly, a built landscape can be designed to be seen at a particular pace, such as motorway art.

Bridges are used as a motif throughout the building but most notably in the permanent exhibition. They are an example of the designed use

Figure 5 The Hall of Witness. © Mairi Johnson.

of movement and also of repetition. Their origin in terms of the design of the museum came from seeing pictures of the Warsaw ghetto that showed wooden bridges for Jews built over the streets below so that the body politic would not be infected by the disease of Judaism. They are examples of a symbol of movement, of transport, and in some instances of landscapes that are intended to be seen at walking speed.

There are long bridges linking the permanent display galleries on either side of the building. These bridges have a glass block floor and glass walls, what Freed describes as a 'dangerous path'. Etched into the glass walls of the bridges are names. One bridge has the family names of people who were killed in the Holocaust, the other has the names of villages that no longer exist. This is the landscape to be seen through movement. In stepping out across the bridge the names are not immediately obvious; the gaze grazes the view out over the skylight or down onto the crowds milling in the Hall of Witness below. As the blur of names becomes arresting, one stops to read the names, to think about them and then to look with more scrutiny at the view beyond the glass wall. It is a device which shows the relationship between the surface of a building and its architectural arrangement and is effective in maintaining concentration on the reason for the building and the purpose of the visit.

Because the building is so tailored to the needs of its different users it is difficult to pass through an undesigned sequence of spaces. There is not an obvious hierarchy of importance to the spaces when the Hall of Witness, which is a gathering and circulating area, is as loaded with symbolism and as sequentially controlled as the Hall of Remembrance. Even the cafeteria has a waiting area, an ascent to a partially obscured dining area and then the resolution as the corner at the top of the stairs is turned and the food counter revealed before you. Presumably workers in the building become immune to the significance of their every step over time but for museum visitors there is little respite from the barrage of meaning.

Never Never Land, the second sign on the right – buildings that set out to tell a story

For a building to suspend disbelief and tell a story, the implication is that the new story inside the building will not allude to the 'real' world outside. Such a building would also have to use an architectural language that originated from the story or its vehicle, or the leap from the everyday to the fantastic would still be grounded in the world of the real. There is an assumption that the world to which a fantasy building does refer is known by those visiting the building, otherwise it will be misunderstood or not understood at all.

The world of the Holocaust is a world far removed from Washington DC and within the Holocaust Memorial Museum the permanent exhibition, designed by Ralph Appelbaum, is a doorway between these two concepts. Inside the permanent exhibition galleries the suspension of disbelief is made easy because the events to which the exhibition refers are slightly re-enacted as part of the telling. The actual experience of being delivered to the camps is recreated within the confines of the exhibition by the visitors themselves. The museum is very popular and is able to deliberately utilize its crowds almost as an architectural device. A ticket to the museum has a time printed on it for entry into the permanent exhibition so there are very precise controls as to how many people are at any place in the exhibition at any time. There are throngs of people in all points along the exhibition all the time and they shuffle along with turgid inevitability, shifted by the pressure from behind.

The first stage of entering the exhibition is a queue. If not a queue of Disneyland proportions, the wait is long enough to make visitors become aware of the time. At Disneyland one is in a queue for most of the day so there is a dualism here – the queue could be for a theme park type experience or not, the reason for the wait is not immediately revealed. This brings to mind the meticulous suspension of disbelief that was employed in the gas chambers. People would climb off the train, be told they were going to have a disinfecting wash and then would be processed en masse into the 'shower room' that appeared genuine even to the extent of having duck boards on the floor. The first realization that all was not as it seemed was when lethal gas was emitted from the jets on the ceiling.

At last, entry is permitted into the waiting area in front of the lifts. Here there are dispensers of facsimile identity cards, detailing someone who was imprisoned in the camps. The idea is that these are the 'Holocaust double' of people entering the exhibition, emphasizing the point that it is only by chance that one person dies and another visits a museum.

The lifts themselves are exposed steel and frighteningly crowded. During the journey to the third floor a video monitor plays footage of the American soldiers as they first came upon one of the camps, 'we don't know what it is, some kind of prison,' a grim analogy with the experience being undergone by the visitors at that moment.

The exhibition is organized chronologically and charts the fate of all those persecuted, not just the Jews. The lighting is always quite dim which adds to the sense of claustrophobia. The detailing is the most raw of anywhere in the building with no attempt to hide or feature wires and ducting.

Beginning with the rise of Nazism in 1933, the display progresses to the implementation of the Final Solution and ends with post-war efforts to resettle survivors. The design relies heavily on black and white moving and still images arranged along the route that is always clogged with people. It treads a thin line between story-telling and history; impression and analysis.

What is interesting is the way the process of viewing such material becomes an enactment of the events. Due to a narrow approach you have to wait and push and be squeezed in line to go through a genuine cattle truck, and the entire audience flow slows and congeals when it comes to the central operative moment of the museum, the display about the gas chambers of Auschwitz. This is what the museum exists for, this is where the story comes to its impenetrable conclusion, but as an audience the relief is palpable when one can go on to the next exhibit in the inevitability of the system.[11]

As well as the images and texts the route is interspersed with tableaux of the victims' possessions. Amongst the late twentieth century techno-telling these take on a real poignancy which is based on both historic nostalgia and alarming familiarity. The contents of pockets are incredibly individual and personal, but then the room filled with mouldering shoes smelling of mildew and leather cries out for the many, for the millions that were slaughtered. The sizes and styles of the shoes reinforce the fact that the victims were ordinary people. Other artefacts include part of a barracks from Auschwitz, one of the box cars that carried people to their death and canisters of Zyklon-B gas, reminders of the collusion of industry in the massacre.

One of the most architecturally poetic displays is a three-storey funnel-shaped tower covered from top to bottom with photographs of life in the Polish village of Ejszyszki, a town of 3500 people, only 29 of whom were left after it was decimated by the Nazis. It was one of these 29 who collected the photographs which now bear testimony to a lost world. In themselves the photographs are not particularly interesting, but the dim 'chimney,' crossed by bridges at every floor with natural light filtering down from the narrow top into the dark base below, lends them their power.

To move through the exhibition at the speed of the crowd takes about three hours. It is exhausting and harrowing, at the very limit of what the public can take physically, emotionally and intellectually. The Hall of Remembrance is situated just outside the exit doors to receive visitors who arrive staggering for a place to sit down. But the space does not welcome them; its emptiness and icy hardness intimidate rather than offer a place to rest and an opportunity for contemplation. The Hall of Remembrance taken out of the sequence of the exhibition, seems to be a space in need of a ritual to fill it, something for people to take part in. (Public ceremonies do take place there on Commemorative days.) But within the sequence, for visitors having just gone through the communal experience of the permanent exhibition, the sudden space and isolation of the Hall are a definite conclusion, if not the one sought at the time.

If this is a deliberate device it is a very sophisticated one, an effective monument to the Holocaust. This is what Freed aimed for in his deliberately uncomfortable spaces and awkward details. It is a long hard manipulation but ultimately it works.

Conclusion – living happily ever after

Reality and historical concepts no longer exist as binary opposites held in place by the structure of historical time. Therefore the difference between fictional and historical narrative is no longer obvious. Baudrillard writes of the Holocaust in *Simulacra and Simulation* that the 'forgetting is part of the extermination'. Once the slaughter is forgotten then the obliteration is complete. The people and the violence never existed. Baudrillard argues that for late twentieth century society 'the forgetting is still too close to the original extermination and must be effaced by an artificial memory.'[12]

We live in a world where there is more and more information and less and less meaning. Against this background the Holocaust is one event among many that has been subsumed into narrative and inevitably metamorphosed into a historical myth. If the Palestinian/Israeli conflict can finally be peacefully resolved the place of the Holocaust in public discourse will alter. The survivors who have been central in promoting the Holocaust will soon be dying. The second generation will not have the irresistible moral authority of their parents. The injunctions 'Remember!' and 'Never Forget!' are still completely appropriate but the problem of giving form to this memory will remain.

The Holocaust, it is said, sensitizes us to oppression and atrocity. In principle it may – no doubt it sometimes does. But making it the touchstone of such actions can easily trivialize crimes of lesser magnitude,[13] for example the daily shame of homelessness, poverty and racism. The difficulty for the museum institution is in deciding how much it should use its facilities to involve itself with world politics, particularly instances of genocide. For example, at the time of writing, the museum did not have a definite policy on whether its special exhibition galleries could be used for a display about Bosnia. Because the institution is so closely tied to government politics it seems unlikely that such a remit would ever be issued and so the long term future for the museum is the recycling of the same information in forms appealing to future generations as they emerge.

The example of the Holocaust has shown that the memory of history is not static. The Holocaust Memorial Museum was designed to resonate with the memory of the Holocaust events as that memory was perceived at the time the museum was built. 'Intrinsically, the intentions are all greater than the reality. It is not meant to be an architectural walk, or a walk through memory, or an exposition of emotions. Odd or quiet is not enough. It must be intestinal, visceral, it must take you in its grip. This is an indeterminate thing to do, and we are not saying that we are using architecture to do it.'[14] 'The way the memorial is built may never come across to anyone, and it doesn't have to because the whole entourage is what must come across.'[15]

As the events of the Holocaust recede still further into the past it will be interesting to see if Freed's architecture is able to retain its links with its original associations. The awkward idiosyncrasies of the building that can now be justified by the current relationship to the events, may over time become read just as awkward architecture. The possibility exists that the building itself could become a historical curio. In the most extreme scenario the architectural language developed in the Holocaust Memorial Museum could be used in the way that classicism has been, as a reference to be reinterpreted itself.

References

1 James Freed, 'The United States Holocaust Memorial Museum,' *Assemblage*, 9 (June 1989), pp.58–79.

2 *Ibid.*, p.64.

3 Bernard Tschumi, 'Sequences,' *Architecture and Disjunction* (London: Massachusetts Institute of Technology, 1994), p.164.

4 Peter Novick, 'Holocaust Memory in America,' in James E. Young (ed.) *The Art of Memory: Holocaust Memorial in History* (New York: Prestel-Verlag, 1994), p.162.

5 Jennifer Bloomer, *Architecture and the Text: the Scr(y)pts of Joyce and Piranesi* (New Haven: Yale University Press, 1993), p.43.

6 Walter Benjamin quoted in Bloomer, *Architecture and the Text*, p.45.

7 Roland Barthes, 'The Imagination of the Sign,' in Susan Sontag (ed.), *A Roland Barthes Reader* (London: Vintage, 1993), p.213.

8 Freed, 'The United States Holocaust Memorial Museum,' p.65.

9 *Ibid.*, p.61.

10 *Ibid.*, p.73.

11 Adrian Dannatt, 'Bearing Witness,' *Building Design*, 1131 (2 July 1993), p.10.

12 Jean Baudrillard, *Simulacra and Simulation*, translated by Sheila Faria Glaser (Chicago: University of Michigan, 1994), p.79.

13 Novick, 'Holocaust Memory in America', p.163.

14 Freed, 'The United States Holocaust Memorial Museum,' p.73.

15 *Ibid.*, p.64.

Joanna Rapp

A Geometrical Analysis of Multiple Viewpoint Perspective in the Work of Giovanni Battista Piranesi: an Application of Geometric Restitution of Perspective

Abstract

This paper is a study of the work of the eighteenth-century Italian artist Giovanni Battista Piranesi. In it, selected etchings by Piranesi have been analysed by means of geometric restitution of perspective. Using this method it will be proved that the drawings of Ponte Fabrizio and Ponte Ferrato have been composed from multiple viewpoints. Piranesi has manipulated the conventional rules of perspective in order to produce a more believable and compelling representation of reality and subtly to influence our understanding of it. The paper presents a specific and detailed analysis of Piranesi's technique and reveals the sophisticated approach to perspective which he employed. It also gives an historical insight into the method of geometric restitution, explains how it operates and why it is useful, by employing it to analyse a series of etchings by Piranesi. It demonstrates that using precise geometrical methods may lead to new and exciting discoveries in the analysis of works of art.

It is assumed that the reader has a basic understanding of the principles and constructions for vertical perspective. For more information refer to 'The basic constructions of perspective'.[1] This will frame our way of thinking about perspective and provide an understanding of the projection methods.

Introduction

This paper is a study of the eighteenth-century Italian artist Giovanni Battista Piranesi. Known predominantly for his *Carceri* etchings and reputedly himself a colourful and interesting character, Piranesi was also one of the great recorders of eighteenth-century Rome. This article attempts to show how, in addition to being a highly skilled draftsman, he also manipulated reality in these drawings to enhance (or falsify) our view of Rome. To do this I have applied a now little-used technique known as *restitution*. A process pioneered by the eighteenth-century German mathematician Johann Heinrich Lambert, restitution uses descriptive geometry to derive the metrical proportions of objects depicted in perspective. The paper will explain how it operates, and why it is useful, by employing it to analyse a series of etchings by Piranesi. This analysis clearly shows how the artist manipulated perspective to control its visual impact on the viewer.

Not only an innovative exponent of etching techniques, Piranesi was also extremely creative in his use of perspective and composition. Many sources talk about the artist's manipulation of reality, referring mostly to exaggeration of scale, moving buildings to suit the composition, falsifying proportions between the human figure and the monuments, or perspective foreshortening. That he composed views by combining different viewing positions is noted in the RIBA catalogue: *Piranesi, Rome Recorded*.[2] One of the entries in the catalogue briefly points out that topographic view painters would often 'compose' their image from a number of viewing points and also that the manipulation of perspective was a common practice amongst the *Vedutisti* painters. The RIBA catalogue goes on to explain that only occasionally is this issue addressed in modern accounts of his work. But despite being given relatively little attention, this device remains an important clue to understanding the sophisticated approach employed by Piranesi. The aim here has therefore been to present a more specific and detailed analysis of his technique. The intention is to reveal exactly how Piranesi composed his perspectives and confirm his profound knowledge of geometry and skill in using it to manipulate his works of art.

1. Giovanni Battista Piranesi

Giovanni Battista Piranesi was born on the 4th of October, 1720, in Molino near Mestre and was baptised in the Church of San Moise in Venice. His eye, imagination and character were moulded in Venice, a city built on swampland and raised on timber piles, where buildings were constructed lightly, and predominantly using materials such as brick, wood and stucco. Here, marble and stone were present only to face the grander buildings and were rarely more than a thin veneer over brick. The light in this environment was also unique with façades illuminated by the light reflected off the water.

The particular quality of Venice undoubtedly contributed to Piranesi's artistic vision, but his own family experience also had an impact on developing various aspects of his future artistic life. His father, who was a stone mason, gave his son basic technical knowledge; his brother, a Carthusian monk, stimulated his younger brother's enthusiasm for antiquity; and his uncle, Matteo Lucchesi, introduced him as an apprentice to the world of architecture and archaeology in his workshop.[3] But the culture and art of Venice inspired Piranesi's mind: paintings by Tiepolo, Guarini, Canaletto and Piazzeta; the theatre of Goldoni and Gozzi; and the music of Vivaldi. Piranesi experienced the atmosphere of the Venetian theatre, its scenography and the fantastic world of exotic fables, *capricci*-architectural fantasies and Arcadian landscapes.

Very different to the ephemeral Venetian atmosphere at that time was Rome, where a twenty-year-old Piranesi arrived in 1740 in the retinue of the Venetian ambassador. The heavy stone blocks constituting the surface of the Via Appia; the giant foundations of Hadrian's Mausoleum and the ancient walls of the city were overgrown and decaying, but still endured. Shining in the still light of noon or sinking in the deep shadows of dusk—it seems reasonable to assume that these edifices charmed the artist. In comparison with the smooth floors of Venetian palaces, the ragged earth of Rome from which rose the greatest monuments of the City, almost certainly had an impact on Piranesi. In one of his etchings the earth is scored by carts in the Piazza del Popolo and is reminiscent more of a field in the countryside than of the surface of a square of the 'Eternal City'. We can see similar uneven terrain in the etchings of the Quirinal Hill, Piazza Navona and in front of the Pantheon, while the Forum Romanum lies fallow. On this ground sculpted by rain and sun Piranesi built his own Rome. Every drawing holds one, inimitable moment of life. Apart from squares and buildings, there are stalls and wells, horsemen, rococo carts, clergymen, antiquarians, beggars, dogs, goats, cows and everything that Piranesi saw when walking through Rome.[4]

In nearly a thousand visionary drawings, Piranesi froze the city of Rome at a particular moment in the eighteenth century, in all its banal and incredible aspects.[5] He was depicting ancient monuments not only because he was looking for an attractive view that he could sell in his shop in Via del Corso, but also to discover the secrets of their coming into existence, to learn and show how they were built. He was an archaeologist in times when this word was not yet in common use. In the preface to the *Antichita Romane*[6] he explains his concern for the preservation of this heritage:

> When I first saw the remains of the ancient buildings of Rome laying as they do in cultivated fields or gardens and wasting away under the ravages of time, or being destroyed by greedy owners who sell them as materials for modern buildings, I [was] determined to preserve them for ever by means of my engravings.[7]

Their merit is even greater because we do not have equivalent documentation of previous epochs, before Piranesi. He was very meticulous in preparing his views with numbers and descriptions of each monument, parts of the building and ornamentation. But despite this textbook-like exactness, the aesthetic and expressive qualities of his work are never jeopardised. With his careful and precise observation of monuments and their details, he created marvellous and visionary masterpieces. Indeed, he preserved and celebrated the achievements of Rome in his works. Since then, about a third of the monuments drawn by Piranesi have disappeared from the Roman landscape.[8]

Giovanni Battista Piranesi's work undoubtedly makes him one of the greatest artists in the history of etching and the *Vedute* genre. He was however also an architect and he believed that his profession was able to change the world and the spaces it represented. He was not given much opportunity to build, but he was a man of great artistic ambitions and etching was the device with which he demonstrated this.[9] He was using the tools of an architect to convey the ideas he could never build. From his architectural education Piranesi acquired the skill of systematised thinking and an understanding of structural rules and construction. And although limited by the technical demands of etching, it seems this hidden passion for building enabled him to convey the same confident expression in his depictions of Roman monuments as that which had inspired their original construction.

Piranesi's prints showed things in an original and unprecedented way. With his extraordinary observational skills and wild imagination he created an unknown image of Rome designed to inform the way we think about this Ancient City. He drew it dramatic and gigantic in comparison with tiny human figures. He was also interested in Roman building techniques and frequently recorded examples of engineering in detail. He enhanced the idea of Rome and its ruins through his picturesque and expressive views, strengthened by his choice of viewpoints and perspective. Exploring how Piranesi used perspective as a compositional device and as a tool through which to manipulate the depicted topography will provide an insight into the mind behind these dramatic images.

Unfortunately, only a handful of his preparatory drawings, showing compositional structure, have survived. He usually prepared initial sketches in black chalk, with red chalk on top of it to emphasise tonal colour, and a few examples of these sketches have been found at the back of trial proofs of his prints or on odd scraps of paper. It seems that this was the style of working that Piranesi adopted and he resolved the details of the composition straight onto the copper plate. His biographer Legrand wrote:

> Piranesi never produced finished sketches, a rough study in red chalk, reworked with pen or brush and even then only in parts, being sufficient to secure his ideas. It is almost impossible to distinguish his thoughts on paper because it is nothing but a chaos from which he only extracted a few elements for his plate with consummate skill.[10]

And then he cites Piranesi himself:

> Can't you see that if my drawing were finished my plate would become nothing more than a copy while, on [the] contrary, I create the impression straight on to the copper making an original work.[11]

There is also, of course, the possibility that Piranesi destroyed his preparatory sketches in order to protect the 'secrets' of his craft, but for whatever reason, few of these drawings have survived and as a result it remains unclear as to how he mapped out his subject on the plate before the etching.[12] Yet we can perhaps look for clues somewhere else and there is one unquestionable hint to be found in Piranesi's words:

> In truth . . . anyone who does not see the use of [perspective] and its necessity in Architecture, does not yet know whence she draws her greatest and most substantial beauty.[13]

This statement emphasises the importance of perspective in his designs. Studying perspective was a fundamental part of Piranesi's training. He was taught perspective by Carlo Zucchi (an average etcher, seal-engraver and also an author of a treatise on perspective) but he also underwent a formal training with the Valeriani family of stage designers. Stage design was a popular field in which many great artists were involved, and inspired by experimenting with linear perspective and its potential for creating illusionary effects. Indeed, it had a great impact on some of the most prolific architects of the Baroque, such as Bernini and Juvarra, and was obviously present in the art of Tiepolo in Venice, where, since Tintoretto and Veronese, a long tradition of spectacle had been established. The person who transformed stage design in Italy was Ferdinando Galli da Bibiena with his treatise of 1711, *Architettura Civile*.[14] His *Scena per Angolo* changed the 'nature of perspective representation and its relation to reality'. In *Scena per Angolo* a commonly used one-point perspective (frontal view) was replaced by two-point perspective which creates a greater illusion of reality. Abandoning the traditional central viewpoint enables the scene to open further vistas and makes it richer spatially.

Piranesi certainly knew Bibiena's treatise[15] and in his training he would also include Bibiena's handbook for students entitled *Direzioni a Giovani Studenti nel Disegno dell'Architettura Civile*.[16] This book first introduces geometry, proceeds with the five orders after Vitruvius, Serlio and Palladio and continues with Bibiena's own *Divisions in Architecture*. *Prima Parte di Architetture e Prospettive* indicates how important Piranesi's background in stage design was for his ideas. Although his plates are not presented by him as stage designs, most of them are clearly influenced by the imaginary architecture typical of such designs. In several drawings in *Prima Parte* we can see the relationship to stage designs from Bibiena's treatise. In this first publication of his etchings, Piranesi, as a young artist, may possibly have wanted to demonstrate his proficiency in solving problems of composition and to show that his talent exceeded that of his masters.

But despite the strong influence of stage design on Piranesi we can see differences in style emerging even in his early drawings. Piranesi refined Bibiena's overloaded compositions and reduced the excessive ornamentation that obscured the lines of the buildings. His drawings show greater structural clarity and portray massiveness of individual forms more convincingly. At the same time, Piranesi is very precise in controlling his etching technique, using lines that vary in width, and creating a more natural atmosphere for the scene. This broad range of line widths and densities allows contrasts of black and white, light and shadow as well as the gradual fading of forms in the distance. The values that make Piranesi a great master of his era are: elegance of line; perspective drawing controlled to perfection; the composition of subjects enriched by the presence of the landscape and the human figure; balance between the shadow and light; and drawing precision.

Piranesi belonged to the group of painters known as *Vedutisti* (view painters) which originated in Italy and included such famous names as Luca Carlevaris, Michele Marieschi, Giovanni Paolo Pannini, Antonio Canal (Canaletto), Francesco Guardi and Bernardo Bellotto. This group of painters deserves to be recognised as great perspectivists. The predominant characteristic of *Vedute* painting was not only linear perspective but also natural atmospheric and tonal perspective. This kind of painting is as realistic as possible, and so, in a sense, similar to modern photography in its primary objective. Indeed, *Vedute* and landscape painters have been associated with various methods of work based on using perspective drawing aids.

But clearly, tools used by artists to achieve their artistic aims should not change the way we value their work. Painters have always sought devices to help them in their work and this continues today. Even if we take an extreme position and assume that the better a piece of art imitates reality the better it is, we would have to ask which or even whose reality it is. Every artist reproduces his own, subjective visual reality, his own object and his own view of it. Imitation of reality is extremely individual and it results in an unlimited variety of representations. In this lies the precise content and sense of art. Even picturing reality by means of photography gives results dependant on the way the object is framed and the techniques used which produce very varied effects.

The value of the work of art is independent of any drawing aid. Talent is greater than the most sophisticated reproduction technique and the eye and mind of the artist is something more subtle than even the most sophisticated photographic lens.

In many ways this truth also applies to the perspective of the *Vedutisti* painters regardless of whether we are considering linear, natural atmospheric or tonal perspective. Piranesi belonged to the group of artists whose work struck wonder in observers even if it illustrated landscapes that were already famous or monuments familiar to European culture. It represented Piranesi's own view of art. His striking contrasts of light and dark, incredible skies disrupting the scenes and frightful characters populating them, have had a major impact on the way we imagine eighteenth-century Rome. And hence, when we look at photographs of some of the monuments that Piranesi depicted, our sense of excitement is often diminished.

Other artists such as John Flaxman, who was a draughtsman and sculptor; and the great precursor of romanticism, Wolfgang Goethe, are among those who were disappointed when they saw the ruins of Rome after their imaginations had been stimulated by the drawings of Piranesi.[17] In these emotional illustrations of ancient Rome he never sacrificed the precision of perspective. Piranesi was a brilliant and intelligent exponent of perspective techniques, not in any way limited by the application of this science. The key to our understanding of Piranesi's approach is, as Manfredo Tafuri described it, the use of 'imagination as an instrument, to control the space and the relationship between past and present'.[18] Piranesi, it might be said, acknowledged that our experience of the world is essentially perspectival and took licence to control it.[19]

2. Projective geometry

Although predominantly a representational convention, the theory of perspective is closely related to other sciences such as optics, physiology, psychology and geometry, especially the principles of projection. The history of perspective, when considered as a defined artistic practice, began in the fifteenth century and many prominent artists and architects such as Filippo Brunelleschi, Piero della Francesca, Paolo Ucello, Leonardo da Vinci, Albrecht Dürer and Rafael Santi, contributed to the exploration of its theoretical and practical implications. Leonardo da Vinci defined three concepts in the theory of perspective, and his considerations are still valid today:[20]

- Linear perspective
- Perspective of air and light
- Analysis of the sharpness of contours and contrasts depending on the spatial depth

Perspective, conceived as an image captured on a vertical plane, is evident in the work of a number of practical exponents of the drawing, including Albrecht Dürer and Andrea Pozzo—in particular, Pozzo's influential treatise provided a systematised theory of perspective. But it was not until the late-eighteenth century that Gaspard Monge created descriptive geometry as a separate domain of mathematics, and since that time it has been possible to develop further the theory of perspective based on projective geometry. He described descriptive geometry in this way: 'It is a means of investigating truth; it perpetually offers examples of passing from the known to the unknown.'[21]

Projective geometry is essentially an extension of a Euclidean definition of space. However, when central projection (otherwise known as perspective) is considered within the limits of projective geometry some peculiarities emerge, and it becomes necessary to represent points which do not technically exist. In Euclidian geometry, parallel lines, even if extended indefinitely, will never intersect. In perspective, however, such lines will inevitably meet and their point of intersection, the perspective vanishing point, will have a real representation on the picture plane. Since this point can have no real position in Euclidian space it has been called an *improper point*. On the picture plane the vanishing point is a real point that is equivalent to a point at infinity in Euclidean space, but such a point is impossible to represent in Euclidean geometry. Euclidean space is insufficient, but it can be extended by adding *improper points*. As a result we obtain a new richer and more general projective space. Such a procedure (extending) is often used in mathematics to define more general objects.

In projective geometry, parallelism, the measure of angles, the length of segments and the order of points are not preserved; however, rectilinearity and tangential relations are. For example, in Euclidean geometry the ratio of the length of segments is preserved while in projective geometry this relation and proportionality is not maintained. The so-called *cross ratio* of four points is preserved in projective geometry and will prove to be useful later in this analysis.

Although it is based on rules, restrictions imposed by perspective do not limit the artist but in fact allow him greater freedom of expression. Piranesi's drawings testify that thorough knowledge of perspective can overcome conventional limitations and find a fuller expression of visual experiences. The use of traditional perspective construction as a tool for a flat representation of three-dimensional form may well have originated from the architectural convention of drawing in plan and elevation. We construct a perspective of an object from its plan and elevation positioned on the drawing in a way that they correspond with each other, and with a specific viewing position. Perspective is, in this sense, a measured drawing and if constructed accurately, it is of course possible to reverse this process, and in doing so, reveal the foundations upon which the drawing has been built. This technique will also prove to be useful in an analysis of Piranesi's drawings.

The question of how Piranesi used and exploited perspective in his art, and how he overcame its rules, can be investigated by means of *geometric restitution*. Using this method it is possible to focus on his perspective images, work backwards and find his notional position as an observer. This will provide an insight into the devices used by Piranesi to construct his views of Rome.

3. The geometric restitution of perspective

Geometric restitution of perspective (or *the inverse method of perspective*) is a technique for reconstructing the base elements of perspective, which are: the centre of projection (the position of the eye), the depth of sight (the distance from the eye to the picture plane), the horizon line and the base line (the ground line). Consequently, we can reconstruct the shape, size and position of the object as it would be in real space, based on its perspective. This is the opposite process to projecting the object in real space onto a picture plane. In other words, the real shape of the object can be derived from its perspective image. Restitution can therefore serve as a very valuable method for investigating the geometric properties of perspective in works of art.

The aims of *restitution* can be extensive. It can be used to survey the dimensions of unreachable (or difficult to reach) building fragments—for example, those in danger of collapsing—and also in surveying and reconstructing the shapes and sizes of sculptures, monuments, architectural details or the spatial planning of new buildings into the existing urban fabric. Restitution can also be used to explore the more general pre-planning of appearance and composition; in which case, sketches or drawings can provide a sufficient starting point. For technical surveying, or detailed architectural or archaeological investigations, it is essential to base geometric restitution only on reliable data such as photographs taken with suitable cameras to retrieve exact information. Therefore, for special purposes such as detailed technical documentation, that has to be produced in architectural surveying with a high degree of graphic precision and metric accuracy, the use of *photogrammetry* rather than *restitution* is necessary.[22, 23]

There are also different requirements on perspective projection depending on why one wants to prepare the restitution. To reconstruct only a general geometric outline of an object one can use even a simplified perspective image. It is, however, easier to establish base elements of perspective (centre of projection, the depth and line of sight, horizon line, vanishing points and the ground line), if the perspective projection is characterised by slightly exaggerated perspective. It should also be clear from the image whether it is a one-point central perspective, two-point or three-point inclined perspective. For better results the image should be clear and sharp with legible edges to the objects and sufficient depth in the picture.

The methods of perspective restitution used in the analysis of Piranesi's etchings are presented in *The Basic Constructions of Perspective*.[24] In this paper, in particular, two methods of restitution of the base elements of perspective have been used.

In the first method, the base for the restitution is the perspective of the rectangle derived in the horizontal plane from the perspective image (Fig. 1). Here the given elements are: the perspective of the rectangle, the ratio between the sides (angle a between the side of the rectangle and its diagonal) and the length of one of the sides of the rectangle. The ratio between the sides of the rectangle permits one to establish the position of the eye and the distance of the eye from the picture plane. Knowing the length of one of the sides of the rectangle allows one to establish the ground line position.

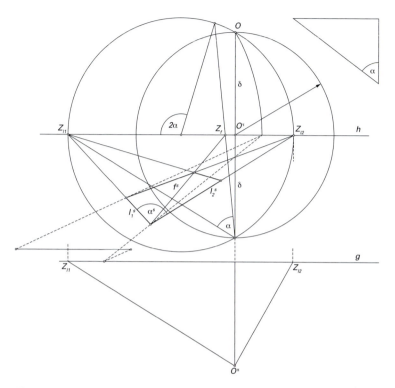

Figure 1 Restitution based on the rectangle derived in the horizontal plane from the perspective image. (Drawn by the author.)

In the second method, the base of the restitution is the perspective of a given parallelepiped where at least one vertical wall is a square (Fig. 2). On the basis of this information one can establish the position of the eye and its distance from the picture plane. The intersection points of the projected sides of the base rectangle determine the vanishing points Z_1 and Z_2 for the horizontal lines parallel to the rectangle sides. The line between the Z_1 and Z_2 is the horizon line. Because the sides of the rectangle are perpendicular in relation to each other, the eye must be located on the circle between Z_1 and Z_2. Furthermore, one assumes that the vertical squares have a vanishing point Z_1, whilst the vanishing points of the diagonals of these squares are located on the vertical line intersecting the point Z_1. These points can be denoted Z_t (top) and Z_b (bottom). The points Z_t and Z_b are located symmetrically in relation to the horizon line because both diagonals are inclined relative to the ground at 45 degrees. Due to the diagonals being perpendicular to each other, the eye must be located on the circle between Z_t and Z_b. Therefore the eye must be situated on the intersection of both circles.

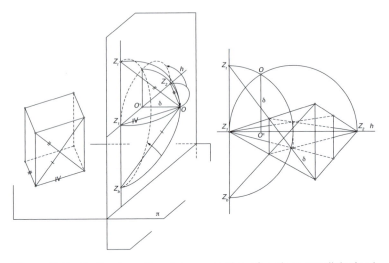

Figure 2 Restitution based on the perspective of a given parallelepiped where at least one vertical wall is a square. (Drawn by the author.)

4. Lambert's contribution to the method of geometric restitution of perspective

The first person to explain the concepts upon which geometric restitution is based was Johann Heinrich Lambert (1728–1777). One of the eighteenth century's most distinguished mathematicians, Lambert was also an accomplished scientist and philosopher who wrote extensively on perspective. One of his most significant works on perspective was *Free Perspective* in which he began to develop a unified perspective theory.[25] Lambert was interested in the relationship between the orthogonal plan and its perspective image. And his writings were certainly influenced by some of the earlier works on this subject, especially those of Andrea Pozzo and Ferdinando Galli da Bibiena. But uniquely, Lambert wanted to understand the geometric properties of perspective and how he could deduce the viewing position of an artist from it. He believed that perspective derived from optics is a natural way to depict the world.[26] His aim was to prove that we do not need to start with the orthogonal plan to generate perspective. Combining optics with geometry, he concluded that from the perspective image we can measure the real angles of the object and derive its specific viewpoint.

As demonstrated by Bibiena, perspective applied to the theatre stage becomes a model for the natural way to see the world—a notion which directly impacted Lambert's treatise, in its most important chapter: *On the Inverse Rules of Perspective*.[27] Here, he explains how to find the centre of the projection and the horizon line based simply on the points of convergence of parallel lines from the perspective image. Lambert goes on to show the geometric relationship between the plan, elevation and perspective by proving that not only is it possible to turn a plan of the object into its perspective, but also to work out a plan of the object from the perspective image. This discovery is the key to our understanding the process of geometric restitution and how useful it can be potentially.

Writing more than a century before the invention of photography, Lambert could not have predicted the importance of this entirely theoretical and idealistic geometric study, but through his work on perspective, Lambert is also now regarded as a creator of theoretical *photogrammetry*.[28] As a result of his geometric sensibility and idealistic mathematical thinking, he recognised the possibility of reconstructing an orthogonal plan and the viewing position from the perspective image. He demonstrated the basic methodology used to work out this information. The tasks of restitution and the way we solve them, remain essentially the same as Lambert presented them in the eighteenth century. Differences, such as there are, lie in the language he used and his method of explanation. For the most part Lambert's language is very general and sometimes imprecise. His commentary on geometrical constructions has a very descriptive character, mainly providing step-by-step instructions like recipes, while not entirely explaining why they should be done in this way. Relative to modern scientific language, the language employed by Lambert can make it difficult fully to understand the precise rationale behind the method. At the time when he wrote his treatise, it probably meant that only a handful of people could understand his texts and perhaps he intentionally aimed them at a very sophisticated audience.

In his monumental treatise *Free Perspective*, in the last chapter (no. 8) entitled *On the inverse rules of perspective*, Lambert presents seventeen propositions in relation to restitution of the base elements of perspective. He illustrates these propositions with six examples: special attention will be paid here to two of these examples (Figs. 3 & 4). The main task (usually the most difficult) to resolve in these examples is the restitution of the position of the eye. These examples are worth analysing because the geometric constructions presented in them are models for the kind of constructions that are used today, including within this paper.

5. Analysis of selected Piranesi etchings

By using geometric restitution the aim is to analyse a work of art and characterise the perspective used by Piranesi. In this case there is less interest in deducing the real dimensions of the depicted objects and more interest in establishing the relationships between them, or their relative proportions. Geometric restitution requires not only the

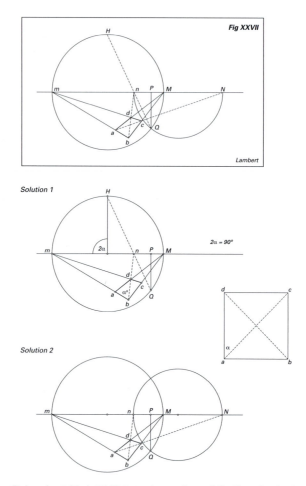

Figure 3 *Lambert, Task 21.* This task consists of finding the horizon line, position of the eye and its distance from the picture plane, if the perspective of a square is given. Lambert gives two solutions to this task, but he presents them both in one drawing denoted: Fig. XXVII (number according to Lambert). *Solution 1.* An angle between the diagonal and the side of the square is α = 45 degrees. Therefore the solution is a special case of the construction shown in Fig. 1. *Solution 2.* In this solution one wishes to determine vanishing points *m* and *M* of the perpendicular sides of the square and vanishing points *n* and *N* of the perpendicular diagonals of the square. As a result the eye *Q* must be located in the point of intersection of the circles determined by *mM* and *nN*. (Drawn by the author.)

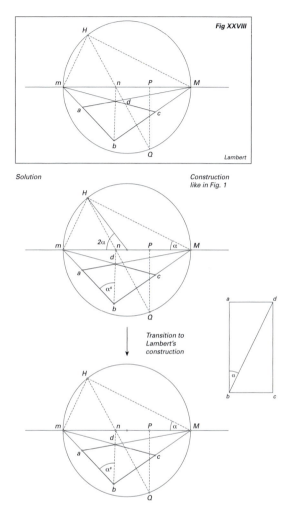

Figure 4 *Lambert, Task 22*. This task consists in finding the horizon line, position of the eye and its distance from the picture plane if the perspective of a rectangle and the ratio of its sides is given. *Solution.* In Fig. XXVIII (number according to Lambert) Lambert presents a solution for a special case if the ratio of the sides of the rectangle equals 1:2. In the general case for a given rectangle one can determine the angle α. Lambert's construction follows the construction shown in Fig. 1 in a way illustrated in the diagram underneath Fig. XXVIII. In both examples, points *m* and *M* determine the horizon, point *Q* is a mirrored image of the eye position and the segment *PQ* is the distance between the eye and the picture plane. Lambert did not present the construction shown in Fig. 2 used for the restitution of the perspective *Ponte Fabrizio*. (Drawn by the author.)

perspective drawing but also some additional information. This may include the real size of an element of an object, its position in space or some kind of proportional information. For this reason, not only the perspectives drawn by Piranesi are used but also the measured plans and elevations of these objects drawn by the artist.

Fully to understand the perspective used by Piranesi (assuming that the picture plane is vertical) requires above all deciding whether the picture has one or more centres of projection and therefore if it has more than one horizon line. When the existence of one centre of projection is established it is then possible to find the depth of sight and the angle from which the image can be seen. Establishing the view points in Piranesi's drawing may prove particularly revealing and help understanding of how Piranesi decided the best angle from which to view these monuments, to impress observers and thereby alter their perception of ancient Rome.

It seems reasonable, then, to assume that the method of geometric restitution will offer some insight into the artist's intentions and the results of the analysis of his drawings will provide reliable information about how Piranesi composed his perspectives. This will not only illustrate the usefulness of restitution as an analytical tool but will also make it possible to step into Piranesi's mind and imagine what practical decisions he made while preparing his etchings.

Some early analysis of the etchings proved that Piranesi's perspectives are geometrically accurate and that they fulfil the requirements of restitution (Fig. 5). These drawings are suitable for restitution, because it is possible to determine the vanishing points exactly. The precise use of perspective within his etchings means that they could even be used as evidence in more specific investigations of the buildings depicted. This is an indication of a solid and rigorous training in perspective, and demonstrates that Piranesi could freely move within the perspective space and manipulate it to achieve new levels of expression.

So far as can be established, an investigation into Piranesi's work, by means of geometric reconstruction of perspective, has not previously been attempted. The benefit of such a study is to provide an insight into the process and thinking behind Piranesi's drawings.

First comes the analysis of the drawing *Ponte Ferrato, called The Bridge of Cestius*.[29] The bridge takes its name from Lucius Cestio, governor of Rome, who had it built in 26 BC to link Tiber Island with the right bank of the River Tiber. The bridge was completely demolished one hundred years after Piranesi depicted it. Today's structure is completely different from the original, except for some blocks of stone used for rebuilding the central arch (Fig. 6).

In relation to the technique of restitution, this example is interesting because the monument no longer exists and this etching could serve as the starting point for a survey. However, for the purposes of this paper, there is no particular interest in reconstructing the exact

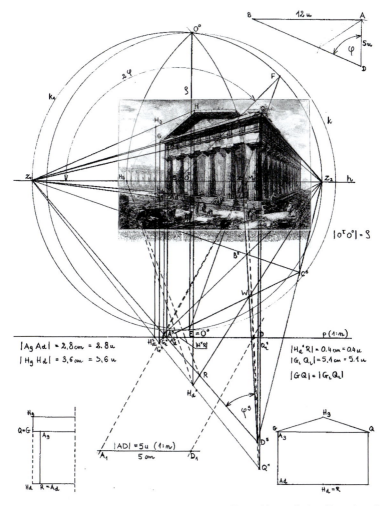

Figure 5 Perspective restitution of Piranesi's etching of the *Temple of Neptune*. (Drawn by the author.)

dimensions of the bridge and the focus instead is upon the nature of Piranesi's drawing.

The first restitution is based on the perspective of the rectangle *ABCD* derived in the horizontal plane from the perspective image of the central span (Fig. 7). The perspective of the rectangle *ABCD* lowered to an appropriate comparison level is denoted by $A^5B^5C^5D^5$. In this case restitution of the base elements of perspective has been performed according to constructions shown in Fig. 1.

Figure 6 Current view of the Ponte Ferrato, 2006. (Photograph by the author.)

On first inspection, the drawing seems like a perfectly reasonable view, but analysis indicates that Piranesi's perspective has some extraordinary qualities. For example, a reconstructed plan of the bridge shown in (Fig. 7) does not correspond with the plan of the real monument. There are differences in the proportions of the lateral spans of the bridge depending on their proximity to the eye. The perspective of the bridge drawn from the reconstructed viewing position does not precisely match the image which is depicted in the etching. In particular, the span of the arcade located furthest from the eye is too large, and the span of the nearer arcade is too small. So in this respect, despite constructing an apparently coherent scene, Piranesi's drawing is not, in fact, a correctly drawn perspective from one established position of the eye. This could be either a result of a mistake made by the artist or his deliberate and conscious action. Knowing Piranesi's mastery, it is difficult to believe that he could unintentionally make mistakes of this magnitude. One should therefore look at the drawings again and try to understand the rationale behind such inconsistencies. The approach to restitution of this drawing could also be different and these alternatives should be considered in greater detail.

In this context Lambert can perhaps provide some further insight into how accurate information might be retrieved from the perspective image. Under the influence of mathematical studies, supported by his

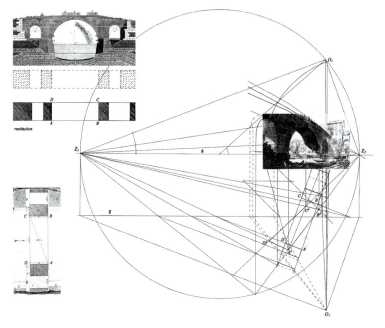

Figure 7 Perspective restitution of Piranesi's etching *Ponte Ferrato*. (Drawn by the author.)

exploration in physics, astronomy, and philosophy, Lambert takes an approach typical for German philosophers of the Enlightenment, that of a 'careful observer'.[30] In relation to restitution, he wrote about the necessity of finding the right element of perspective as a foundation for the analysis:

> We must first take care of these elements, as the basis, for which we can find what we are looking for.[31]

The first analysis of Piranesi's drawing has distinguished a rectangle determined by the inner corners of the central span of the bridge as the base for all the following constructions. Possibly, one should look for a different element of the drawing that will provide a more geometrically accurate starting point for the restitution. Lambert goes on to state:

> What is required in all cases, if we are to solve and apply the inverse tasks in conformity with the rules of perspective, is that the picture must be drawn correctly, according to these rules, because it will form the basis for the conclusions that we will draw from it.[32]

This means that the restitution is only worth as much as the element from which it is built. Perhaps the result of the first analysis of *Ponte Ferrato* is not reliable and the approach to the restitution was wrong. Piranesi did not make a mistake and there is a danger of a misinterpretation of the artist's intentions. The rectangles derived from Piranesi's perspective seem to be falsified, as will soon be discovered, and so they cannot serve as the basis for the correct restitution of the whole of the Ponte Ferrato.

Lambert's comments on the reliability of restitution are the key to understanding why the reconstructed plan does not correspond with the real plan of the bridge. And since it might reasonably be suspected that these inconsistencies may also occur in the other etchings by Piranesi, at this point the etching of the Ponte Ferrato will be put aside and another drawing will be considered which may serve better for a detailed analysis and may more clearly illustrate the problem. The Ponte Ferrato will be returned to later.

The next etching is that of another bridge, *Ponte Fabrizio, today called Quattro Capi*[33] which is from the collection *Antichita Romane* (1756) and shows the Roman bridge which connects the Tiberina island with the east bank of Rome. This ancient bridge was built in 62 BC by the Consul Lucius Fabricius and has remained almost intact until now (Fig. 8). As indicated by Lambert, one must start by looking for a suitable component to form the basis for the analysis.

Figure 8 Current view of the Ponte Fabrizio, 2006. (Photograph by the author.)

In this case, a square in the vertical plane will be used for the restitution instead of an horizontal rectangle. From the elevation (Fig. 9) it can be seen that the arches of the bridge are circular. The circles determining the spans are equal and lie in the same vertical plane. This implies that the diagonals of a square circumscribed on each circle are perpendicular and parallel in pairs. These circles in perspective transform into the ellipses. The examination of the drawing *Ponte Fabrizio* indicates that the only representative elements for the restitution are these ellipses, determined by the arches of the bridge. In this case, restitution of the base elements of the perspective has been performed according to constructions shown in Fig. 2. As shown, we can exactly match the ellipses to the shapes of the arches drawn by Piranesi: see Fig. 9. The top and bottom tangents to both ellipses intersect in one point on the horizon line and this point is the vanishing point. This looks like a correct perspective. In the next step the vanishing points of the diagonals of the trapeziums (perspectives of the squares) have been determined, circumscribed on the ellipses (perspectives of the circles). These vanishing points Z_3, Z_4 and Z_5, Z_6 lie on the vertical line that intersects the left vanishing point Z_1.

This reveals that the adequate pairs of the diagonals, parallel in reality, do not have the same vanishing point in the perspective drawing! And therefore, knowing that the *Ponte Fabrizio* is symmetrical and its spans are circular it is evident that Piranesi's ellipses are not perspectives of two circles located in the same plane. Indeed, using the construction from Fig. 2, two separate positions of the eye are determined, O_1 for the left part of the bridge and O_2 for the right part: see Fig. 9. All of which leads to the inescapable conclusion that Piranesi's drawing is a composition of two perspectives drawn from two different positions of the eye. After completing the restitution of the plan of the bridge from both eye positions, it is clear that it has been drawn for two different picture planes. These planes are inclined relative to each other. The rays drawn from both eye positions through the middle of the bridge pillar intersect on the ground line *g*. Piranesi's drawing is a symmetrical composition of the left and right part of the bridge. This drawing has been composed with incredible precision; the secret of Piranesi's craft is now becoming evident.

Idea, talent and excellent knowledge of the art of perspective permitted Piranesi to compose two perspectives in such a way that they have the same vanishing points on the horizon. This was a necessary condition of the success of this undertaking, which resulted in the drawing looking so deceptively like one perspective of one object. Both parts of the bridge, left and right, look very natural, because they are seen at a quite narrow angle. Furthermore, cutting the right span of the bridge more or less in the middle allowed Piranesi to avoid exaggeration of the bridge at the closest part to the eye. It should also be noted that for two diverse viewing positions, one gets the same ground line at

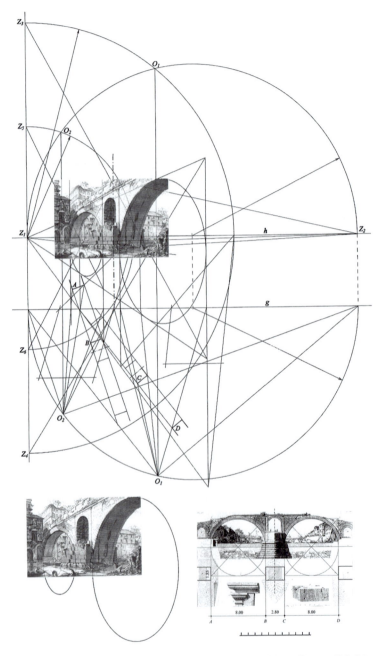

Figure 9 Perspective restitution of Piranesi's etching *Ponte Fabrizio.*
(Drawn by the author.)

the same scale within Piranesi's drawing. This indicates that Piranesi selected the views in such a way that for different view points he got the same scale for the same ground line.

Although technically highly skilled, Piranesi was first and foremost an artist, and by means of his drawings, including this bridge, he manipulated reality to artistic effect. He was not just a recorder of history, he created new artistic visions of the buildings that really exist but in a different shape. In his drawings he places great emphasis on detail, yet at the same time he wanted to show the larger scene. Combining two perspectives allowed him to show the detail, but still to keep the whole drawing well proportioned. One can therefore argue (from the artistic point of view) that Piranesi was right to compose his etching from two different perspectives. And one can appreciate Piranesi's choice if one sees how the bridge would look if drawn from one position of the eye. It seems Piranesi anticipated that if he had drawn the scene from one viewing point the bridge might look distorted or disproportionate. The investigation will continue by looking at how the bridge would appear if it was drawn 'properly' from each of the two viewing positions which Piranesi combined to create his etching.

First, it is assumed that Piranesi is standing at position O_1 (Fig. 10). The perspective of the right span of the bridge fits the etching. The left side of the bridge is reconstructed according to Piranesi's plan. This immediately reveals that the arch of the bridge located further away from the eye would be much narrower than that depicted by the artist. Through the slim opening under the arch one would not be able to see the buildings behind the bridge. If one then traces the left arch as represented by Piranesi onto the elevation it can be seen how extremely elongated and incorrect it would appear. The width of the central pillar and the left span increases as shown in Fig. 10. It is quite clear that Piranesi has played a sophisticated visual trick on the viewer who, without resort to the kind of analysis described above, would never realise that the image is not a true depiction, let alone imagine the scale of the geometric distortion.

Secondly, in the next drawing it is assumed that Piranesi is standing at position O_2 (Fig. 11). The perspective of the left side of the bridge overlaps with the etching and the right arch, reconstructed from the measured plan of Piranesi, becomes wider and takes the shape of a hyperbola. This restitution clearly shows that if the Ponte Fabrizio was drawn from this point of view the shape of the hyperbolic right arch would be very distorted and uncomfortable to look at. On the other hand, the elevation drawing demonstrates that what Piranesi depicted would be an ellipse much narrower than the real circular span of the bridge.

With reference to this reconstruction of the bridge from the eye position O_2 it is worth demonstrating that the right part of the bridge takes the shape of a hyperbola. This can be verified geometrically (as shown in Fig. 11) as well as analytically using the term of the *cross ratio*.

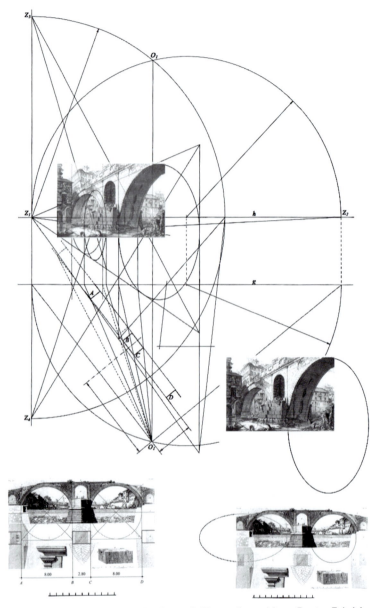

Figure 10 Perspective restitution of Piranesi's etching *Ponte Fabrizio,* viewing position O_1. (Drawn by the author.)

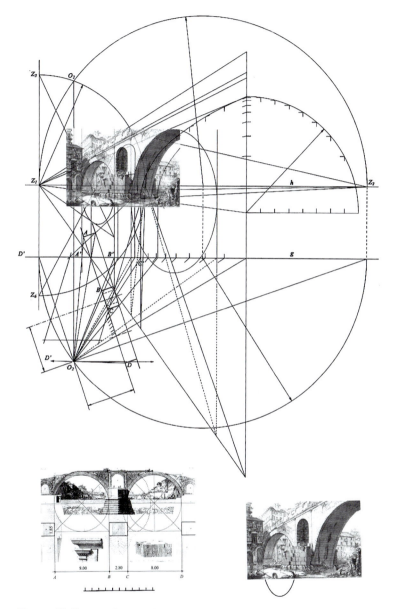

Figure 11 Perspective restitution of Piranesi's etching *Ponte Fabrizio,* viewing position O_2. (Drawn by the author.)

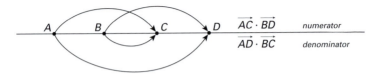

Figure 12 The *cross ratio* [A,B,C,D] of four distinct points A, B, C, D on a Euclidian line. (Drawn by the author.)

On the plan of the bridge, the points defining the left span are denoted A and B, the points defining the right span by C and D (see Fig. 11). The central projection from the point O_2 onto a ground line transforms points A, B, C, D into A', B', C', D'. The point D' is located on the left, outside of the drawing, because it is an intersection point of the ray O_2D and the ground line. The rays coming out from point O_2 and going through the circle CD of the right span create a cone. The intersection of the cone and the picture plane is a hyperbola. One part of the hyperbola is situated on the right side of the point C'. This part of the hyperbola is a perspective of the arch of the right span of the bridge, the second part is located on the left side of the point D' outside of the drawing. The location of the point D' can also be calculated using the *cross ratio*.[34]

The *cross ratio* [A,B,C,D] of four distinct points A, B, C, D on a Euclidian line is (Fig. 12)

$$[A,B,C,D] \frac{\overrightarrow{AC}}{\overrightarrow{AD}} \frac{\overrightarrow{BD}}{\overrightarrow{BC}} \tag{1}$$

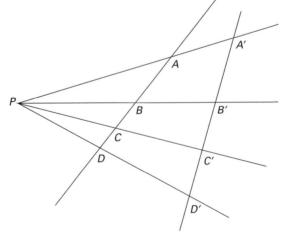

Figure 13 The *cross ratio* is an invariant of the central projection. (Drawn by the author.)

The cross ratio is an invariant of the central projection. This means that (Fig. 13): If A', B', C', D' are the projections, respectively, of A, B, C, D then

$$[A',B',C',D']=[A,B,C,D] \tag{2}$$

For points A, B, C, D on the plan one has (Fig. 9)

$$\overrightarrow{AC}=10.80$$

$$\overrightarrow{BD}=10.80$$

$$\overrightarrow{AD}=18.80$$

$$\overrightarrow{BC}=2.80$$

Therefore:

$$[A,B,C,D]=\frac{10.80\times10.80}{18.80\times2.80}=2.216 \tag{3}$$

Now it is assumed that the point D' is located in the x distance from the point C'. Measuring segments on the ground line in Fig. 11 one gets

$$\overrightarrow{A'C}=8.72$$

$$\overrightarrow{B'D}=3.95+x$$

$$\overrightarrow{A'D}=8.72+x$$

$$\overrightarrow{B'C}=3.95$$

Hence the *cross ratio* $[A', B', C', D']$ equals:

$$[A',B',C',D']=\frac{8.72(3.95+x)}{3.95(8.72+x)}=2.216 \tag{4}$$

Substituting (3) and (4) into the condition (2) one obtains:

$$\frac{8.72(3.95+x)}{3.95(8.72+x)}=2.216 \tag{5}$$

The solution to the equation (5) is:

$$x=-1261$$

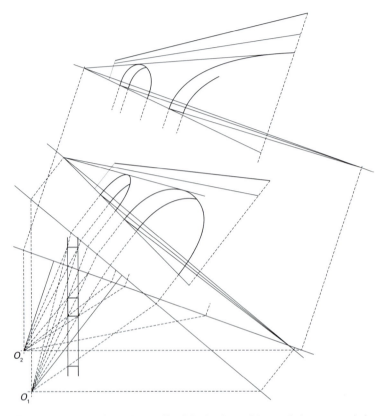

Figure 14 Plan of the *Ponte Fabrizio*, both positions of the eye and the corresponding perspective views. (Drawn by the author.)

The negative value of x indicates that the point D' is located on the left side of the point C'. The result corresponds with the geometric construction.

To sum up the above investigation, it is possible to present on one drawing a plan of the bridge, both positions of the eye and the corresponding perspective views (Fig. 14).

Piranesi was an expert in perspective and he clearly had a good understanding of its techniques. The restitution of the etching *Ponte Fabrizio* shows that if Piranesi had drawn the perspective of the bridge from one point of view, quite close to the object, the drawing would appear distorted because it would be seen at a very wide angle. Some parts of the bridge close to the eye would be significantly enlarged while others would stay very small. He liked to show precise details in his etchings so he had to station the view point at close proximity to the bridge. Seen as a whole, this would lead to an unnatural perspective distortion and to avoid this, it therefore appears that the artist decided

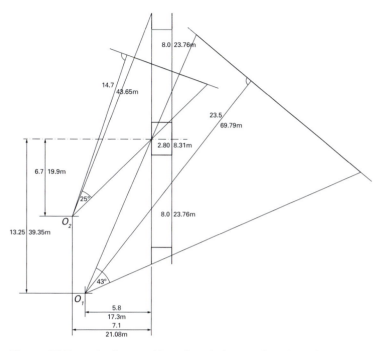

Figure 15 Two viewing positions in relation to the plan of the *Ponte Fabrizio*. (Drawn by the author.)

to combine two perspectives into one. Standing quite near to the bridge, he chose viewing positions in which both parts of the bridge, the left and the right, could be seen at a beneficial angle of less than 60 degrees (Fig. 15). The left part of the bridge is seen from the eye position O_1 at an angle of 25 degrees and the right one is seen from the position O_2 at an angle of 43 degrees. Each part of the bridge is thus seen at a comfortable viewing angle and one at which the bridge is aesthetically pleasing.

Piranesi's etching looks like a perspective of a single object. But the outcome of the completed restitution of *Ponte Fabrizio* indicates that Piranesi's drawing can only be a perspective from a single viewpoint if the bridge is asymmetrical. It might be asked, however, whether the drawing could ever be a perspective of some symmetrical bridge with two elliptical arches? To find out, it is necessary to examine whether a suitable point exists on the circle described by all possible eye positions.[35] In perspective, measuring the lengths of segments on the horizontal plane must be done by means of *measuring points* (Fig. 16). Between the eye position and the measuring point exists a one-to-one relationship which means that the eye position defines exactly the position of the measuring point and vice versa. Therefore instead of examining the position of the eye one can investigate the position

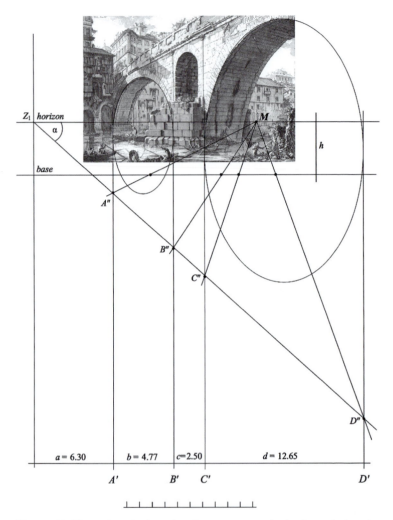

Z_1 horizon

α

base

A''

B''

C''

M

h

D''

$a = 6.30$

$b = 4.77$

$c = 2.50$

$d = 12.65$

A'

B' C'

D'

Figure 16 Measuring the lengths of segments on the horizontal plane by means of *measuring points*. (Drawn by the author.)

of the measuring point M on the horizon line. It is possible to create a geometric mechanism (Fig. 17) that will help to establish whether the bridge depicted by Piranesi can ever be symmetrical.

In Fig. 18 the horizon line and the ground line are determined. Also established are the perspectives of points A, B, C, D projected onto a ground plane and they are denoted A'', B'', C'', D''. For the given position of the measuring point M distances d_{AB}, d_{BC}, d_{CD} between the points A,B,C,D are established on the ground line (see Fig. 17).

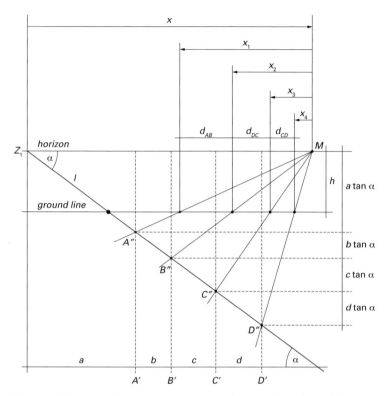

Figure 17 It is possible to create a geometric mechanism that will help to establish whether the bridge depicted by Piranesi can ever be symmetrical. (Drawn by the author.)

The search now is for such location of the measuring point M on the horizon line at which the bridge would be symmetrical, which means $d_{AB} = d_{CD}$. Let x denote the position of the measuring point M on the horizon line. From Fig. 17 the following proportions are obtained:

$$\left.\begin{aligned}
\frac{X_1}{h} &= \frac{x-a}{a\tan\alpha'} \\[6pt]
\frac{X_2}{h} &= \frac{x-(a+b)}{(a+b)\tan\alpha'} \\[6pt]
\frac{X_3}{h} &= \frac{x-(a+b+c)}{(a+b+C)\tan\alpha'} \\[6pt]
\frac{X_4}{h} &= \frac{x-(a+b+c+d)}{(a+b+c+d)\tan\alpha'}
\end{aligned}\right\} \qquad (6)$$

Hence is obtained:

$$
\left.
\begin{aligned}
x_1 &= \frac{h(x-a)}{a\tan\alpha} = \frac{hx}{a\tan\alpha} - \frac{h}{\tan\alpha'} \\
x_2 &= \frac{h(x-(a+b))}{(a+b)\tan\alpha} = \frac{hx}{(a+b)\tan\alpha} - \frac{h}{\tan\alpha'} \\
x_3 &= \frac{h(x-(a+b+c))}{(a+b+c)\tan\alpha} \\
&= \frac{hx}{(a+b+c)\tan\alpha} - \frac{h}{\tan\alpha'} \\
x_4 &= \frac{h(x-(a+b+c+d))}{(a+b+c+d)\tan\alpha} \\
&= \frac{hx}{(a+b+c+d)\tan\alpha} - \frac{h}{\tan\alpha}
\end{aligned}
\right\} \tag{7}
$$

The distances d_{AB}, d_{BC}, d_{CD} can be determined by the following formulae:

$$
d_{AB} = x_1 - x_2,\ d_{BC} = x_2 - x_3,\ d_{CD} = x_3 - x_4 \tag{8}
$$

The bridge is symmetrical if:

$$
d_{AB} = d_{CD} \tag{9}
$$

In other words if:

$$
x_1 - x_2 = x_3 - x_4 \tag{10}
$$

Using the values x_1, x_2, x_3 and x_4 given by (7) the following equation can be obtained:

$$
\left(\frac{1}{a} - \frac{1}{(a+b)} - \frac{1}{(a+b+c)} + \frac{1}{(a+b+c+d)} \right) \cdot x = 0 \tag{11}
$$

In the considered case from Fig. 16 is taken:

$$
a = 6.30,\ b = 4.77,\ c = 2.50,\ d = 12.65
$$

For this data is calculated:

$$
\begin{aligned}
& \frac{1}{a} - \frac{1}{(a+b)} - \frac{1}{(a+b+c)} + \frac{1}{(a+b+c+d)} \\
&= \frac{1}{6.30} - \frac{1}{6.30+4.77} - \frac{1}{6.30+4.77+2.50} \\
&\quad + \frac{1}{6.30+4.77+2.50+12.65} \\
&= 0.15873 - 0.09033 - 0.07369 + 0.03814 \\
&= 0.03285
\end{aligned} \tag{12}
$$

Therefore the equation (11) takes the form

$$0.03285x = 0 \tag{13}$$

Because the value of the formula (12) is not equal to 0, then the equation (13) is satisfied if and only if $x = 0$. For $x = 0$ the measuring point M is located in the left vanishing point Z_1 (see Fig. 19) and

$$x_1 = x_2 = x_3 = x_4 = -\frac{h}{\tan \alpha}$$

This means that the values of $x_1 = x_2 = x_3 = x_4$, being negative are located on the right side of the calculated measuring point $M = Z_1$. Thus, according to (8) the plan of the bridge is reduced to one point (the large black point in Fig. 17), which is the intersection point of the ground line and the line l. Therefore, the dimensions of the bridge are reduced to 0 and the measuring point M (and also the position of the eye), for which it is possible to reconstruct the symmetrical non-zero dimensions of the bridge, does not exist. Finally, this means that the symmetrical bridge for which the perspective is Piranesi's drawing does not exist.

Neither the measuring point nor the position of the eye exists for which one can reconstruct the symmetrical bridge. If it is assumed that both ellipses are the perspectives of the curves on the same plane, it would mean that one of the ellipses is the perspective of the circle and another one is the perspective of another ellipse (not a circle). In this case the spans of the bridge would not be symmetrical in relation to the middle axis of the central pillar of the bridge.

This implies that in general Piranesi's drawing could be the perspective of an infinite number of bridges with asymmetrical spans for every different position of an eye along the circle. As the above analysis has shown, one of the arches of the bridge is circular, either the left or the right, for the two identified viewing positions. For all other viewing positions bridge spans are elliptical and asymmetrical. In the case being considered, with the established vanishing points, horizon line and the ground line, a viewing position from which the bridge would have symmetrical arches does not exist. Strictly speaking, Piranesi's picture does not depict the Ponte Fabrizio.

Thus, more is now known about Piranesi's approach to composing his views and a brief return may be made to the drawing of the Ponte Ferrato, to determine whether the artist used the same method to set up this etching as he did in *Ponte Fabrizio*. On the elevational view of the bridge drawn by Piranesi it can be seen that the arcades of the central span and the spans on each side have circular shapes (Fig. 18). This means that the ellipses which are the perspectives of these circles can be used for the restitution of the eye position. The geometric constructions are shown in Fig. 18. In the first step, the shape of the central span was approximated by means of the largest ellipse drawn. Then, in a similar process to that used in the case of *Ponte Fabrizio*, the position of the eye O_1 was established based on the ellipse. This position, it turns out, is exactly the same as the one determined before on the basis of the rectangle in the horizontal plane. Achieved conformity is a proof for the correctness of the geometrical construction used and makes the result credible.

In the next steps, the arches of the side spans have been approximated using ellipses and subsequently two other positions of the eye were established O_2 and O_3. Three different eye positions and three inclined picture planes are shown on the plan of the bridge and demonstrate that therefore Piranesi's drawing is a composition of three perspectives of each span of the bridge. The arrangement of viewing positions and the background planes indicates a logical sequence ensuring good visibility of each part of the bridge (Figs. 19 & 20). This etching will not be analysed any further, because the results will be similar to the detailed

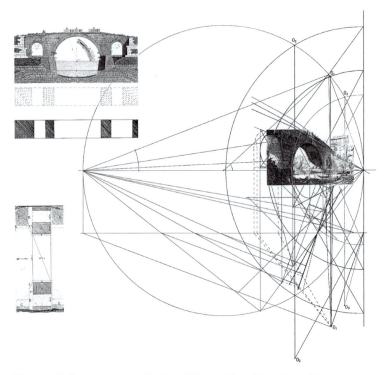

Figure 18 Perspective restitution of Piranesi's etching *Ponte Ferrato* – three different viewing positions. (Drawn by the author.)

analysis of *Ponte Fabrizio*. However, this quick examination confirms the results achieved before and indicates that the artist used this practice on more than one occasion.

6. Conclusions

Piranesi did not leave behind many sketches or notes explaining the way in which he planned his etchings, but the geometric analysis presented here reveals how the artist could have been thinking when composing these views. With his excellent understanding of perspective techniques, he would have considered the implications of drawing the bridge from one viewing position. Ultimately, however, his primary concern was for the quality of the drawing and he was, it seems, prepared to manipulate the conventional rules of perspective in order to produce a more believable and compelling representation. In so doing he converted the traditional topographical view and instead of just providing factual information he used it as a tool to interpret reality and in a very subtle way, influence the understanding of it.

This study presents just a small sample of Piranesi's work but it gives some insight into what may have gone on behind the scenes when he was constructing his images of Rome. Piranesi's work was not accidental; everything he did was planned carefully, to the smallest detail. Otherwise, he would never have been able to achieve the expression in his etching that deceived so many romantics. He composed his perspectives with such precision, that it made it feasible to employ a precise geometric tool to analyse his work, and although it has clearly been proved that the images do not reflect reality (from a single viewpoint), it has been possible to prove that they are distorted using precise geometrical constructions. Even if it is assumed that the restitution drawings which have been constructed may have some minor imprecisions, the results are strikingly exact and everything falls in place perfectly. The final evidence that confirms both the accuracy of the restitution and Piranesi's meticulous planning is the fact that the rays drawn from two viewing positions through the middle of the bridge's central pillar intersect exactly at the same point on the ground line (see Fig. 9).

Many have accused Piranesi of insufficient knowledge of the art of perspective, while others perceive the mastery or even virtuoso skills that led him to the brave and unusual compositions in the *Carceri* drawings.[36] It has also been observed that when preparing the *Carceri* series 'he almost seems to have attacked the plate direct without any preliminary drawings', but such an approach would not have been possible in his constructed views of Rome.[37] In etchings such as the image of the Ponte Fabrizio, he must have put a considerable amount of time and effort into planning the composition. Successful execution of these drawings must have been supported by an excellent and detailed knowledge

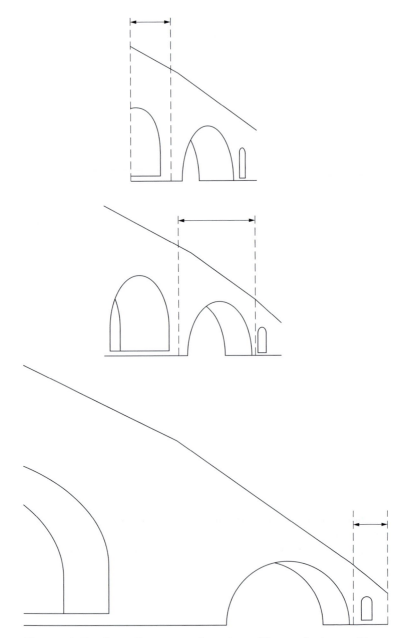

Figure 19 The *Ponte Ferrato* seen from three different viewing positions. (Drawn by the author.)

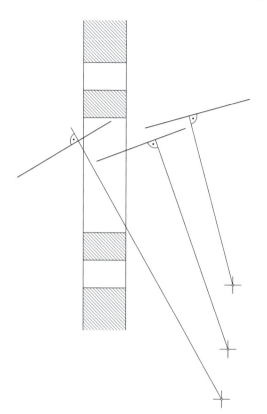

Figure 20 Three positions of the eye in relation to the plan of the *Ponte Ferrato*. (Drawn by the author.)

of perspective and combined with very good judgement which enabled him to determine what would be detectable by the viewer.

Many artists before him were inspired by Rome and were painting its classical motifs and famous landmarks, but Piranesi captured both the antique beauty of the city and its mediaeval ruins, as well as modern Rome in all its richness. He harmonised varied themes into a coherent and innovative portrayal of Rome. He used surveyed plans, archaeological finds and his own thoughts to develop his very own artistic vision. Sometimes he enriched the existing elements with additions imagined by him that do not exist in reality. He used the restricting medium of etching with virtuosity and originality, creating new techniques allowing him to use it beyond its traditional limitations.[38]

Even if it is believed that the better a work of art reflects reality then the better it is, the exactness of representation has its limits. These limitations will depend upon the tools and techniques used by the artist both to construct the image as well as the techniques used to provide its textual and visual qualities. No matter how the picture is constructed, there will always be a difference between the picture and reality. Even if the work of art is entirely created by the artist's imagination and his own vision, he will certainly have been influenced by observations throughout his life. Perspective need not be just a schematic model of reality but it can be used to represent the way that vision is transformed into a picture.

Perspective is not only a geometric concept; it provides also the key to satisfying the physiological and psychological needs of people's eyes. The subjective curves, increasing perspective divisions, distortions and even anamorphosis can occur especially when an image is viewed from a wide angle. All of these experiences contradict geometry from one stationary view point. If the scene is drawn from a narrow angle the picture will not have great depth, and perspective cannot, of course, take into consideration binocular vision. The artist has to look for solutions to all these contradictions between the appearance of drawings and the true shape of the object. He needs to restrict himself to the method, but at the same time he has to find ways to deceive the eye of the viewer and best recreate the illusion of reality. His strategy needs to be sophisticated and his tricks must be cleverly hidden from the person looking at the picture. Of course, he will have to make some compromise between his subjective vision and the possibilities of its graphic representation.

There have been many debates throughout the twentieth century about whether perspective is an adequate tool for representing reality. Criticisms by modern painters and philosophers include the argument that perspective is deceptive and that it does not really give the viewer a true picture of reality.[39] It has also been claimed that it does not reflect the true way in which the world is seen, and so perspective has become just a convention blindly used by artists. Cubist painters, for example, believed that perspective confines the artist's imagination and this limitation is an unnecessary constraint.

Experience of perspective may not be exactly the same as its image, but on the other hand it is the best graphic tool so far invented. Linear perspective and the retinal image are not identical but the difference between them is not significant enough for a casual observer to be aware of. Equally, although the complex dynamics of perception are not replicated in the static drawing, the image drawn by means of geometrical perspective will be similar enough to the visual experience and so its value should not be underestimated. In fact, Piranesi's etchings demonstrate that the eye cannot detect the fact that these drawings are compositions of several view points, without a comparison with photographs or a detailed analysis. Piranesi proves that despite being a much-regulated method, perspective can be extremely versatile. It is true that it has a set of rules, but as a geometrical tool it must have. Despite this, Piranesi used these rules very creatively to convey his message about the city of Rome. He did not breach the rules of perspective, but used them in a very ingenious way. By composing the view from different viewing positions he did not want to undermine the technique, but rather to use its potential to communicate more in a single image.

Piranesi has often been accused of being untruthful in his representation of Rome, which refers mainly to the fact he sometimes moved things around and exaggerated the scale of monuments.[40] Yet his interpretations of the Roman monuments, despite the changes he made, seem to breathe life into them instead of just being mere documents. Piranesi's use of perspective and in particular the use of multiple view points has been compared to the cubist deconstruction of Euclidian space.[41] Referring to Piranesi's work being an anticipation of the cubist movement and to how he 'exploded and restructured the homogenous space and linear time implied by perspective' can be tempting, but in this case, does not seem quite true.[42]

Piranesi's space was coherent rather than fragmented like analytic cubism. He did not mean to break the space by composing multiple viewpoints but instead to make it even more legible and articulate. His montage of perspectives was deliberate, but not with the intention of undermining 'the perspective logic'.[43] It is difficult to imagine a more logical and precise composition of these views than that used by Piranesi. If he did not understand and follow the rules of perspective it could lead to disproportionate images. In contrast to modern painters, Piranesi saw perspective not as a restricting medium, but as an extremely valuable and effective tool which helped him to achieve a better proportion in his art.

The secret of Piranesi's genius lies in the fact that he could bring together fact and detail with incomparable levels of emotional expression. Above all, he believed in the beauty of the ancient ruins and he was capable of representing them with grandeur and splendour in a way that impresses the viewer. Piranesi had a passion for understanding the methods of Roman builders and he examined the construction of ancient walls, the principles of building bridges and other ancient monuments. He reflected this knowledge within his etchings which were also based on direct observation and scrupulous archaeological work. The ancient sites and ruins, and their detailed investigation, were a creative inspiration for his artistic work, while the dynamism of his perspectives was clearly influenced by Baroque scenography and the shapes of spaces in his etchings have a lot in common with the Baroque architecture of Rome.

The dramatic compositions of his etchings are also a sign of the early influence of Venice, one of the most theatrical of Italian cities, and the home of Piranesi's artistic identity and birth. He achieved magical and mysterious views of Rome in a perfect combination between the perspective, theatrical composition and play between light and shade. He used the technique of *chiaroscuro* to create striking tonal effects like a painter. He was in full control of perspective which he used to show the architecture in the most interesting and stunning way. He would not want his beloved monuments of Rome to look distorted, so instead of using a single potentially uncomfortable viewing position he used multiple views.

Various positions of the eye and different directions of looking at the scene (different picture planes) give Piranesi's perspectives a dynamic character. Panofsky described the qualities of Piranesi's drawings as 'the boldest abstractions in the history of art'. Namely, 'looking with one static eye' and 'creating an entirely rational and homogenous space'. Space around Piranesi becomes a continuation of direct experiences.[44] The effect of changing the viewing position can be interpreted as if looking at the object in motion (see Figs. 15 & 20). In particular, Piranesi's bridges can be seen as a sequence of frames of the different parts of the object joined into one entity, similar to the effect of a film camera panning across the scene. This interpretation concerns not only the bridges. It is also valid in relation to the drawings, where Piranesi changed the scale, proportions or the distances between the buildings. Therefore, in general, Piranesi's etchings are not static but have movement hidden in them.

Indeed, movement in Piranesi's etchings is ever-present and has a diverse character. It is an ordinary movement based on the changes in the viewing position and the picture plane for one object or the manipulation of dimensions and relative position of objects to each other. But, it is also a movement of impressions, mood and emotions, characteristic, for example, of the geometrically irrational drawings of Prisons.

Horace Walpole praised Piranesi's imagination:

> The sublime dreams of Piranesi, who seems to have conceived visions of Rome beyond what it boasted even in the meridian of its splendour. Savage as Salvator Rosa, fierce as Michael Angelo, and exuberant as Rubens, he has imagined scenes that would startle geometry, and exhaust the Indies to realise.[45]

The analysis demonstrated throughout this paper confirms the importance of imagination to an artist even when it comes to such a 'conventional' method as perspective. Piranesi reveals his imaginative power and talent not only in his masterly use of etching techniques but also in his extraordinary use of perspective. Piranesi embraced perspective as one of his most precious tools.

Acknowledgement

This article is based on the dissertation written in 2007 at the University of Westminster, London, under the guidance of Richard Difford.

References

1. Joanna Rapp, The basic constructions of perspective. A geometrical background to the article: "A geometrical analysis of multiple viewpoint perspective in the work of Giovanni Battista Piranesi". (This can be accessed in the multimedia section of the online version of this article, available via www.tandfonline.com/loi/rjar20.)

2. *Piranesi – Rome recorded*, a complete edition of Giovanni Battista Piranesi's *Vedute di Roma* from the collection of the Arthur Ross Foundation, third rev. ed. (London: Royal Institute of British Architects, 1991); various authors, pp.10–11.

3. Extensive information about the early formative years of the artist and the importance of his Venetian origin can be found in John Wilton-Ely, *The Mind and Art of Giovanni Battista Piranesi* (London: Thames and Hudson, 1978); Jonathan Scott, *Piranesi* (London/New York: Academy Editions/St Martins Press, 1975); or Luigi Ficacci, *Piranesi – The Complete Etchings* (Cologne: Taschen, 2000).

4. Bohdan Paczkowski, 'Tworcze paradoksy Piranesiego', *Zobaczyc* (Gdansk: slowo/obraz terytoria, 2005).

5. Marguerite Yourcenar, *Le Cerveau noir de Piranesi* (Gdansk: slowo/obraz terytoria, 2004).

6. In English, 'Roman Antiquities'.

7. Wilton-Ely, *The Mind and Art of Giovanni Battista Piranesi*, p.35; original source: G.B. Piranesi, *Le Antichita Romane*, I, 'Prefazione agli studiosi delle antichita Romane' (1756).

8. Elzbieta Jastrzebowska, *Rzym Antyczny w oczach Piranesiego i dzis* ('Antique Rome in Piranesi's eyes and today') (Warsaw: Wydawnictwo DIG, 2005).

9. There are different opinions relating to whether Piranesi really wanted to build buildings. Some commentators believe that he was not motivated to find architectural commissions along with the real world constraints that these projects would entail.

10. Wilton-Ely, *The Mind and Art of Giovanni Battista Piranesi.*, p.38; original source: J. G. Legrand, *Nouvelles de l'estampe*, p.202.

11. *Ibid.*, p.38; Original source: *ibid.*, p.220.

12. After Piranesi's death his sons inherited his business and for a while continued printing their father's work as well as their own, but during the Napoleonic wars the family moved to France. However, although they tried to take all the copper plates and prints with them, they might have had to leave some behind and subsequently these were lost. More information about the continuation of Piranesi's business by his sons can be found in Wilton-Ely, *The Mind and Art of Giovanni Battista Piranesi*, or Scott, *Piranesi.*

13. G.B. Piranesi, dedication letter printed in most issues of the *Prima Parte di Architetture e Prospettive* (Rome: Stamperia de Fratelli Pagliarini, 1743).

14. Ferdinando Galli da Bibiena, L'Architettura Civile Preparata su la Geometria, e ridotta alle prospettive. Considerazioni pratiche di Ferdinando Galli da Bibiena Cittadino Bolognese architetto primario, capo maestro maggiore, e pittore di camera, e feste di teatro della maestra di Carlo III. Il monarca delle Spagne dessegnate, e descritte in cinque parti . . . Dedicata Alla Sacra Cattolica Real Maestra di Carlo III Re delle Spagne, d'Ungheria, Boemia Ec. (Parma: Per Paolo Monti, 1711).

15 Ibid.

16 Ferdinando Galli da Bibiena, Direzioni a Giovani Studenti nel Disegno dell'Architettura Civile: nell'Accademia clementina dell'Instituto delle scienze unite da Ferdinando Galli da Bibiena (Bologna: Lelio della Volpe, 1725).

17 Scott, Piranesi.

18 Manfredo Tafuri, The Sphere and the Labyrinth: Avant-Gardes and Architecture from Piranesi to the 1970's (Massachusetts Institute of Technology, 1987), p.29.

19 Alberto Perez-Gomez, Louise Pelletier, Architectural Representation and the Perspective Hinge (Cambridge, Mass:, The MIT Press, 2000), p.216.

20 Various sources: see, for example, Jose M. Parramon and Muntsa Calbo, Perspektywa w Rysunku i w Malastwie (original title: El Gran Libro de la Perspectiva), (Warsaw: Wydawnictwa Szkolne i Pedagogiczne, 1993); Martin Kemp, The Science of Art (New Haven and London: Yale University Press, 1990).

21 Kemp, The Science of Art, p.225.

22 Zbigniew Brzosko: Wykreslna Restytucja Perspektywy ('Descriptive Restitution of Perspective'), (Warsaw: Wydawnictwa Naukowo Techniczne, 1995).

23 Kazimierz Bartel, Perspektywa Malarska ('Painter's Perspective') (Warsaw: Panstwowe Wydawnictwo Naukowe, 1958).

24 Rapp, The basic constructions of perspective.

25 Johann Heinrich Lambert, Die Freye Perspektive (Zurich: Ben Heidegger und Compagnie, 1759).

26 Perez-Gomez, Pelletier, Architectural Representation and the Perspective Hinge, p.77.

27 German original title: Umgekehrte Aufgaben der Perspektive.

28 Published and with a commentary by Max Steck, Johann Heinrich Lambert — Shriften Zur Perspective (Berlin: Dr. Georg Luttke Verlag, 1943); notes to Lambert's text, chapter 8, p.438.

29 Veduta del Ponte Ferrato dagl'Antiquari detto Cestio.

30 Radoslaw Kuliniak, Tomaz Malyszek, Johann Heinrich Lambert — Rozprawa o Criterium Veritas (Wroclaw: Wydawnictwo Uniwersytetu Wroclawskiego, 2001).

31 Steck, Johann Heinrich Lambert — Schriften Zur Perspective, p.289; translation, Joanna Rapp.

32 Ibid., p.289; translation, Joanna Rapp.

33 Veduta del Ponte Fabrizio oggi detto quattro Capi.

34 The full mathematical explanation of the term can be found, for example, in George A. Jennings, Modern Geometry with Applications (New York: Springer-Verlag, 1994).

35 It is not possible to move away from the circle because then the eye would have to be positioned on another circle between different vanishing points, which would mean that it would be a different perspective from that drawn by Piranesi.

36 Ulya Vogt-Goknil, Giovanni Battista Piranesi — Carceri (Zurich: Origo Verlag, 1598).

37 Scott, Piranesi, p.53.

38 He learned basic etching in six months in C. Zucchi's workshop, but he soon introduced innovations to the technique: not only would he employ a variety of techniques in parallel with pure etching but he also made use of copper

plates larger than the conventional veduta. He used to re-bite his plates with acid and also used tools for engraving to 'scratch, stipple and burnish his plates'.

39 Further reading on perspective critiques can be found in Robin Evans, *The Projective Cast — Architecture and its Three Geometries* (Cambridge, Mass.: The MIT Press, 2000).

40 Or, to enhance the monumentality of the architecture, he reduced the size of the human figures.

41 Perez-Gomez, Pelletier, *Architectural Representation and the Perspective Hinge*, p.77.

42 *Ibid.*

43 *Ibid.*

44 Vogt-Goknil, *Giovanni Battista Piranesi — Carceri.*

45 Cited in Peter Murray, Walter Neurath Memorial Lecture, 'Piranesi and the Grandeur of Ancient Rome' (London: Thames and Hudson, 1971), pp.56 and 58.

Amy Thomas

'Mart of the World': An Architectural and Geographical History of the London Stock Exchange

Abstract

A stock exchange is a spatial contradiction. Conceived as a marketplace for the trade in securities and other financial instruments, it is intended to provide a regulated forum as a fair and free market for its members: an open economic environment made possible by institutional confinement. Once the largest and most influential in the world, the London Stock Exchange (LSE) embodied this contradiction. Established in the heart of the imperial metropolis, the LSE emerged at the core of a global financial network that sustained Britain's territorial and 'informal' Empire. Concurrently, its self-regulated standing within the City of London and reliance on an esoteric world of gentlemanly connections positioned it as an establishment shaped and assisted by its locality.

Established to finance overseas trade in the seventeenth century, the London stock market materialised as the informal appendage of commodity markets in the alleyways surrounding the Royal Exchange. The next three hundred years saw the consolidation and growth of the LSE from classicising institutional grandeur, concrete monolith in the 1970s, and most recently, to the corporate serenity of Paternoster Square.

In mapping the movement of global markets alongside the shifting terrain of the LSE buildings, this paper addresses the manner in which the latter reflects the geographical scope of Britain's capital accumulation throughout the last three centuries. The LSE is looked at in the context of the rise and fall of the British Empire and in its more recent role as channel for international (and offshore) capital, in order to assess whether its architectural choices might reflect shifting attitudes towards economic expansion. At present there are no dedicated architectural accounts of the LSE at any point of its existence. This paper intends to traverse the gap between economic geography and architectural history via a methodology of spatial scales, moving from the cartographic to the bodily. In producing a dialogue between macroscopic and microscopic analysis, this enquiry intends to expose more tangible interpretations of an immaterial system that increasingly distorts our material reality.

Even as the architecture of a nation is an index of its character, that of the Stock Exchange is intimately related to its history of never-ceasing growth. Structural extension has always been

going on in all directions; it is going on now at its centenary and
presumably always will be going on.

Charles Duguid, 1901[1]

Synthesizing Spatial Scales

A stock exchange is a spatial contradiction. Conceived as a marketplace
for the trade in securities and other financial instruments, it is intended
to provide a regulated forum as a fair and free market for its members:
an open economic environment made possible by institutional
confinement. Once the largest and most influential in the world, the
London Stock Exchange (LSE) embodied this contradiction. Established
in the heart of the imperial metropolis, the LSE emerged at the core of a
global financial network that sustained Britain's territorial and economic
empire. Concurrently, its self-regulated standing within the City of
London and reliance on an esoteric world of gentlemanly connections
positioned it as an establishment shaped and assisted by its locality.

Established to finance overseas trade in the seventeenth century, the
London stock market materialised as the informal appendage of commodity markets in the alleyways of the Bank area of the City. A microcosm of international trade, this dense web of conduits encompassed a
network of coffee houses operating as unofficial temporal and spatial
extensions of the neighbouring Royal Exchange. The trade in securities
initially took place within the alleys themselves, acting as channels for
the distribution of financial information: an incorporeal market defined
by immaterial place. Towards the end of the century the money markets
acquired a more fixed geography at Garraway's and Jonathan's coffee
houses, and in 1761 a group of stockbrokers set up what could be termed
the first consolidated stock exchange at the latter.

The rapid expansion of the Empire in the next two centuries led to
the growth of London's financial infrastructure, positioning the LSE at
the economic core of Britain's hegemony, expressed in its architectural
consolidation. Beginning with small premises in 1773 in Sweetings
Alley, followed by the construction of a functional basilica form edifice
by James Peacock in 1801 in Capel Court, the building soon grew in
scale and grandeur with subsequent rebuilding by Thomas Allason
in 1853 and dramatic enlargement by J.J. Cole in 1885, shifting from
marketplace to monument. Accommodating thousands of brokers and
jobbers at any one time, the gargantuan domed trading floor became
an icon of the City, witnessing the boom and bust cycles of imperial
expansion, a pressure gauge for the nation.

The increasing internationalisation of finance and technological
advancements in trading that occurred throughout the first half of the
twentieth century resulted in the move to rebuild in 1966, in a concrete,
modernist idiom that radically departed from the institutional classicism
of the last two centuries. Designed by architects Lloyd Llewelyn Davies,
Fitzroy Robinson & Partners and Weeks, Forestier-Walker & Bor, the new

concrete monolith was completed in 1979 (officially opened in 1972), reaching 26 stories. However, despite a superficial gesture towards modernity (and almost £11 million later), the Big Bang and abolition of open outcry trading in 1986 would ensure that the gleaming 23,500ft^2 trading floor would be abandoned in less than a decade.

Over the next thirty years, the LSE decreased in scale and prominence with the global expansion of the securities market, digitization of trading and the loss of its regulatory powers to the Financial Services Authority (FSA) in 2000. Now acting as a virtual platform for equity markets and as publisher of financial information, the institution has sacrificed its symbolic edifice in favour of practicality, residing in leased, trading-floor-free offices in Paternoster Square. Built in 2003 as a component in William Whitfield's master plan by architects Eric Parry and Sheppard Robson in a restrained modernist style, the edifice was subsequently fitted for the LSE in 2004 by interior architects Gensler with an aura of corporate serenity that is a far cry from the chaotic marketplace of centuries before.

In mapping the movement of global markets alongside the shifting terrain of the LSE buildings, this paper addresses the manner in which the latter reflects the geographical scope of Britain's capital accumulation throughout the last three centuries. The LSE will be looked at in the context of the rise and fall of the British Empire and in its more recent role as channel for international (and offshore) capital, in order to assess whether its architectural choices might reflect shifting attitudes towards economic expansion. Whilst a plethora of institutional and economic historians have produced intricate investigations of the LSE and its mechanisms,[2] at present there are no dedicated architectural accounts of the LSE at any point of its existence. This paper intends to traverse the gap between economic geography and architectural history, in the specific context of the LSE, and in doing so articulate the link between global finance and the financial institution: a marriage of geographical space and architectural place that is often neglected by both disciplines for want of obeying or renouncing systemic devices.[3]

This paper does not intend to provide a complete architectural survey nor historical narrative of the LSE but rather to align key moments in both histories to the development of financial markets. In order to encompass the topographical and chronological breadth in question, the enquiry will implement a methodology of spatial scales. Beginning with a telescopic assessment of the symbiosis between imperial expansion and subsequent globalisation of the economy, and the cartography and scalar shifts of the LSE buildings, the focus narrows to the LSE as marketplace, the institutional interior, and finally, the bodily and psychological interaction of the trader with the architectural environment of the LSE. In producing a dialogue between macroscopic and microscopic analysis, this enquiry intends to expose more tangible interpretations of an immaterial system that has been so influential in shaping our material reality.

Geographical entanglement

The London stock market emerged at the end of the seventeenth century in the heart of the City, at a time when the latter was fast becoming the centre of international trade in an increasingly centralised British imperial economy. The 1690s witnessed a financial revolution in which the emergence of specialist merchant banks, the growth of the mortgage and insurance market, and the birth of the financial press completely transformed the economic landscape of London. The increase in the number of joint-stock companies, most notably the East India Company and later the Hudson's Bay Company, and their expansion, opened up new investment opportunities,[4] whilst the rise in overseas military endeavour increased the National Debt, providing long-term repositories for capital. The result was the strengthening of Britain's credit network, producing a spectacular increase in so-called 'invisible earnings', enabling large merchant companies to free up capital for long-distance trade.[5] London's port became a major source of employment in the capital, whilst "the growth of its trading wealth enabled the city itself to develop as a centre of consumption and to dominate English society."[6]

By the start of the next century, London had come to hold a unique position in the context of Britain and Europe. Its geographical, political and economic proximity to government and the Bank of England, alongside its distinctive overseas orientation and a long-term capital market, positioned London at the core of the emerging financial infrastructure that grew with Britain's imperial web.[7] The tangible result was an urban environment that was not only responsive to economic growth but also linked through commercial, imperial and military channels to a global terrain. The surge of trading in foreign commodities in the Royal Exchange and its environs increased land values in the area,[8] causing a bout of speculative building in the early eighteenth century, whilst the consolidation of informal markets into prominent establishments, such as Lloyds Insurance (1687–8) and the Bank of England (1691), provoked an increase in institutional architecture in the capital, exemplifying a shift in scale that would intensify with the imperial grandeur of the next century. With the Austrian War of Succession and the Seven Years War in the mid century, and the increased involvement of the British government and Crown in Indian affairs, government borrowing increased dramatically with a concomitant rise of securities traded on the stock market. These developments led to the first official confederation of stockbrokers at Jonathan's in 1761. Coming together from the disparate and mobile marketplace within the alleys, the small group of traders paid a large subscription of £8 per year to the owner of Jonathan's to have sole occupancy of the building once a day, to accommodate the increased demand in trading.[9]

The second half of the eighteenth century witnessed a remarkable increase in public debt and influx of European capital to London that

Figure 1 'An historical, emblematical, patriotical and political print representing the English Balloon or National Debt in the year 1782.' (London Metropolitan Archives.)

would irrevocably alter the shape of the stock market and in turn, its architectural expression. A satirical print made in 1785 shows the first purpose built Stock Exchange, constructed in 1773 in Sweetings Alley in response to the increase in government borrowing [Fig. 1]. The Exchange is depicted with a 'proportionable ball of gold the specific size of all the money we have to pay it with supposing that to be twenty millions of pounds sterling' surmounting the building; the financial burden was paradoxically Britain's crowning glory that would continue to grow, freeing up capital for worldwide expansion and defence of the realm. Pitt's economic policy during the Napoleonic wars saw the debt increase in unseen proportions, rising from £245m in 1783 to £700m in 1815.[10] The concomitant closure of the continental bourses throughout this period of unrest in Europe, including Paris (1793), Amsterdam (1795), and turmoil in Germany, triggered a mass exodus of business to London, rendering it the European centre for trade in securities.[11] As the state became progressively dependent upon the trade in the public 'Funds' to finance defence in what historians Peter Cain and Anthony Hopkins have called "a form of military-fiscalism . . . that sought to create additional revenues by market-oriented policies",[12] the stock market increasingly came to be affiliated with the wellbeing

Figure 2 New Stock Exchange', 1809; Augustus Charles Pugin. (London Metropolitan Archives.)

of the nation, positioning the LSE at the centre of an emerging British rhetoric in which finance and national security would be inextricably intertwined.

The decision to formalise the Stock Exchange in 1801 in the shape of Peacock's new building in Capel Court occurred alongside its rising prominence in public life and enhanced significance in assisting overseas war efforts and commerce [Fig. 2]. Situated in Bartholomew Lane, between Old Broad Street and Throgmorton Street at approximately 4000ft², the new building was in close proximity to the Royal Exchange, where Foreign Exchange continued to be traded, and the Bank of England, in which Soane's Rotunda was home to the market for government securities until 1834.[13] The foundation stone, now residing in the cafe of the Paternoster Square premises, was inscribed with the total figure of the National Debt at L552,750,924;[14] with the expansion of foreign markets and overseas warfare, Britain's presence abroad became increasingly reliant on financial institutions at home, with the LSE as a fundamental link in the imperial chain.

Throughout the first half of the nineteenth century, the increase in colonial acquisitions accompanied the success of the railways and the birth of the steamship, bringing a rise in foreign trade that caused London's docks to expand dramatically, collectively covering around 440 acres and holding over 1,400 vessels.[15] These changes were felt on a smaller scale further inland, as the Foreign Exchange Market, which currently resided in the Royal Exchange, was incorporated into the LSE in 1822, accommodated in a purpose built "Foreign Room", attached to the main building.[16] As advances in communication brought the rest of the world within Britain's economic grasp, proximity between the domestic and foreign market on the trading floor was essential to profitability.

Despite the increased presence of foreign securities, the bulk of trading remained in domestic investments. As Michie has noted, "in 1850, the London Stock Exchange was the biggest and most important of its kind in the world", which was "mainly a reflection of the strength and vitality of the British economy at this time,"[17] resulting in dramatic surges of trading activity that ultimately grew beyond the capacity of its edifice.[18] The decision to entirely rebuild the LSE in 1853 was testament to the thriving domestic market. With a vast trading floor, the impressive domed structure was designed by Thomas Allason [Fig. 3] to accommodate the expanding market in railway, steamship and mining stocks: Britain's burgeoning industrial prowess that was fuelling its imperial expansion. However, whilst Allason's structure would double the floor space of Peacock's design, with £6,000 being spent on enlarging the site, the edifice would not be sufficient for the dramatic influx of foreign securities that would occur in the second half of the nineteenth century.[19]

Figure 3 'The New London Stock Exchange', *Illustrated London News* (March 25th, 1854).

During this period, the City became the centre of international services and repository for the headquarters of many foreign banks due to its unrivalled financial expertise, military security and lenient tax laws that still are the source of allure for foreign capital today. London at this time was in a perpetual state of reconstruction to accommodate its increased enterprise and imperial administration, with over £7 million spent on public works and building in the City between 1782 and 1861.[20] Concurrently, the LSE was subject to piecemeal enlargement, with acquisitions of existing properties, on the eastern part of the site, in preparation for Cole's enormous extension in 1885.[21] With an additional 8,000ft^2 including new office space, committee rooms and vast central trading area connecting to the original floor, comprising a 70ft wide dome, Cole's addition was both functional in its expansiveness and symbolic in its grandeur [Fig. 4]. As observer Charles Duguid commented in 1901, the LSE now represented a "great institution, the mart of the world, the nerve centre of the politics and finances of its nations," and "the barometer of their prosperity and adversity."[22]

As the 'barometer' of the country's achievements, the LSE's unfaltering architectural colonisation of the surrounding buildings emulated Britain's continuing economic imperial expansion. At a time when it seemed to many that the Empire was actually relinquishing territories, with Canada, Australia, New Zealand and parts of North America on the path to self-governance, the financial reach of the official and

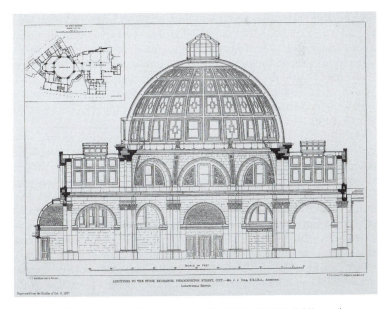

Figure 4 Section of the 'Gorgonzola Hall', 1885. (Guildhall Library.)

'informal' Empire was paradoxically at its most fervent.[23] The dramatic increase in trading in foreign government bonds and imperial securities on the London stock market throughout this period exemplifies this thesis, reflected in its requirements for architectural growth. The escalating physical presence of the LSE in the City was the result of Britain's increasingly invisible, but dominant, existence abroad, assisted by technological advances. The development of international telegraphic communications from the mid nineteenth century onwards meant that the barriers that had formerly maintained the independence of national stock exchanges were removed, resulting in the creation of a verifiably international securities market. [24] As various exchanges began to be increasingly specialised, the LSE became the central marketplace for almost all non-European securities, as it "possessed the necessary contracts, experience and communication facilities."[25] Furthermore, as the improved speed of international communication obliterated mercantile monopolies and increased profits abroad, investment in British-owned overseas enterprises on the London stock market increased,[26] an influx that was assisted by the acceleration of transactions in the LSE, brought about by the new technology.

Unlike the markets it housed, the LSE remained largely unchanged throughout the first half of the twentieth century, with the exception of minor extensions and marginal war damage. However, within the LSE markets changed radically during the wars, with severe reductions in foreign investment in the American market and heavy restrictions on domestic markets.[27] The decline of the British Empire proper and its impact on the London stock market during this period is an extensive discussion that will not be explored in any great depth in this paper.[28] However, the financial measures taken in an attempt to hold on to the Empire, such as the securing of the Sterling Area (the Empire-based currency zone) during and after the two World Wars, and the emergence of the Euromarket, would have a profound impact on London as a financial centre, the LSE and its architecture.

In the 1950s confidence in the Sterling Area began to shrink with decolonisation, forcing Britain to engage with Europe and Japan, the emerging dominant centres for trade.[29] Austere post-war regulation continued to fix exchange rates, prohibit trade in foreign currencies, and heavily restrict trading in sterling with non-residents following the loss of its colonies and the Suez Canal crisis in 1957.[30] It is this moment that economist Gary Burn attributes to the emergence of the Euromarket, as City banks who had relied on international lending and suffered massively from the economic restrictions, turned to the use of U.S. dollars, which seemingly avoided Britain's books and concomitant regulations.[31] The result was the formation of an 'invisible' financial network that would transform the mechanisms of London: "as the imperial basis of its strength disappeared, the City survived by transforming itself into an 'offshore island' servicing the business created by the industrial and commercial growth of much more dynamic partners."[32]

Despite the fact that the Euromarket boomed in the next decades to reach around $46 billion by 1970, steadily emerging to become the largest source of capital in the world,[33] the LSE's antiquated structure, requiring all transactions go through its convoluted broker-jobber system, prohibited its participation.[34] It continued to lose its American market, failed to develop one in either Eurobonds or European shares, and retained a presence only in Australian and South African mining securities. None of this was through ignorance, but an unwillingness to allow its members to respond to the needs of the international institutional investors who were interested in such securities.[35] London was attractive to investors because of its decreasing regulation in these markets, whereas the LSE was internally regulated by rules that sought to hold on to the captive domestic market, rendering it unsuited to this type of international transaction.[36]

Consequently, the LSE faced criticisms concerning its reluctance to modernise. Fixed commission rates and single capacity (the required separation of jobbers and brokers) were viewed as activities that prevented competition, whilst its selective British-only membership policy prohibited the participation of international investors. Concurrently, its building was becoming overcrowded (with as many as 8,000 people having access to the floor at any one time by the mid 1960s) and increasingly technologically outmoded.[37] The demolition and rebuilding that began in 1966 by Llewelyn Davies et al., was an attempt to rectify the Exchange's technological deficit in a radically modern architectural idiom, producing one of the first icons of the newly emerging City skyline [Fig. 5].[38] However, despite the architectural gesture and attempts to make the LSE the largest and most efficient market in Europe throughout the 1970s, the Exchange was listed on the Office of Fair Trading Restrictive Practices register in 1979. With its absence from the Euromarket and increasing international competition from the likes of the New York Stock Exchange, the LSE continued to fall behind in a city where even the biggest institutions were increasingly based upon Japanese, American or European capital.[39]

Britain's entry into the European Community in 1973, the abolition of exchange controls in 1979 and the computer revolution throughout the next decade led to a dramatic increase in overseas investment and international presence in the City. The OPEC price rise in the 1970s and concomitant flow of petrodollars through the City (expanding the Euromarket) rendered London an attractive destination for US and foreign banks to set up headquarters,[40] whilst a change in legislation now permitted foreign-securities houses to set up in London.[41] The result was a boom in the physical and economic presence of foreign institutions, posing a strong threat to the London market and the longstanding monopoly of the LSE. The response was the deal between

Figure 5 London Stock Exchange Tower in 1970 by the architects Lloyd Llewelyn Davies, Fitzroy Robinson & Partners and Weeks, Forestier-Walker & Bor. (London Metropolitan Archives.)

Thatcher's *laissez-faire* government and the LSE in 1986 that led to the deregulation of the stock market, the Big Bang. The introduction of Dual Capacity, abolition of fixed commissions, and admission of overseas and large institutional members, led to various mergers between its jobbing and broking firms, and the growth of financial conglomerates (predominantly from the US and Japan) "combining banking, dealing and currency trading ... and buying up the expertise of the Stock Exchange firms to become the new 'market makers' of 1986."[42]

The result was the flight of its expanded member firms from the LSE floor to large new offices in Canary Wharf and other commercial developments throughout the City that emerged in the boom of post-regulatory finance. In addition, the introduction of a new electronic trading system SEAQ (Stock Exchange Automated Quotations), modelled on its NYSE rival NASDAQ, instigated the abandonment of face-to-face, or open-outcry, trading. Accessible both remotely and on the floor itself, for the few small firms that continued to use the floor, it became cheaper to utilise the technology from their own offices via telephone and computers. Barely a decade old, the LSE's 'modern' trading floor was completely empty within a matter of months. The international expansion of the London stock market had led to the withering of its physical prominence in the City.

In the next two decades, the LSE took advantage of its geographical proximity to Europe and convenient position between Eastern and Western time zones, alongside advances in price-matching technology, to promote itself as "Marketplace to the World."[43] Due to the removal of its regulatory capacity in 2000 by the FSA and the repercussions of the Big Bang, the LSE moved to more suitable premises in Paternoster Square in 2004, requiring computer rooms to run trading platforms, broadcasting studios and offices for programming and marketing, rather than a trading floor [Fig. 6].[44] As the site of Lord Holford's famous post-war scheme and the object of contentious debate between Arup, the Prince of Wales and many others in the architectural community, the recent convoluted history of the square is well known and outside the remit of this paper. However, it is interesting to note that despite its association with 'Britishness', in its recent Royal affiliations and location, the site was taken into the ownership of the "Paternoster Associates" in 1989 (a consortium comprising Greycoat, Park Tower (US) and Mitsubishi Estate Corporation, MEC, (Japan)) and moved solely into the hands of MEC in 1991. Representing what King has called "receptacles for both the national and international surplus", the new premises for the LSE demonstrate the manner in which "the financial function of London's buildings (storing capital rather than people) has been increasingly transnationalized."[45]

According to Cain and Hopkins, the decline in industry towards the end of the British Empire proper occurred in tandem with the necessary growth of the financial sector. The result was such that the UK "inherited from its Empire days a bloated, but politically powerful financial center in London" that has become a source of allure for international capital.[46] Today the City thrives as part of a strong offshore network comprising sovereign territories and former colonies such as Hong Kong and Singapore, which continue to support its prominence in global geo-fiscal affairs. Whilst the British Empire no longer has an overtly visible geographical presence, its role in the preservation of an elite financial system is stronger than ever. Similarly, the apparent disappearing of the LSE to a benign C21st office building does not represent its declining role, only a shift in the visibility of power structures. Whilst only 23% of the LSE's membership is not UK-based, its international quotient now accounts for 48% of its total market value.[47] Standing on Japanese-owned property, in between two US-based multinationals (Goldman Sachs and CB Richard Ellis), in a City that is predominantly inhabited by international corporations, the geography of the LSE is reflective of its changed role.

Mapping the markets

If the LSE buildings are symbolic of broader trends in the global economy, the architecture must be understood in its capacity to

Figure 6 Aerial view of Paternoster Square. (Photograph by the author.)

Figure 7 Digital media screens in the atrium of the London Stock Exchange during the ceremony of 'Market Open'. (London Stock Exchange.)

accommodate financial exchange, as a marketplace. On entering the LSE today, the absence of a trading floor is emphatic. Unlike its nineteenth-century predecessor, the iconic glazed core is not filled with the visible noise of exchange but by a continuous stream of information delivered via media screens lining the atrium with share prices, flat screen televisions broadcasting business news, and hidden overhead speakers discharging inexorable market updates [Fig. 7]. Information sharing and shifting values are the primary emphasis in the space.

Today, the LSE comprises two equity markets known as the Main Market (hosting the companies listed on the FTSE 100, FTSE 250 and FTSE Small Cap) and the Alternative Investment Market (AIM), as well as the Professional Securities Market (PSM) and Specialist Fund Market. Known as 'secondary markets' (where stocks are traded after a firm makes an Initial Public Offering of its shares and bonds), the virtual distance between the seller, buyer and 'product', and the perpetual shifting of ownership that produces its value, results in a market that is a spatially distorted, to the point of being almost entirely conceptualised. The shrinking of the LSE edifice since 1986 visualises this abstraction; the increase in speed and volume of capital in the last few decades has resulted in the decrease in labour time and space. As Sharon Zukin argues, "today, simultaneous exchanges by electronic media tie together even the smallest places but they destroy the social distance that made experiencing them so distinctive."[48]

Prior to its formalisation in 1773 in Sweetings Alley, 'social distance' was the only defining characteristic of the stock market. Beginning in a parasitical relationship with other commodity markets in the Royal Exchange and the surrounding alleys, brokers and jobbers existed

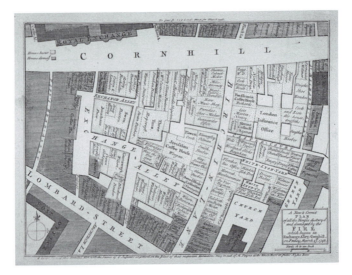

Figure 8 'A new & Correct Plan of all the Houses destroyd [*sic*] and damaged by the Fire which began in Exchange-Alley, Cornhill, on Friday, March 25, 1748.' (London Metropolitan Archives.)

in a fluid capacity, using the passages to facilitate the distribution of financial information [Fig. 8]. Paid on commission, the broker was an intermediary man of connections buying and selling on behalf of a client. Moving freely between coffee houses, he would have a detailed knowledge of raw materials, supplies in port and the requirements of manufacturers.[49] Working as dealers, buying and selling on their own account, jobbers had a more sinister reputation. Frequently accused of confederating to raise the price of stocks and spreading false information to make the market more favourable, multiple acts were enforced to attempt to quell the nefarious activities of jobbers and ban trading in the alleys, which was often said to be the cause of financial catastrophes such as the South Sea Bubble.[50] The movement of the stock market to Sweetings Alley and later Capel Court was an attempt to contain and regulate what had become an extremely volatile market, which, with the growing National Debt, Britain's economic stability increasingly rested upon. For reputable brokers, the complex webs of exchange in the dense network of alleys had come to represent "the clamorous importunity of partial interests"[51] that Adam Smith had warned against. Paradoxically, the way to achieving an efficient, open, free market was via architectural exclusion.

The enclosure of the Capel Court site was enhanced by its diminutive entrances and position in the midst of a dense network of alleys. However, once inside, a more liberal arrangement prevailed in the open trading floor where jobbers' pitches were defined only by their distance from the nearest column, wall, or other notable architectural feature. Its basilica form, with peripheral piers and arches forming recesses for the National Debt commissioners around a large central space,[52] continued the tradition of exchange architecture that was prevalent in Europe, with Domien de Waghemakere's building for the Exchange in Antwerp (1531) and Edward Jarman's designs for the nearby Royal Exchange (1669; Dest.1838) setting a precedent.[53] The open trading floor permitted mobility that was fitting for the volatile nature of its product, exemplified in an intriguing diagram of the interior of the Royal Exchange from 1798, revealing the zoning of traders according to commodity or its country of origin [Fig. 9]. Known as 'walks', these sites were unfixed: if the activity of buying and selling depended on the fluctuations of commodity prices, the merchant and broker would need to move about the room to establish such values, whilst affirming the relationships between brokers and the markets they served. The vacuum provided by the trading floor allowed for an informal method of exchange that

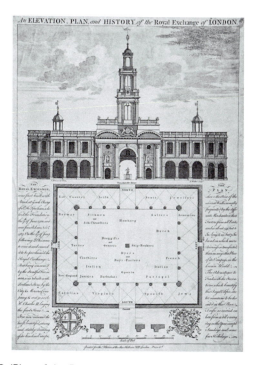

Figure 9 'Plan of the Royal Exchange, shewing [*sic*] the Merchants' Walks on the floor of the building', 1798, Grose's Antiquities. (London Metropolitan Archives.)

permitted the movement of capital between protagonists, in turn dispersing wealth to a mercantile elite, both reflecting and assisting the national web of relationships between industrialists, merchants and financiers that was fuelling Britain's industrialisation.[54]

With the imperial expansion and technological improvements of the nineteenth century, the trading floor of the LSE became increasingly sensitive to conditions beyond its locality, in a quasi-microcosmic fashion. An extraordinary diagram from 1880 by J.J. Cole shows the organisation of the trading floor prior to enlargement using colour-coded sections to represent the markets, defined by curved and perforated lines as if to highlight their flux and instability [Fig. 10]. A subsequent pamphlet written in 1884 "to confer on the arrangements of the Market on the opening of the Eastern addition" uses the drawing as a reference for the proposed reorganisation of the floor in the 'New House',[55] providing a rare insight into the link between the trading floor and the global marketplace. The Sub-Committee's proposal to bring "the Colonial Market into close unity with the Consols Market" (British government bonds) due to their "certain affinity", is telling of the deepened involvement of British government and Crown in the affairs of the colonies following the removal of trade monopolies from joint-stock companies, such as the East India Company, in the middle of the century.

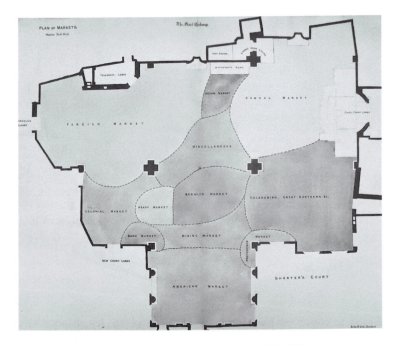

Figure 10 'Plan of the markets' by J. J. Cole. (Guildhall Library.)

Similarly, the decision to make space "for the American Market to expand" anticipates Britain's increasing role as creditor to the US for its major infrastructural projects and industry. It is also likely that the suggested movement of the Foreign Market to a larger space "under the new dome" and the increased scale of the Colonial Market, would have owed itself to the improved communications within Europe and the Empire following the introduction of the telegraph and first price-sharing system in 1872.[56] Technological improvements not only required Cole's attention in the accommodation of new communication facilities, but also in predicting the impact it would have on the markets so as to allow the correct spatial provision. These documents reveal an architectural synergy with the markets that went beyond the purely functional; like its members, Cole and the Committee were required to speculate in order to accommodate future economic shifts. Like the international marketplace it represented, markets on the floor were in constant flux, yet relied up on a certain topographical arrangement to assist the processes of exchange. As the link between market and place was being severed by the increasingly global free market, its movements were mapped on the floor of the LSE.

The design for the floor in the 1970s took on an entirely different, fixed character with freestanding, hexagonal jobbers' booths filling the central space, and brokers' boxes placed on split levels at the Periphery [Fig. 11]. The booths remained generic without any visible signification of market, presumably in the same spirit of speculation exhibited in Capel Court, yet the social distance that had formerly defined the ordering of markets had been replaced by architectural categorisation. The LSE's unique broker-jobber system, which was soon to be eliminated with the introduction of dual capacity in 1986, had been preserved in the fabric of the building. A broker would go to a 'booth' to receive quotations from a jobber, who was now effectively a wholesaler, before agreeing a price and returning to their 'box' to process the transaction. However, it was noted by a contemporary reporter that due to the rapidly changing share prices on the new electronic system, brokers were often required to run between booth and box, and as such, Llewelyn Davies et al. were requested to ensure the distances between jobber and broker were such that no firm had an unfair advantage by virtue of proximity, thereby guaranteeing fair competition.[57]

The uneasy marriage of technological speed and institutional stasis reflected the inability of the committee to have predicted the colossal metamorphoses that would take place in finance in the next decade, encapsulated by the rapid redundancy of the trading floor after the Big Bang. As London's growing link with international markets became increasingly reliant upon technology, it grew difficult to build flexibly for the future around the LSE's rigid values. Global economic shifts

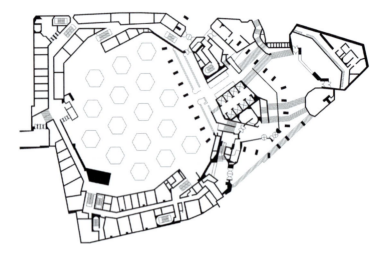

Figure 11 Ground plan of the London Stock Exchange trading floor, 1972. (© Danielle Willkens.)

were not alone in shaping its architecture; self-representation, aimed at both its members and the public, was equally influential in the layout and style of all the LSE's buildings.

Identity: an architectural construct

On the 1970s trading floor, the spatial connection between the market and marketplace had been severed by the temporal incompatibility between the pace of technology and the pull of tradition; a desire to modernise materially was hampered by the preservation of the LSE's two hundred year-old social structure. Whilst the 1970s building was evidently a radical departure from the classicism of its predecessor, upon closer inspection, both plan form and design pointed to tradition. Despite concrete and stainless steel touches and a geometrically bold layout, the repeated tessellated hexagon motif, in plan, light fixtures, ceiling coffers and jobbers' booths, was almost baroque in its ornamental consistency. Coupled with the use of travertine marble on the walls, the design referenced the geometric grandeur of Cole's dome, whilst the honeycomb structure evoked institutional unity. Furthermore, the "mean and cramped" fenestration of the tower and its "grim and fortresslike"[58] concrete exterior presented a bold statement that simultaneously excluded as it drew attention. As one member of the architectural press wrote in 1972, "although imaginative in plan shape . . . there is an overpowering feeling of gloom. The architectural profession may only be commissioned to design one stock exchange per century and may consequently feel it has to provide a battleship of a building to stay the course."[59]

The internal layout of the tower continues the established order. With the trading floor connected on the ground and first floors, but adjacent (to keep the floor free of load-bearing columns), the seven-sided tower comprised a central service core circumvented by ring corridors and office space at the perimeter, with five floors for the Exchange at the top of the building and settlement rooms at the first floor, sandwiching ten floors of maintenance and lettable space in between. The levels for the Council and Committee were given prominence by their 1.5 storey height, filled with ceremonial banqueting and conference spaces, whilst the organisation of offices on the administrative floors reads like a set of royal apartments, as interconnecting rooms progress in order of professional status: with large open clerical offices, enclosed secretarial areas, detached executive offices and even a private apartment for the Chairman, the arrangement exhibits what Frank Duffy has called a "gradual unfolding of rewards ... the universal currency of space standards."[60] The tiered ordering of space preserved a hierarchical and gendered social system that was becoming rapidly under threat.[61]

At this time the club-like world of the City received intense criticism from both Conservative and Labour governments. Thatcherites in particular were hostile towards a "paternalist Tory tradition"[62] that preserved monopolies and privileges via an old-boys network that had existed for centuries. Seen as undermining Britain's potential in the forum of international capitalism, the LSE's two-century-old membership policy was brought under scrutiny, which permitted only jobber and broker firms to apply (within which all partners had to join and could have no other occupation), and until 1967, prohibited members from having seats on any foreign stock exchange.[63] Despite being considered restrictive to the economy, the privacy and exclusivity permitted by the LSE's membership policy was integral to the self-regulation that defined it, whilst architectural enclosure was essential to its preservation. The 1970s "battleship" would defend "the operations of a complex system, which even today in its preoccupations and language remains mystifying and impenetrable to the outsider."[64]

The spatial segregation of the LSE had always been fundamental to its operation, beginning with its geographical disassociation from the speculative malpractice of so-called "alleymen" at its formation in the eighteenth century.[65] In the eyes of legitimate traders, the alleys formed the material gulf between profit and professionalism, with shady courts and clandestine corners assisting reprehensible transactions. However, for over a century, this intimate web of coffee houses had permitted a form of social interaction that was necessary for the mechanisms of the stock market and continued well into the late twentieth century. The absorption of Hercules' Tavern into Capel Court in 1801, via a specially constructed back entrance,[66] and the movement of Maybey's restaurant to the ground floor in 1872 provided an unceremonious extension of the trading floor in which dialogue would facilitate business. "Many a daring deal has been arranged over those tables and over those fine wines",[67] wrote Duguid in 1901, a sentiment that prevailed in the 1980s as one member recalls, "on the Stock Exchange floor you were expected to go across to the bar and have several drinks at twelve o'clock ... Some people were known to enjoy several glasses of brandy after lunch, having had two gin and tonics before and several glasses of wine."[68] As a method of keeping the interiority (and perhaps integrity) of the LSE intact, activities that would usually remain extraneous to the workplace were permitted, catered for, and even encouraged within its walls. The success of the institution had always relied upon a closed system of trust that combined business with entertainment, akin to that of a gentleman's club: "its prestige was enhanced by the informality of its proceedings."[69]

This style of business was an extension of the 'gentlemanly capitalism' that defined the operations of the City, and indeed the Empire.[70] Developed by Cain and Hopkins, the term refers to a system that emerged following the financial reforms of the late seventeenth century, in which the consolidation of power of the landed interest, as well as the growth of a merchant oligarchy and 'commercial dynasties', resulted in the professionalising of private sector occupations, such as banking and later stockbroking.[71] With the simultaneous emergence of new departments in government like the Treasury and Board of Trade, and the assimilation of the National Debt with the wellbeing of Britain over the next century, finance increasingly became associated with public duty, which in turn became the "hallmark of gentility".[72] As the investment industry boomed at the beginning of the nineteenth century, City elites grew more influential in government, and the City became a world in which the operations of politicians and financiers were rapturously intertwined.[73]

The ambiguous relationship between the LSE and government came to reveal itself fervently in the second half of the nineteenth century with the economic and social reforms taking place in Britain. Gladstone's liberal policies and emphatic push towards free trade had instigated a departure from the inward-looking, aristocratic allegiances that characterised Britain's financial elite. In taking economic management out of the hands of party politicians and into the control of the Bank of England and Treasury, the City flourished, and whilst many Stock Exchange members did suffer from the abolition of the 'Old Corruption', this encouraged entry into international markets, in which they had great success.[74] The concomitant growth of the international markets was articulated in the expansion of the site during this phase and the addition of a more prominent frontage on Throgmorton Street. Forming the first major articulation of the LSE to the public gaze since its construction, the facade would have heightened popular awareness of a once concealed establishment, visibly and geographically aligning it with the nearby Bank of England.

The LSE's affiliations with the might of the Empire surged during this period with the burgeoning trade in foreign securities; the grandeur of Cole's extension in 1885 was not a purely functional expansion but symbolised the wealth of the nation. Described vividly in a chapter entitled "The Stock Exchange Militant and Loyal", Duguid highlights the mass of the structure "marked by a solidity and reality" with "many of the stones being more than three tons in weight," going on at length to describe the various marbles including those "from the Roman quarries near Carthage."[75] Echoing the plethora of grand imperial institutional buildings that had emerged throughout the metropolis during this period, including the Foreign, Colonial and India Offices, and Admiralty buildings in Whitehall,[76] the luxuriousness, weight, and classical provenance of the materials used in the LSE represented the might of the Empire and the splendour of antiquity.

As Cain and Hopkins have noted, the separation of government and the City during this period of economic reform, "together with the esoteric nature of financial management gave these gentlemanly institutions a certain political invisibility."[77] The success of the LSE now resided in its institutional independence, placing it at the heart of Britain's gentlemanly imperial financial web. A photograph of the hall from 1900, taken during the celebration of the Relief of Mafeking during the Boer War, was one of many instances in which the LSE publicised the collective celebration of national events in the grandeur of the Gorgonzola Hall.[78] The stereoscopic technique in this image deliberately enhances the illusion of depth, forming a sea of suited gentlemen facing the camera, reinforcing the overwhelming scale of the LSE and the significance of the individual within the institutional, and imperial, whole. Here, the building was a wholly contrived setting for the theatre of Empire, which was only as strong as its gentlemanly connections.

The staged nature of this photograph betrays a highly considered public image of the institution that exerts the institution's exclusivity. The 1950s witnessed a shift in the LSE's attitude towards self-representation as it began to expose its inner workings to the general public. During these years, its organisational structure changed to become a mutual company, giving LSE members part ownership.[79] Concurrently, new services were offered to non-members, such as settlement and publishing of information, as a way of generating profits. With the democratisation of its internal structure and increased public role, the LSE began to focus on its image in promotional terms. Beginning with the acquisition of a PR advisor in 1947, followed by the opening of the building in 1951 as part of the Festival of Britain, and the addition of a public viewing gallery in 1953 to be open on Saturdays,[80] the LSE participated in a form of institutional tourism that was swept along by the verve for nationalisation in the post-war period. However, a staged photograph or empty edifice on the weekend could only say so much; architecture was the optimum vehicle for cautious self-representation insofar as it revealed as much as it concealed. The LSE remained a closed world, which would only be reinforced by the new building in the 1970s.

The switch to corporate membership in 1986 and replacement of the LSE's governing Council by a Board of Directors in 1991, represented its move into the commercial domain, crystallised by its conversion to a Public Limited Company in 2000 and listing on its own Main Market in 2001. The move to Paternoster Square in 2004 accompanied an entire overhaul of the LSE's image, provided by Gensler's design rhetoric of "openness and transparency,"[81] permeable open office space and glazed partitions. Using the new location "as a graphic mechanism to refer to the world's other global financial centres",[82] Gensler's interior branding utilises coloured squares to denote cartographic co-ordinates, on the doors, walls and glass divisions of each meeting room, articulating its 'global' reach. Furthermore, the first floor, which was initially intended by Parry to be a trading floor, has been converted into a media centre, with a glass-walled broadcasting studio, lecture theatre and conference rooms, described by Gensler as the LSE's "public face . . . where market intelligence is relayed to the financial community",[83] representing the seamless worldwide transmission of information.

Despite the semblance of openness, the current LSE building expresses selective disclosure. Designed by Parry to accommodate a generic financial institution, the ground floor fenestration of the building uses opaque glass to visually exclude in tandem with a highly secure entrance,[84] whilst the self-supporting limestone "skin" has the effect of screening the interior, allowing it to recede behind a benign yet resilient external structure: the building's 'shell and core' form provides accidental discretion [Figs. 12 & 13]. The choice of Paternoster Square, with its architectural history and proximity to St Pauls, provides a setting that is rooted in the history of the City and Britain. As Whitfield put it, the project "is not so much about the architecture as place-making."[85] Parry's restrained modernist exterior, with its classicising loggia, suited the LSE's desire to be modern in outlook but traditional in its values, namely as a safe marketplace for its members. Once again, the LSE selectively conveys its image as one that is publicly private.

Internally, there are aspects of the design that reiterate the LSE's longstanding rhetoric of institutional enclosure. In contrast to the global "graphic mechanisms" littered throughout the interior space, the terminology used to describe different parts of the Paternoster building communicates something more fundamental. With "The Source" installation in the entrance, "The Foundation" restaurant (where the original 1801 foundation stone is displayed), "The Hub" meeting area, and "The Summit" executive rooms on the top floor, the nomenclature of each space alludes to knowledge, or more specifically, to esotericism. To its

Figure 12 Exterior of the London Stock Exchange; Architects: Eric Parry; SheppardRobson. (© Nick Kane Photography.)

members, one major advantage of trading on the LSE is that it grants privileged access to financial data unavailable to outsiders. The containment of specialist information within its membership is a defining characteristic of the institution. Where previously the boundaries confining this knowledge were prescribed by the architectural limits of the LSE, today they take the form of symbol and metaphor in accordance with the virtual nature of the market.

Building Exchange relationships

Running throughout the LSE's buildings is a representational conflict between a unified public entity, and a social system that relies on a network of individuals. The ordering of space within the 1970s tower, the integration of Hercules Tavern into Capel Court and the symbolism in Paternoster Square point to an institution that relies upon the communication of its members. Whether in the gentlemanly camaraderie of the trading floor or the corporate privacy of the current building, the modus operandi of exchange has been at the root of the LSE's self-representation and defined its architectural form.

According to Gensler, the open plan fit-out for the current LSE would contribute to "an energizing workspace that embraces new work

Figure 13 Exterior of the London Stock Exchange; Architects: Eric Parry; SheppardRobson. (© Nick Kane Photography.)

patterns, technologies and strategic purposes," assisted by sporadic and sheltered seating areas for "dialogue and impromptu meetings."[86] Certain sections of the building, such as the executive meeting rooms and HR offices, are glazed with opaque, soundproof glass to offer "audio privacy,"[87] whilst the waiting areas outside them have variants of 'lounge music' softly playing to reinforce this. The atmosphere in the building is one of cynical quietude, far removed from the visceral scenes of trading in former buildings, representative of the technological unravelling of verbal and financial exchange that emerged in 1986.

Prior to the implementation of fixed booths and boxes in 1974, jobbers and brokers were dependent upon proximity and flexibility on the floor, communicating via gesture, dialogue and lip-reading. The result was an uncomfortably crowded, chaotic trading floor, but as Hennessey has noted, "this was not always seen as a disadvantage," as "if you were close to where the leading brokers passed . . . this brought opportunities to quote a price and *form a judgment* about the business."[88] Visibility and propinquity enabled traders to assess the validity of the information offered on account of the integrity of the man offering it; spatial relationships were integral to a network of trust. As financial psychologist David Tuckett points out, "human relationships of exchange involve a story being told to create a belief that continued attachment to the relationship will be excitingly rewarding or a source of danger and disadvantage. The word 'credit' is actually based on the Latin verb 'to believe'."[89] The exchange value of securities was intimately connected to the character of the man selling them: on the floor, brokers and jobbers were not merely trading in financial products, but advertising their own personality in order to create strong exchange relationships. Failure to live up to this bond of trust, by defaulting on a deal, would result in immediate expulsion, "and their characters blasted by the suspension of a blackboard in a conspicuous part of the House on which their names are painted at full length."[90] The open trading floor was an arena that enabled surveillance and the visible condemnation of those who ruptured the unofficial system of trust. A man's contract was only ever as good as his word, hence the Stock Exchange motto, "dictum meum pactum."

The informality of proceedings on the floor meant that success arose from the ability to be spontaneous. Having a small and mobile pitch was fundamental, as it allowed traders "to grab a better vantage point"[91] when occasions arose, meaning that smaller jobbers firms would often lose out due to a visible presence that was proportionate to their reputation.[92] In the late 1960s, the informal layout of the trading floor was consequently viewed as the architectural aid to the LSE's 'restrictive' system that was increasingly the object of public criticism. It was believed that the integration of fixed booths and boxes into the new trading floor would improve efficiency and accommodate the implementation of the first electronic trading system TALISMAN (Transfer Accounting and Lodgement for Investors, Stock Management for jobbers). Chosen by the jobbers themselves, the hexagonal booths had rings of seats inside where the clerks would carry out their business, providing a less flexible but more equal method of trading, ensuring that smaller firms would have a higher stake in the market. Such changes were made at a time when the stock market was becoming increasingly stringent in its professional requirements, with the introduction of exams for stockbrokers in the 1970s, and greater emphasis on specialisation within stockbroking firms, including departments for research and analysis.[93] As the

LSE's aims and methods became progressively scientific, so the floor became a diagrammatic and knowable environment; the architectural cleansing of an old system.

Up to this point, exchange in Capel Court had been a messy business, with traders darting around the floor and messengers running to and from the Bank to communicate changes in the bank rate.[94] All of this took its toll on the building and its traders, with the oak flooring wearing down "at an estimated rate of 1¾ inches per decade" and the build up of extreme temperatures in the summer due to the mass of bodies.[95] The 1970s design took various measures to avoid the bodily chaos of former years, including the use of rubber flooring to prevent erosion. Physical exertion also dissipated as each member firm's office outside the LSE was connected to the floor via its own telephone communication point, equipped with a 'Market Price Display Service' whereby information was displayed on television screens connected to a central computer.[96] Described by a contemporary observer as "a small town within a city,"[97] the LSE created a community beyond its walls, reducing the friction of face-to-face trading.

However, there was a conflict between the new technology and the Exchange's refusal to abandon its anachronistic jobber-broker system, which resulted in impractical solutions. In the new building, traders were supplied with 'bleepers' to replace the deafening voice calling each member to the floor.[98] One consequence of this was that the overall volume in the room would be lowered, inadvertently exposing private conversations and verbal agreements between members. In order to reassert aural privacy the architects were requested to preserve a level of background noise, which was achieved by the use of hardwearing materials on the interior to produce a resounding echo to drown out individual conversations.[99] The acoustic legacy of Capel Court's cavernous interior had been subsumed into the operation of the LSE. So long as trading was to be performed by verbal exchange, noise was a feature that would need to be incorporated, and if necessary fabricated, architecturally.

Historically, outsiders had referred to the noise of traders on the floor in pejorative terms as an audible reflection of the apparent animal disorder within, whereas to the trader, it was an important component of the mechanisms of the market. As a journalist in 1933 perceptively put it, "to the untrained listener the noise will probably sound like senseless babble: and by way of assistance to a more intelligent appreciation of its quality I can only suggest … the resultant sound may be compared to the steady hum of a dynamo."[100] Much like the turmoil of the virtual marketplace today, to the outsider, the sonic chaos of the trading floor rendered the performance of products or the integrity of the trader difficult to assess, blurring the boundary between speculative chance and good judgement. As Tuckett puts it, "feedback given to investors is 'noisy', in the sense that it is extremely difficult to determine cause and effect and so to draw any secure conclusions about whether an investor's efforts in buying, holding and selling them is a result of skill or luck."[101]

This audible confusion was to be enhanced by the visual enclosure of the LSE, as public surveillance was prohibited by the absence of windows at eye line. For members inside, the lack of visible fenestration and centric location of the floor focused the gaze inwards, forming a theatrical space for the visceral spectacle of exchange. As Duffy notes, on the trading floor "no view is a good view . . . all attention is within."[102] Today, the drama of open-outcry has been replaced by the theatre of ritual in the ceremony of 'market open' in which all staff in the LSE line the glass walls of its central atrium to watch a newly-listed member begin the day's trading [Fig. 7]. At one minute to eight, the member firm stand on a ceremonial balcony and insert a glass plaque engraved with the company's name into a plinth, originally triggering the movement of a dynamic installation named 'The Source'.[103] Designed by the artists' collective Greyworld, the installation was conceived as an alternative to the bell at the start of trading. Formed by a square grid of 162 cables reaching all eight stories of the atrium, nine spheres would run up and down each cable to form shapes, such as the rising sun in the morning and the name and position of share prices throughout the day, behaving like pixels to produce three-dimensional images [Fig. 14].[104] Linked to the Internet to capture the movement of the market in real-time, the installation was intended by the collective to be a "microcosm of activity, a living reflection of market forces."[105]

This highly symbolic structure positions the market as an autonomous phenomenon at the centre of the LSE's operations. Its ethereal form celebrates the seamless transmission of information, highlighting the collision of "two fetish beliefs in technological and spatio-temporal fixes" in a world in which "capital moves faster and faster and where distances of interaction are compressed."[106] In the broader context, the result of this technological shift has been a public perception of the market as disassociated from human agency, an abstract automaton, shaping our politico-economic and geographical environment, rather than the reverse. At the institutional level, the collapsing of social distance has ensured that it is now technology, rather than traders, that define the LSE and warp its architectural form. Historically, the LSE expanded commensurately with the size of the market; today the underlying fundamentals have become distorted to such an extent that the concept of the marketplace has been entirely restructured.

Conflicts through space and time

The inability of any one LSE building to accommodate the medium and long-term shifts in international markets, and the incompatibility between the speed of transactions and institutional stasis, demonstrate

Figure 14 'The Source', installation by Greyworld. (London Stock Exchange private collection.)

that the *spatial* history of the LSE has been defined by the continual need to overcome fundamental *temporal* incongruences. Its architecture has been required to exist in a divided state, building for the past yet designing for the future, with inert structures housing persistent oscillations in market trends, share prices and technology. Capel Court underwent continued and piecemeal extensions across nearly two centuries: "continuous progress and adaptation to the times has necessitated addition, alteration, and enlargement," Duguid observed in 1901, "the shape of the Stock Exchange is shapeless."[107] In the 1970s, Llewelyn Davies et al were required to cater for an institution in transition, in which traditional values had not caught up with technological ambition, producing a building that would be all but redundant within a decade. Today, the Paternoster premises are speculative architecture in the most literal sense: with the current rate of transaction at 6 milliseconds,[108] it seems only rational that the interior layout should have the capacity to be altered within a matter of weeks. Much like the brokers who are required to make decisions based on continued uncertainty and conjecture, the architecture of the LSE has been in an unending position of instability. As Tuckett puts it, "uncertainty about the future value of assets creates inherent and irresolvable conflicts . . . at the first decision moment but also at ongoing dynamic ones. The experience of conflict through time, therefore, is at the heart of the financial system."[109]

At the core of these temporal-architectural contradictions has been the struggle for profit-driven efficiency. If an exchange is an institutional platform to facilitate free trade, then its architecture must provide a friction-free arena within which the speed of transaction is paramount. As Marx once argued, fundamental to capital accumulation is the ability to surmount geographical boundaries, "tear down every spatial barrier to intercourse, i.e., to exchange, and conquer the whole earth for its market."[110] Within the buildings of the LSE, space has been the primary obstacle to productivity. The attempted solutions in overcoming such hindrances have been twofold: firstly, to assist movement within the building, exemplified in the architectural and technological cleansing of the floor in the 1970s; and secondly, to display greater command over the space, illustrated by Cole's plan of the markets in 1880. The architectural strategies to increase financial production thus mimic the broader geopolitical strategies that create and sustain its markets.

As David Harvey has articulated, historically, "urban-based merchants and traders learned that their power to survive within a land-based feudal or imperial power lay in cultivating a superior ability to manoeuvre in space", whilst today "the capitalist class and its agents . . . maintain much of their power of domination by virtue of superior command over and mobility in space."[111] Just as the Victorians sought to increase trade profits by developing railways, canals and telegraphs to reduce "the frictions of distance or speeding up capital circulation",[112] so the trading floor would need to mirror the conquering of space through temporal and technological means, in order to accommodate the increase in trade such improvements would bring. If the productivity of capital relies on what Harvey calls 'time-space compression', it has been the role of the LSE to paradoxically condense the global reach of an ever-expanding market within its walls to ensure its continual growth.

The methodological shift in scales within this paper has attempted to highlight the capability of global financial markets, as essentially immaterial systems, to distort our material environment. It is within this theoretical context that architecture of the LSE becomes the point of contact, or perhaps rupture, between global and local networks, invisible and visible forces, use value and exchange value. Inadvertently, my visit to the LSE on 4th August 2011 coincided with the day that almost £50 billion was wiped from the value of the UK's 100 largest companies, as fears surrounding the US economy and the worsening Eurozone crisis sent shockwaves of panic across the financial world. If the architecture of the Exchange is the point of distortion in this space-time compression, it is then hardly surprising that on the most tumultuous day on the global stock market since 2008, I saw but three people wandering through its serene, vacant atrium.

Acknowledgements

I would like to thank Professor Iain Borden, without whom this paper would not have been possible. This work was supported by the Schools Competition Act Settlement Trust (SCAST) Postgraduate Research Scholarship.

References

1   Duguid, C. 1901, p.308
2   For detailed economic accounts see Ranald Michie (1999), George Blakey (2007), and E.V. Morgan & W.A. Thomas (1962); Hennessey, E. (2001), Duguid, C. (1901) and Jenkins, A. (1973) provide entertaining anecdotal accounts of the institution at different phases of its existence; Frank Duffy's work (1980; 1986; 1997) is apposite in tracing the metamorphosis of financial architecture following the Big Bang but unfortunately pays little attention to the LSE either historically or presently
3   Anthony D. King's research into *Post Imperialism and the Internationalisation of London* (1990) is exemplary of the former. Whilst an insightful and compelling account of the spatial connection between British imperial economy, urban development and even architectural typology, King's thesis neglects more focused analysis of the architecture itself
4   Between 1690 and 1695 the number of joint-stock companies increased from 15 to 140 with a corresponding increase in total capitalisation from £0.9m to £4.5m. Hennessey, E. 2001, p.7
5   Cain, P. and Hopkins, A.G. 2001, p.72
6   King, A.D. 1990, p.73
7   Ibid, pp.70–72
8   Keene, D. 'The Setting of the Royal Exchange: continuity and change in the financial district of the City of London 1300–1871' in Saunders, A. 1999, p.260
9   Hennessey, E. 2001, p.16–17
10 Hennessey, E. 2001, p.19 The loss of the American colonies in 1783, increase in Indian trade following Pitt's India Act of 1784 also had a dramatic impact on the scale of the National Debt
11 Ibid
12 Cain, P. and Hopkins, A.G. 2001, p.77

13 Hennessey, E. 2001, p.18
14 This is particularly poignant when we consider that interest payments on the Debt "swallowed more than 50 per cent of public expenditure in peace time . . . equivalent to about half the value of total exports in the eighteenth century." Cain, P. and Hopkins, A.G. 2001, p.79
15 King, A.D. 1990, p.74
16 With the gradual integration of the market into the mechanisms of the Stock Exchange culminating in an official merger of 1835, the room soon lost its specific purpose becoming the place for any deals extraneous to the National Debt. Hennessey, E. 2001, p.43
17 Michie, R. 1999, p.70
18 A period of great booms, the first half of the century also bore witness to a number of dramatic busts, led by the railways as well as the defaulting of South American loans and 'American Panic' of the 1830s
19 Michie, R. 1999, p.70
20 King, A.D. 1990, p.78
21 The volume of trading had increased to such a degree that in 1873, the settlement room in the basement used for the 'clearing' of stocks and clerical organisation of payment and delivery, had to be moved to an entirely separate site in Drapers' Gardens
22 Duguid, C. 1901, p.1
23 Cain, P. and Hopkins, A.G. 1993b, p.3
24 Michie, R. 'Different in Name Only? The London Stock Exchange and Foreign Bourses c.1850–1914' in Michie, R. (ed.) 2000 p. 282
25 Ibid
26 Cain, P. and Hopkins, A.G. 1993a, p.185
27 Hennessey, E. 2001, p.101
28 See Brendon, P. 2007 *The decline and fall of the British Empire: 1781–1997* (London: Jonathan Cape); Darwin, J. 1991 *The end of the British Empire: the historical debate* (Oxford: Basil Blackwell); Douglas, R. 2002 *Liquidation of empire: the decline of the British Empire* (Basingstoke: Palgrave)
29 Michie, R. 2000, p.281
30 Shaxson, N. 2011, p.80; Palan, R. 2010, p.160
31 Burn, G. 2005, *The Re-emergence of Global Finance* (Basingstoke: Palgrave); see Palan, R. 2010 pp.160–161
32 Cain, P. and Hopkins, A.G. 2001, p.642.
33 Shaxson, N. 2011, p.92
34 As Michie notes, "By 1968 it was estimated that 60 per cent of the trading in Euro-Currency Bonds was in London . . . but only 1 per cent passed through the London Stock Exchange" Michie, R. 1999, p.466
35 Ibid, p.472
36 Ibid
37 Hennessey, E. 2001, p.144 There had been attempts at drawing up plans for new buildings in 1948 by the Exchange's Surveyor, G.J. Buckingham, although insufficient funds meant this could not take place. Ibid p.143
38 The reluctance to move the Exchange was largely due to the prestige of the area and lack of space elsewhere, which Anthony King attributes to the increasing financial specialisation of land within the Square Mile, "suggesting the rapidly increasing dependence of the City of London on its continued role in the capitalist world-economy." King, A.D. 1990, p.96

39 Cain, P. and Hopkins, A.G. 2001, p.642

40 King, A.D. 1990, p.90

41 Ibid, p.93

42 Ibid, p.94

43 John Kemp-Welch in Hennessey, E. 2001, p.194. During this period the LSE embarked on various attempts at consolidation with other international exchanges. These include the launch of the 'access package' for the top three hundred European firms to trade in Frankfurt and London in 1999, as well as failed mergers with NASDAQ in 2005 and the Toronto Stock Exchange (TMX) in 2011

44 Sandler, L. and Sukumar, N. 'London Stock Exchange New Building Aims to Project Fresh Image' *Bloomberg*, August 30, 2004

45 King, A.D. 1990, p.104

46 Palan, R. 2010, p.164

47 LSE Website [www.londonstockexchange.com/exchange/traders-and-brokers/membership/member-firm-directory/member-firm-directory-search.html]

48 Zukin, S. 1991, p.12

49 Daunton, M. 1995, p.337

50 Morgan, E.V. and Thomas, W.A. 1962, p.30; Smith, C.F. 1929, p.218

51 Daunton, M.J. 1995, p.534

52 Hennessey, E. 2001, p.24

53 For a detailed account of the genesis of exchange architecture, see Pevsner, N. 1976, *A History of Building Types* (London: Thames & Hudson), pp.193–212

54 Daunton, M.J. 1995, p.246

55 The pamphlet describes a new plan to go with the written description, which unfortunately does not appear to be archived. LSE: 'Minutes of the Sub-Committee formed to confer on the arrangements of the Market on the opening of the Eastern addition', 22nd August 1884

56 Duguid, C. 1901, p.216

57 'Dictum Meum Pactum: the new Stock Exchange building' *Architects' Journal* v. 156, n. 45, 1972 Nov. 8, p. 1041

58 Ibid

59 Ibid

60 Duffy, F. 1997 p.17

61 Despite the (albeit belated) entry of women into the Stock Exchange in 1973, female toilet provision on the floor of the Council was only a fifth of the men's, with no washrooms on the trading floor for potential new female members

62 Cain, P. and Hopkins, A.G. 2001, p.642

63 Hennessey, E. 2001, p.157

64 Keene, D. 'The Setting of the Royal Exchange: continuity and change in the financial district of the City of London 1300–1871' in Saunders, A. 1997, p.260

65 Alleymen encompassed "broken down merchants' clerks, decayed tradesmen who have lost money by speculation, and others whose pretensions to honesty and character it would be difficult to describe" Evans, D.M. 1852, p.52

66 Hennessey, E. 2001, p.24

67 Duguid, C. 1901, p.181–2

68 George Nissen in Augar, P. 2001, p.38

69 Cain, P. and Hopkins, A.G. 1993a, p.129; In the tradition of the gentleman's club, dealings were often carried out over dinner or at shoots in the country.

70 Cain, P. and Hopkins, A.G. 2001, p.31

71 Ibid, p.69

72 Ibid. As Cain and Hopkins have pointed out, the response to the new monied interest was divided, as "to some observers, the new financiers were patriots whose expertise in organising low-cost credit funded the defence of the realm, overseas expansion and domestic employment. To others, they were upstarts who threatened to undermine the established social order by imposing 'avarice' into a world that depended on 'virtue' to guarantee good government." Ibid, p.72

73 Ibid p.73

74 Cain, P. and Hopkins, A.G. 1993a, p.149; During the 1870s the Exchange was subject to inspection by a Royal Commission due to a series of scandals surrounding foreign loans in the previous decade. Publicized widely by the press, public accusations were rife: "secrecy permeates every branch", one observer wrote, "and shrouds the arcana of that mighty body – secrecy is the inherent and palpable cause of all its misdoings in the past." See Hennessey, E. 2001, p.62–74

75 Duguid, C. 1901, p.303

76 King, A.D. 1990, p.78–9; For a detailed account of Britain's imperial architecture at home, see Bremner, G. A. 'Nation and Empire in the Government Architecture of Mid-Victorian London: the Foreign and India Office Reconsidered', *Historical Journal*, Vol. 48:3 (2005), pp.703–742

77 Cain, P. and Hopkins, A.G. 1993a, p.149

78 Duguid situates the extension of the Stock Exchange in the context of various national events such as Queen Victoria's Diamond Jubilee and death, as well as imperial victories. Duguid, C. 1901, p.303

79 In planning for the construction of a new building, the Exchange's 4,000 proprietors were unwilling to offer the money required. As a result, a scheme was developed to convert the shares into annuities to raise funds. The Committee for General Purposes and Committee of Trustees and Managers, which had traditionally controlled the operations of the Exchange, were dissolved and all responsibility for transactions, business, assets and property were taken over by a newly centralised Council, comprising its shareholders. Hennessey, E. 2001, p.143

80 Ibid, p.138–9

81 www.gensler.com/#projects/54

82 www.gensler.com/#projects/15

83 Ibid

84 With only one functioning entrance, the security to the building is extremely high, with two sets of guards either side of the doors, a bag scanning device and turnstiles once inside. The back entrance onto Newgate Street mimics this form but remains unused for maximum surveillance

85 Powell, K. 2003 'Squaring up; Masterplanner: Sir William Whitfield' *AJ*, Vol. 218, October 30, 2003, p.36

86 www.gensler.com/#projects/54

87 Sandler, L. and Sukumar, N., 2004

88 Hennessey, E. 2001, p.144

89 Tuckett, D. 2001, p.1

90 Duguid, C. 1901, p.177
91 Hennessey, E. 2001, p.144
92 Ibid
93 Hennessey, E. 2001, p. 146; Jenkins, A. 1973, p.176
94 Ibid, p.141
95 Jenkins, A. 1973, p.97
96 Ibid. p.180
97 Ibid p.181
98 Ibid p.182
99 'Dictum Meum Pactum: the new Stock Exchange building' *Architects' Journal* v. 156, n. 45, 1972 Nov. 8, p. 1041–2
100 'Midas' of *Financial News* 1933 in Hennessey, E. 2001, p.122
101 Tuckett, D. 2011, p.22
102 Duffy, F. and Waters, B. 'Squaring up for the Big Bang: redesign the office' *Building* vol. 250, no. 13, 1986 Mar. 28, p. 30–34; p. 32
103 A lack-luster inflated sphere now takes its place, onto which the name of the company is projected
104 *Greyworld* [http://greyworld.org/]
105 Ibid
106 Harvey, D. 2010, p.158
107 Duguid, C. 1901, p.309
108 LSE Rulebook [www.londonstockexchange.com/traders-and-brokers/membership/faqs/rulebook-faq/rulebook-faqs.htm]
109 Tuckett, D. 2011, p.20
110 Karl Marx in Harvey, D. 2010, p.157
111 Ibid, p.155
112 Ibid, p.158

Select Bibliography

Augar, P. 2001 *The Death of Gentlemanly Capitalism: The Rise and Fall of London's Investment Banks* (London: Penguin Books)
Bowen, H.V. 2006 *The Business of Empire: the East India Company and imperial Britain, 1756–1833* (Cambridge: Cambridge University Press)
Blakey. G. 2008, *A History of the London Stock Market* (London: Harriman House)
Cain, P. and Hopkins, A.G. 1993a *British Imperialism: Innovation and Expansion 1688–1914* (London: Longman)
———— *British Imperialism: Crisis and Deconstruction 1914–1990* (London: Longman)
———— 2002, *British Imperialism 1688–2000* (London: Longman)
Daunton, M.J. 1995 *Progress and poverty: an economic and social history of Britain, 1700–1850* (Oxford: Oxford University Press)
Duguid, C. 1901 *The Story of the Stock Exchange* (London: Grant Richards)
Duffy, F. 1997 *The New Office* (London: Conran Octopus)
Evans, D.M. 1852 *The City: or, the Physiology of London business; with Sketches on 'Change, and at the Coffee Houses* (London: Groombridge & Sons)
Hennessy, E. 2001 *Coffee House to Cyber Market* (London: Ebury Press)
Greater London Council: City of London: Building Act case file (Stock Exchange; Fitzroy Robinson et al), 1967–1974
Harvey, D. 2010 *The Enigma of Capital and the Crisis of Capitalism* (London: Profile Books)

Jenkins, A. 1973 *The Stock Exchange Story* (London: Heinemann)

King, A.D. (ed.) 1980 *Buildings and Society: Essays on the societal development of the built environment* (London: Routledge & Keagan Paul)

—— 1990 Global Cities: *Post-Imperialism and the Internationalization of London* (London: Routledge)

London Stock Exchange (hereafter LSE): Committee for General Purposes and various sub-committees; Trustees and Managers Minutes; Council Minutes; specifications, plans and elevations of Exchange buildings' 1798–1990

Lillywhite, B. 1963, *London Coffee Houses: A reference book of coffee houses of the seventeenth, eighteenth and nineteenth centuries* (London Allen & Unwin)

Michie, R. C. 2001 *The London Stock Exchange: A History* (Oxford: Oxford University Press)

—— (ed.) 2000 *The Development of London as a Financial Centre* (London: I.B. Taurus)

Morgan, E.V. and Thomas, W.A. 1987 *The Stock Exchange: Its History and Functions* (London: Elek)

Palan, R. 'International Financial Centres: The British Empire, City States and Commercially Oriented Politics', *Theoretical Inquiries in Law*, Vol. 11, n. 149, 2010 pp. 149–176

Pevsner, N. 1979 *A History of Building Types* (London: Thames & Hudson)

Saunders, A. 1997, *The Royal Exchange* (London: London Topographical Society)

Shaxson, N. 2011 *Treasure Islands: Tax Havens and the men who stole the world* (London: Bodley Head)

Smith, C.F. 1929, 'The Early History of the London Stock Exchange', *The American Economic Review*, Vol. 19, No. 2, pp. 206–216

Tuckett, D. 2011 *Minding the Markets: An Emotional View of Financial Instability* (London: Palgrave)

Zukin, S. 1991 *Landscapes of Power* (Oxford: University of California)

Dissertation Authors

Joseph Godlewski's dissertation was completed as part of the MSc Architecture programme at the College of Environmental Design, University of California, Berkeley, USA, in 2009. It was published as a Special Article in *Traditional Dwelling and Settlement Review*, v.21 n.2 (2010), pp. 7–19 (www.iaste.berkeley.edu/category/tdsr), and the research later formed the basis of his doctoral studies at Berkeley. Joseph Godlewski is currently Assistant Professor at Syracuse University's School of Architecture, USA.

Ocean Howell's thesis was completed as part of the MSc Architecture programme at the University of California, Berkeley, USA, in 2005. One chapter was published as "The 'Creative Class' and the Gentrifying City" in the *Journal of Architectural Education*, v.59 n.2 (2005), pp. 32–42 (reprinted here), and a second chapter as "Skatepark as Neoliberal Playground: Urban Governance, Recreation Space and the Cultivation of Personal Responsibility," *Space and Culture* v.11 n.4 (2008), pp. 475-96. Ocean Howell is currently Assistant Professor of History and Architectural History in the Clark Honors College at the University of Oregon, USA.

Mairi Johnson's dissertation was completed as part of the Graduate Diploma Architecture programme at the Bartlett School of Architecture, University College London (UCL), UK, in 1995. The work won the RIBA President's Prize for Dissertation in 1995 and was published in *The Journal of Architecture*, v.1 n.3 (1996), pp. 207–25 (www.tandfonline.com/loi/rjar20). Mairi Johnson is currently Deputy Director for Design at the UK's Education Funding Agency.

Joanna Rapp's dissertation was completed as part of the Graduate Diploma Architecture programme at the University of Westminster, UK, in 2007. The work won the RIBA President's Medal for Dissertation in 2007 and was published in *The Journal of Architecture*, v.13 n.6 (2008), pp. 701–36 (www.tandfonline.com/loi/rjar20). Formerly an architect at SOM Chicago in the USA, Joanna Rapp is currently based in the UK.

Amy Thomas's dissertation was completed as part of the MA Architectural History programme at the Bartlett School of Architecture, Univeristy College London (UCL), UK, in 2010. The work won the RIBA President's Award for Outstanding Masters Thesis in 2012 and was published in *The Journal of Architecture*, v.17 n.6 (10 December 2012), pp.1009–48 (www.tandfonline.com/loi/rjar20). Amy Thomas is currently a doctoral student at the Bartlett School of Architecture and teaches Architectural History at UCL, Queen Mary University of London and Regents University London, UK.

Index